DEBT
AND THE
ENVIRONMENT:

CONVERGING CRISES

DEBT
AND THE
ENVIRONMENT:

CONVERGING CRISES

MORRIS MILLER

United Nations Publications

The opinions in this publication
are the authors and do not necessarily reflect
the views or policies of the Secretariat

United Nations Publications
United Nations
Room DC2-853
New York, N.Y. 10017, U.S.A.

United Nations Publications
Palais des Nations
1211 Geneva 10,
Switzerland

Sales No. E.91.I.17

ISBN 92-1-100457-8

CONTENTS

PREFACE

The eminent architectural critic, Ada Louise Huxtable, once characterized the present period as "one of the greatest most challenging periods of history, the age in which man has reached first the clouds and then the moon. . . . (and) has turned the dream of a better world into a fouled environment." If she wrote critically, she remarked, it was "as a concerned observer in search of possibilities for a positive interpretation of the present."[1]

This observation strikes a responsive chord. Having been engaged for most of my working life in dealing with the contentious and frustrating issues related to development, the role of critic comes easily. It is a constant but essential struggle to maintain a positive outlook, to be, in a phrase, a *constructive* critic. Only with that frame of mind can one continue to work for a better future. Despite the regression of the past decade, the hope is based on confidence that our human capacity to build can and, in the end, will surmount our capacity to destroy and to indulge in short-sighted self-interest. We cannot be unmindful of the consequences of this self-indulgence both for contemporary fellow beings on this small planet and for the generations to come. This book is written with this underlying premise of hope—and with a sense of danger that lends urgency to the task.

Despite some steps backward, there is ample historical evidence to support this optimistic view and to turn a deaf ear to the cynics and the fatalists who are self-styled "realists." Although there has been enormous progress, it is even more important to recognize that so much more is possible, that we are far short of realizing the full potential of human ingenuity so evident in the phenomenal scientific and technological achievements of the present era. This success has not been matched as yet on the socio-political side. So we face the challenge of changing our institutions and policies to enable us to deal in a much more effective and compassionate fashion with the many down-side aspects of this progress.

The focus of concern for those engaged in trying to promote "development with a human face" is centred both on reducing the gross inequities of *wide and widening* income gaps between the rich and poor nations and between classes within them, and on the environmental degradation that is a by-product of our past and present *manner* of development. Thus before we can wipe out the scourges of poverty and famine and environmental damage, there are many serious problems to contend with, among which the global environmental and debt crises are central. Given the interdependent nature and global scope of these crises, resolving them will call for, among other things, the forging of new forms of governance at the international level. This institutional aspect merits more attention than it has so far received if the global-scale problems are to be addressed head-on with a vigour commensurate with the scope and urgency of the challenge.

But first there is a need to raise the public's consciousness of the troubling trends and their implications and of the possibility to change them. The challenge is to sound the warning with credibility so that it is not only heard but heeded, and then to *point* the way in terms of realizable objectives and feasible modalities. This is useful even if it does not go so far as to entail the preparation of a strategic plan or programme with the detailed social engineering necessary to achieve movement in the suggested direction. This book starts with this constraint; there is no blueprint for action. The hope is that this book can provide useful insights for devising the bold, far-reaching policies and institutional changes needed to address the present global *problematique* as reflected in the symbiotically related crises of debt and environment.

The book is structured to provide an understanding about how the two crises reached their present dimensions, particularly focusing on how the prevailing institutional arrangements might have either encouraged or permitted these trends to build to a point where corrective action on a global scale has become necessary. For expository and analytic purposes, as a guide to policy-making and to institutional changes, the approach taken thus focuses first on the global debt and environmental crises as separate issues with special emphasis on their trends and on their linkages. The feasibility and adequacy of the proposals to address these crises, whether conventional and modest or bold and imaginative, can be gauged only partly on the basis of an understanding of the *dynamic* of the situation that indicates the scope and degree of urgency called for. Thus the first item on this book's agenda—**Part I (chapters 1** and **2)**—provides a broad-brush sketch of the magnitude and the dynamic of the debt and environmental trends and their implications, including the large and growing United States debt that has been characterized as "the second debt crisis."

This is followed in **Part II** by **chapters 3** to **5** that focus on a short list of the key *necessary* conditions for achieving the desired outcome. This list includes the leadership required to tackle the current extraordinary global problems. Identifying and assessing these necessary conditions constitutes the first part of the agenda. This descriptive-analytic exercise helps define the roles incumbent on the United States, on the other major economic-financial powers, and on the world community-at-large and thereby provides the criteria for assessing their capacity and willingness to play the required roles.

Part III (chapter 6) is devoted to identifying and assessing the major obstacles to change—to doing "the right thing." Robert Kuttner, the economics correspondent for *The New Republic*, recently made the point about the gap between intentions and performance by paraphrasing Shakespeare's Hotspur: "It is easy enough to call forth policies from the vasty deep; the trick is to get them to come when you call." If they are to come at all, there are obstacles that need to be identified, the better to surmount them.

Chapters 7 to **9** of **Part IV** are devoted to the proposals for tackling both the debt and the environmental facets of the global crisis, including consideration of institutional and policy implications as they pertain to the menu of new financial instruments designed to ease debt burdens and at the same time discourage environmentally harmful practices.

The discussion in **Part V, chapters 10 to 14**, is focused on the rules or system by which the "international public good" can be provided **(chapter 10)**, on the agenda for easing and resolving the debt and environmental crises **(chapters 11** and **12)**, and on the roles of the United Nations and its specialized agencies, of the multilateral development banks (MDBs), of the International Monetary Fund (IMF), and of new global institutions, policies and agreements **(chapters 13** and **14)**.

An **epilogue** provides a summation and assessment that bears on future prospects.

"We seem at present to be backing into the future, one crisis at a time. . . . Who among us is confident that the existing international economic machinery will get us safely through to the end of the century? (Who among us is confident that) our current international economic institutions will be able to ensure adequate international liquidity, a smooth adjustment to irreversible economic change, confidence in our financial systems, reasonable overall stability and growth, and equitable sharing in the fruits of such progress?"

—Professor Gerald K. Helleiner
"An agenda for a new Bretton Woods,"
Foreign Policy Journal, Winter 1987-88

"To deserve a hearing among his fellows . . . (one) must seek to anticipate and supplement the insights of fellow men into the problems of their adjustment to reality."

—Walter Lippmann

INTRODUCTION

Alarm bells about the global debt and environmental crises have been ringing louder and louder since the beginning of the last decade. The warnings have been heard and partially heeded, but not as yet with action on the scale and in the manner commensurate with the threats that these crises pose separately and together. The *denouement* can be significantly less painful and less prejudicial to our future welfare as a global community if the response is as bold and cooperative as the current global situation, in its dynamic and danger, warrants.

There was widespread anxiety about an ''international debt crisis'' when Mexico and Brazil in the summer of 1982 defiantly announced that they could not or would not service their debts on a business-as-usual basis. Within a year the panic subsided. There is, after all, little news-value in accounts of declining living standards, abandoned hope and rising tensions in the far-away, heavily debt-burdened third world countries, unless there are reports of violent rioting in debtor countries. Readers of the business columns and journals were maintaining a low level of concern as they learned about the continuing bitter stand-offs in negotiations between major debtors and their creditor banks, about mounting arrears of unpaid interest and shrinking book values of third world debts that were weakening many of the major banks but in no case threatening to lead to their collapse.

During the decade of the 1980s, however, another related development was being watched with mounting worry: the transformation of the United States from creditor to debtor status and from the mid-1980s an exceptionally rapid increase in United States foreign indebtedness. The focus began to shift from third world debt to what came to be labeled as ''the second global debt crisis,'' a crisis that manifested itself in less dramatic ways but, in the view of many commentators, held much greater potential for global damage and danger. The United States foreign debt was becoming an albatross around the neck of United States policy makers, severely limiting the available options of the world's largest economy. This development, therefore, was compromising its leadership capability to do whatever needed to be done to deal with

1

a global economic/financial situation that was in crisis and badly in need of course correction, stabilization and repair.

Meantime, during the decade of the 1980s anxiety about the environment escalated, moving the issue into the limelight as a matter of global concern. The international dimensions of an environmental crisis were dramatized both by large-scale accidents that inflicted serious environmental damage to the oceans and the atmosphere, and by well-publicized scientific findings about the cumulative damage being inflicted on the planet's oceans, lands and atmosphere by human activities. If continued at the present pace and in the present manner, they would likely have damaging implications for life on earth in the foreseeable future. The impressive breadth and depth of the public's environmental consciousness and concern has been reflected by such events as the turnout of an estimated 200 million for Earth Day 1990 demonstrations in 140 countries.

These debt and environmental developments of the 1980s are symptomatic of a massive dysfunctioning of the prevailing global system that threatens to lead to (1) a breakdown of institutional arrangements governing trade and capital flows, a widening of the already large income gaps between the rich and the poor nations and between the rich and the poor within nations, increasing the likelihood of a major world-wide depression, and (2) a lessening of the capacity to address the threat of irreparable environmental damage on a planetary scale. Neither of the economic-financial and the environmental concerns can be significantly eased or solved alone. Their resolution requires simultaneous action on both fronts. They should be treated, therefore, as one big global crisis with two heads, Janus-like.

This book approaches the two topical issues of debt and environment as separate but closely related, mutually reinforcing crises. The concept of ''crisis'' as the dictionary defines the term portends ''an impending change that is abrupt or decisive, in a phrase, a turning point or an unstable situation that is unsustainable, therefore calling for bold decisions. Given the pervasive nature and international scope of both the debt and the environmental trends, the appropriate perspective must be global. Accordingly, the levels of governance for the requisite decisive actions must include also the global, whether through ad hoc agreements or institutionalized cooperative arrangements between nations.

The nature and scope of the crises

A great deal of confusion necessarily results when commentators-analysts use the concept of crisis with different meanings. At one extreme, there are those who question whether there is a global crisis and, if so, doubt that it is serious enough to call for anything beyond modest tinkering. This view can be found in the editorial pages and in the reportage of *The Wall Street Journal* and like-minded media.[1] Then there is the school of thought that sees the crisis as a temporary aberration that will be corrected when the debtors achieve the state of ''creditworthiness'' and can once again attract private capital. This view is best typified by the World Bank. At the end of 1990 it declared in one of its reports that ''the debt crisis is far from over'' and that one of the key objectives with respect to the third world debt crisis is ''to strengthen creditworthiness, thus eventually permitting a resumption of voluntary commercial lending.''[2]

Since the basic premise of this book is that humanity is living in a world in crisis as reflected in the unsustainable global trends with respect to debt and the environment, the issue of definitions goes beyond mere semantics. Crisis is, after all, a term depreciated by overuse and misuse to apply to a wide variety of troubling problems and in general to difficult times and circumstances. The concept needs clarification at the outset. Crisis need not imply cataclysmic collapse as a necessary condition for the change that is impending; that change could be *decisive* without being *abrupt*. It does mean, however, that the crisis-resolving changes must be *transforming* in some *significant* way with regard to *key* institutional aspects of the global economic/financial system. (See Annex A for a fuller treatment of the concept of ''crisis''.)

To characterize the prevailing global conditions as being in a state of crisis is to go well beyond the issue of the difficulties or problems that threaten such phenomena as major bank failures and banking system collapse, sporadic violent rioting induced by belt-tightening structural adjustment policies and localized pollution disasters. These might well be remedied yet leave virtually intact the very conditions that gave rise to the problems and the dangers inherent in a stressed-out global system that is unstable, imbalanced and dysfunctional.

Resolving the global debt and environmental crises, therefore, calls for distinguishing between not only the treatment of symptoms and the treatment of underlying causal factors but also between objectives. Correcting global trends with respect to both the environmental and the debt factors entails the reduction of a wide range of economic-financial imbalances between industrialized countries and between them and the developing countries, and doing so in a manner and to a degree that addresses the deep-seated factors that gave rise to those imbalances in the first place. At the same time, improving the global system entails achieving growth with greater sharing, more stability and enhanced environmental quality with all that that implies about changing the pattern or kind of growth.

From this broader perspective, it can be said that the global crisis manifests itself when some key elements are missing, such as, for example, (1) the attribute of sharing which implies significantly increasing incomes or states of well-being for those who are living at levels of absolute poverty (roughly defined as having incomes of $1 per day), and (2) the leadership required to correct course to avoid catastrophic breakdown and to improve on the prevailing crisis-ridden global state of affairs.

The equity or distributional aspect is highlighted by the asymmetry of the ritualized process that is in place for treating the crisis as it applies to the third world's debtors. On one side, bankers contend with the discomfort of facing reduced profits and the threat of financial failure; on the other side, the debtors face a situation characterized by falling incomes and rising poverty with the suffering exacerbated by an awareness that, for most of the debt-burdened countries, their debts have been mounting to reach a level almost double what they owed at the onset of the global debt crisis, 10 years ago. At the same time, the countries with the preponderant numbers of the desperately poor are transferring more capital to the richer industrialized countries than they are receiving, a direction of flow that is historically unprecedented and unconscionable.

This negative flow has significance for the environment in so far as it exacerbates the plight of the debtors and in so doing, makes them less willing and less able to give "due weight" to environmental considerations. When the "costs" of environmental damage are subtle and in any case felt only in the longer-term, and when the benefits of environmentally-damaging activities are financially tangible and immediate, it is not difficult to fathom which option the stressed-out debtors will choose. Among the immediate financial benefits some would count the enhancement of their ability to service their debts to a degree that keeps them "in the game" or treadmill of the debt-workout process. Even if they were inclined to believe that environmentally benign patterns of growth were preferable, these countries do not have the means, either financially or in available skilled workforce, to adopt the appropriate technologies and patterns of development. Both need specially-tailored, vastly expanded research and, as a follow-through, the transfer of the necessary technology on a major scale.

In any case, the world community has long tolerated desperate poverty and extremes of income distribution, conditions that should not be acceptable on grounds of justice or fairness. Thus the expectation for a significant degree of change *must* rest on the *non-compassionate* grounds of the self-interest of the powers-that-be to maintain the prevailing system in its essential features, that is, to ease the state of crisis. To do so requires reversing trade and capital flows to correct the imbalances that are not only large but persisting and requires changing the pattern of growth towards one that is environmentally benign. All this entails a reversal of many deep-seated trends. The necessary changes must be *transforming*, therefore, with regard to the key institutional features of the prevailing global economic/financial system. This in turn has implications for changes in the cultural/political aspects of the global system that affect policy-making.

Unhappily, as we shall see when we discuss obstacles to change, a traumatic breakdown is too often necessary for motivating societies to work together to make the changes commensurate with the nature and magnitude of challenges such as those posed by the debt and environment crises. This pessimistic observation is a generalized one, but all indications of the response to the current conditions seem to indicate that it is a judgement that applies to both the debt and the environmental crises when a smooth transition requires *enlightened and forceful leadership*.

The United States, as the world's largest economy accounting for about a quarter of the global GNP, must be relied upon to play that leading role— in consort, of course, with others. Yet as a debtor nation, the United States has become increasingly dependent on net capital inflows from Japan, Germany and other countries. As one analyst put it, "Japan, a protectorate, . . . is underwriting American hegemony and prosperity."[3] This dependency severely constrains the exercise of leadership to take the requisite steps such as, for example, those that would significantly lower real interest rates and those that would open up the markets of the industrialized countries to third world exports. Severely constrained leadership makes the global system much more fragile, vulnerable to shocks such as the financial costs of the Gulf War and the bursting of the financial bubble occasioned by the fall in the price of collateralized real estate in both Japan and the United States that has had an adverse impact on a banking system already weakened by depreciated third world debt and other systemic misjudgements. In a phrase, the United States has become part of the problem rather than a contributor to the solution of the global crises, whether the solution is defined in terms of avoiding a catastrophic *denouement* or of contributing to the establishment of a global system that is both more equitable and sustainable, economically and environmentally.

PART ONE

THE CRISES: THEIR URGENCY AND DYNAMIC

CHAPTER 1

THE DEBT CRISIS

"Since 1980, matters have turned from bad to worse: economic
growth rates have slowed, real wages have dropped, and
growth in employment has faltered in most developing
countries. . . . In some the prolonged economic slump is
already more severe than it was during the Great Depression in
the industrial countries. The tide of poverty and misery in those
countries is rising, not receding. . . .
   Without significant changes in policies, the present economic
uncertainty may soon be followed by a world-wide
recession. . . . This is a *fragile* situation–one that could *rapidly*
deteriorate." (Emphasis added).

—*The World Bank's World Development Report*, 1988

"The debt crisis is far from over. . . ."

—*The World Bank's World Debt Tables*, 1990

THE DARKENING THIRD WORLD DEBT OVERHANG

In the summer of 1982 when the Mexican and Brazilian Governments declared
that they could no longer continue to service their foreign debt on a business-
as-usual basis, the announcements and the subsequent actions dramatically
precipitated a world-wide awareness of a "debt crisis" with global ramifications. The fears focussed on the threats that these defaults posed for the
creditor banks that had extended themselves dangerously in lending to these
countries. When in time these banks and the financial system survived this
blow, a mood of complacency returned. The veneer of complacency has been

9

shattered dramatically from time to time by indicators of stress such as un-
controllable debt-related riots that have erupted in countries of almost every
continent over the last few years.

The rioting in the streets of Venezuelan cities and towns in early March
of 1989 endured over four days and claimed several hundred lives. The event
was newsworthy in its own right, but its wider implications became clear
when Venezuela's President, Carlos Andres Perez, exclaimed that "the crisis
we are undergoing has a name written in capital letters, FOREIGN DEBT."
In a spirited editorial in *The New York Times* of 3 March that was headlined:
"Caracas seethes, Washington snoozes," the event was framed in dramatic
terms:

> " 'The IMF set fire to the streets of Caracas' screamed a Venezuelan
> newspaper this week as riots left hundreds dead. . . . This deal (that
> Venezuela had just signed with the International Monetary Fund (IMF))
> merely put a match to a combustible mixture that has been building for
> years, and not just in Venezuela. . . . How long must (Venezuela and
> other debtors) now wait for Washington to wake up to the urgency of the
> crisis by producing a plausible debt relief plan (rather than continuing to)
> offer encouraging rhetoric about the need for new approaches, but no
> plans?''

Each of these debt-related events has given rise to a wave of anxiety, but
the response has always been short-lived. After the excitement has died down,
these occurrences have generally been dismissed as the price that a debtor
country has to pay for its past mistakes. In any case, it should be an expected
consequence of the necessary "belt-tightening" that is usually called for in
the "structural adjustment" the debtor country must undergo to get back to
a condition of "creditworthiness."

Over the subsequent six years—as shown in both Table 1 and Figure 1
—third world debt is still very much with us, having doubled in eight years
to total more than $1,340 billion by the end of 1990. And it is still going up,
by about 6 per cent in 1990.

Apart from the occasional shock of a media-relayed reminder that the debt
overhang is still somewhat troubling to some people somewhere out there on
this planet, there is little awareness and even less concern in the countries
where the major creditor banks are located. In part this view stems from the
fact that the major banks do not appear to be seriously threatened by defaults

Table 1: The growth of external debt, 1982-90
(US$ billions)

Category	1982	1983	1984	1985	1986	1987	1988(a)	1989(b)	1990(c)
Total debt, DRS countries (d)	753	819	856	952	1,047	1,176	1,156	1,165	1,189
Long-term debt	561	644	684	780	882	999	980	995	1,039
Official sources	199	221	234	296	360	440	443	467	517
Private sources	362	423	450	484	522	559	537	528	522
Short-term debt	168	141	134	132	122	135	141	139	127
Use of IMF credit	24	34	36	40	43	43	35	32	23
Total debt, other developing countries	86	86	81	89	99	116	128	125	130
Total external debt, all developing countries	838	905	936	1,041	1,146	1,292	1,284	1,290	1,319

(a) Estimates.
(b) Preliminary estimates.
(c) Projections.
(d) Countries reporting to the World Bank Debtor Reporting System.
Source: World Bank Debtor Reporting System; data for the category "Other developing countries" are estimates
by the Debt and International Finance Division of the World Bank's International Economics Department (IECDI).

or write-downs of the outstanding debt of the 100-odd third world debtor
countries. And in part this complacent view stems from the fact that only a
few of these debtors are large enough to worry about.

Half of the debtor countries are in sub-Saharan Africa, and each has
relatively small debts in global terms. In any case, almost all of it is owed
to Governments and multilateral agencies, or what is known as "official
creditors," rather than to commercial banks. By the end of 1990 their total
debts to both types of creditors amounted to more than $160 billion, which
is about a third of Latin America's. With a total debt of about $155 billion,
Eastern European countries, including the Soviet Union, can be added to this
group of so-called "problem debtors." The Soviet Union is the largest debtor
with $54 billion outstanding, followed closely by Poland ($43 billion), Hun-
gary ($22 billion), Yugoslavia ($19 billion) and Bulgaria ($10 billion). To
complete the picture, there are also the debts owed by developing countries
to other developing countries. This amounts to about $20 billion. Brazil and
China and the oil-exporting countries are the main creditors. The "crisis"
aspect from a global systemic perspective pertains to the debts of a group of
countries labelled "heavily-indebted middle-income" developing countries,
that is, those whose debts are over $20 billion and whose average annual per
capita income is between $480 and $5,999. This group, comprised of 17
countries, accounts for almost half of the third world's debt, over $500 billion
owed to commercial banks.

Figure 1: *Long Term External Dept of Developing Countries.*

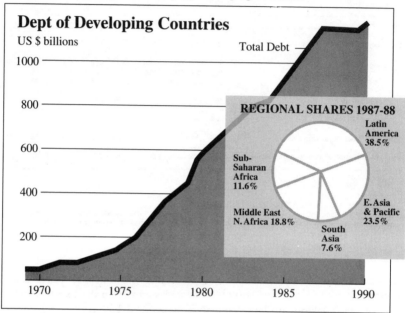

Source: Human Development Report 1990 UNDP

The concern of the private banking community and of the public in the creditor nations has been focused, understandably, on these "problem debtors." The large "problem debtor" countries—those with debts of over $20 billion owed to commercial banks—have held the global limelight; however, the other debtors, whose debts are large relative to their economic size and circumstances, must be brought into the picture when the perspective is broadened beyond the objective of avoiding breakdown to include other equally important objectives, such as: (1) the eradication of poverty that is accentuated by the debt-servicing burden; (2) the lessening of the global environmental damage that ensues from such financial pressure; and (3) the establishment of global conditions for trade and capital flows that are conducive to growth for all with a narrowing of the income/welfare gap between the rich and the poor as well.

The debt numbers, by themselves, provide no clue as to their significance. The $1,340 billion third world debt may be put into perspective, however, by noting that it amounts to roughly half of the combined GNP of the developing countries and is more than 10 times greater (in constant dollars) than the third world debt during the worst years of the Great Depression.[1] Measured in relation to some key indicators, the implications of a debt of that magnitude become clearer. One such benchmark is provided by the percentage of export earnings that has to be devoted to servicing that debt.

- Scheduled debt-service payments of sub-Saharan African countries now absorb about half of their export earnings.
- During the last few years, over one-third of the export earnings of third world debtor countries on average has had to be allocated to debt servicing.
- For many of the debtors, full servicing of their debts according to their contractual obligation would absorb almost all of their foreign exchange earnings.

Little wonder that 30 of the 44 sub-Saharan African countries have had to reschedule their debts in the past eight years, and that arrears of all indebted third world countries have been mounting at an alarming rate, almost tripling in four years, from $27 billion in 1985 to $79 billion by 1989, the year of the Venezuelan riots. The interest arrears alone increased more than four-fold. Of this total, $35 billion was owed just for interest arrears. In 1985 the interest arrears were less than $8 billion.[2]

By the end of 1990, some of the larger debtors had impressive interest arrears: Argentina's was about $8 billion and Brazil's about $9 billion. Brazil has engaged in the bitterest and most protracted of the many debtor/creditor confrontations. In Brazil's latest stand-off with its two dozen creditors, the suspension of interest payments extended for over a year. It has taken on the attributes of a drama and lead a journalist to characterize the confrontation as "the last great showdown of the eight-year old debt crisis."[3] At one time, as many as 24 countries have been in the rescheduling queue, in effect declaring that they could not service their debts on existing terms. The rescheduling queue remains distressingly long, as might be expected when the net outflow from Latin American debtors alone amounted to $22 billion during 1990, a year when their GNP fell by a further 1 per cent and average per capita income levels by a much larger percentage.

The immediate fear in 1982 was, of course, the devastating impact of such threatened defaults and moratoria on the financial viability of the world's major commercial banks, banks with third world "accounts receivable" assets many times greater than their capital assets. This fear gave rise in turn to a reaction that brought on the very developments that were feared: lending by the commercial banks was abruptly cut back, creating a situation even more fragile and frightening. In the five years leading up to 1982 the flow of capital to the developing countries in the form of long-term lending from commercial banks, official lending and concessional aid had amounted to $147 billion; from 1983 onward the flow was reversed to move from the developing countries.

As shown in Table 2 and Figure 2, from 1983 to 1989 the net resource transfers from the developing countries amounted in total to approximately $200 billion. In 1989 alone this outflow rose to its highest annual level, over $50 billion, an amount substantially greater than what they had received that year in official development aid (ODA). This estimate does not include, however, unrecorded capital outflow known as ''capital flight.'' It is estimated to have jumped by over 20 per cent in 1983 and has continued to increase ever since. By the beginning of the 1990s this drain is estimated to be more than 50 per cent of their total net external debt.[4] Meantime, the net annual recorded outflow of payments to creditors has reached a level three times greater than it was during the first year after the onset of the debt crisis.

The increase in these arrears and the continuing length of the rescheduling queues provide warning signals that the limits of tolerance are close to a breakdown. The declining valuations placed on the debts in what is known as a ''secondary market'' is another indicator of growing stress, a condition shared by the creditor banks when they finally agree to accept heavy discounts on these debts. In the last few years, this has resulted in agreements whereby Bolivia could buy back most of its commercial bank debt at 11 cents on a dollar of face value, Costa Rica at 15 cents, Mexico at 65 cents, Venezuela at 35 cents, and Uruguay at 55 cents. Few countries have the foreign exchange to buy back much of their debt, and few bankers are ready to accept the drastic discounts involved. In any case, it is new money that is most needed

Table 2: Long-term debt and financial flows in developing countries, 1982-91
(US$ billions)

Long-term debt and financial flows	1982	1983	1984	1985	1986	1987	1988	1989	Projected 1990	1991
Debt disbursed and outstanding	562.5	644.9	686.7	793.7	893.9	996.3	1121	1143	1190	1230
Disbursements	116.9	97.2	91.6	89.3	87.7	86.7	103	93	110	114
(From private creditors)	84.6	65.0	58.9	57.8	50.8	48.5	–	–	–	–
Debt service	98.7	92.6	101.8	112.2	116.5	124.9	152	145	146	152
Principal repayments	49.7	45.4	48.6	56.4	61.5	70.9	79	75	75	77
Interest	48.9	47.3	53.2	55.8	54.9	54.0	73	70	71	75
Net flows	67.2	51.8	43.0	32.9	26.2	15.8	25	19	35	37
Net transfers	18.2	4.6	-10.2	-22.9	-28.7	-38.1	-45	-51	33	-42

Source: The World Bank, First Supplement World Debt Tables 1989-90.

Figure 2: *Long Term Net Flow & Transfer to Developing Countries, (1982-91)*

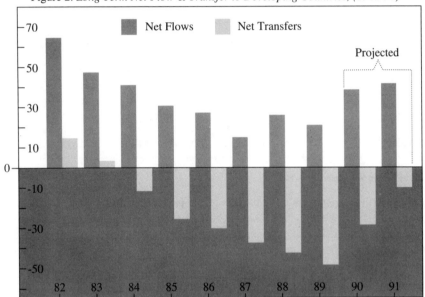

Source: *World Dept Tables 1989-90 edition, The World Bank*

by the debtor countries, and the arrangements arrived at in these buybacks provide little help in this regard. Table 3 and Figure 3 show the downward movement of secondary market prices for six Latin American countries that have been selected as representative.

THE INCREASING DESPAIR OF THE THIRD WORLD DEBTORS

While the stress that is revealed by these indicators of arrears and secondary market prices is felt on the side of both the debtors and the creditors, the impact is not symmetrical: on the bankers' side, the stress is one that can be characterized as discomfort in facing reduced profits and the threat of financial failure for their institution; on the debtors' side, the stress derives not only from falling incomes that were already low but also from an awareness that

Table 3: Falling market prices for developing country debt of selected Latin American countries, 1985-89 (as a percentage of face value)

Country	July 1985	Jan 1986	Jan 1987	Jan 1988	Jan 12 1989	Jan 20 1989
Argentina	60-65%	62-66%	62-65%	30-33%	21-22%	18-19%
Brazil	75-81	75-81	74-76.5	44-47	38-40	34-45
Chile	65-69	65-69	65-68	60-63	58-60	60-61
Mexico	80-82	69-73	54-57	50-52	40-41	38-39
Peru	45-50	25-30	16-19	2-7	5-8	5-8
Venezuela	81-83	80-82	72-74	56-57	38-39	37-38

Source: Shearson-Lehman Hutton Inc.

the burden is growing rather than receding, a psychological factor that intensifies the pain of poverty by removing hope. For most of the debtors the pain of belt tightening has become more acute over time when, after so many years, they cannot see any glimmer of light at the end of the tunnel of their despair.

Some illustrative statistical indicators—as shown in Table 4—reveal the social/economic deterioration process over the decade of the 1980s:

• average per capita incomes fell by about 3 per cent per year in sub-Saharan Africa and by about 1.3 per cent per year in the highly-indebted countries, cumulatively over the decade of the 1980s by as much as 25 per cent for African countries and 10 per cent for Latin American. In many countries, as Figure 4 reveals, the impact already exceeds that of the Great Depression.

• the income gap between the rich and poor nations has grown over a quarter century, with the polarization increasing rapidly after 1980 with sub-Saharan African incomes declining by an annual average rate of 2.4 per cent and Latin American countries by 0.7 per cent, as is evident from an examination of Figure 5.

• the persistently high levels of stress in debt servicing are revealed in relative terms by the changes in the debt–GNP ratios of the highly indebted countries and low-income African countries for the past decade, as shown in Figure 6.

The human aspect of this deterioration in living conditions can be roughly indicated by a "misery index" that is statistically represented in such quality-of-life indicators as life expectancy, infant mortality and illiteracy. Table 5 sets out some salient statistics for a sample of developing countries. The

Figure 3: *The Dept See-Saw for selected Latin American Countries, 1983-1988*

FINANCE

The Dept See-Saw

Total External Dept, $bn

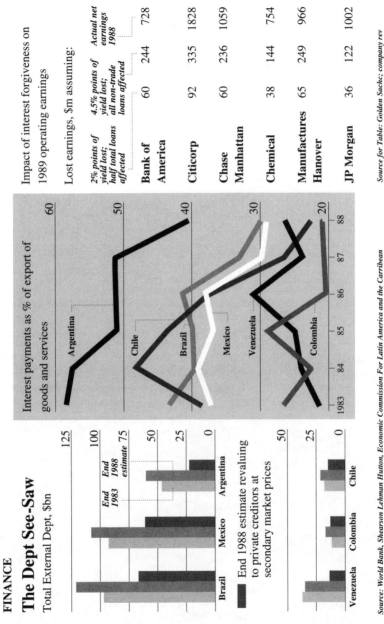

Impact of interest forgiveness on 1989 operating earnings

Lost earnings, $m assuming:

	2% points of yield lost; half total loans affected	4.5% points of yield lost; all non-trade loans affected	Actual net earnings 1988
Bank of America	60	244	728
Citicorp	92	335	1828
Chase Manhattan	60	236	1059
Chemical	38	144	754
Manufactures Hanover	65	249	966
JP Morgan	36	122	1002

Source for Table: Golden Sachs; company rev

Interest payments as % of export of goods and services

End 1988 estimate revaluing to private creditors at secondary market prices

Source: World Bank, Shearson Lehman Hutton, Economic Commission For Latin America and the Caribbean

17

Figure 4: *Per Capita GDP during the Great Depression and the current crisis, 1929-1938 and 1975-1986*

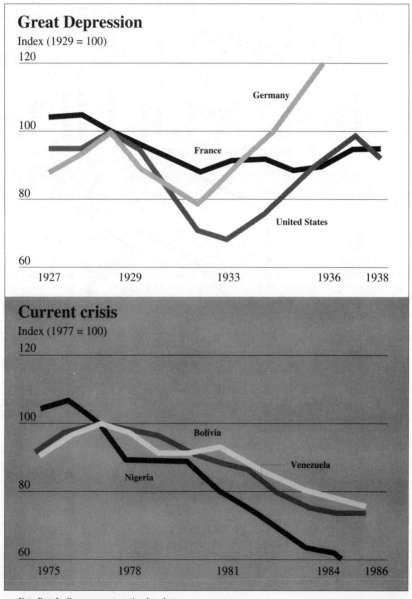

Note: Data for Germany are net national product.
Source: Mitchell 1975. United States Government 1975, and World Bank data.

Table 4: Growth of GDP per capita in developing countries by regions. 1960-1990
(Percentage)

Country group	Average annual rate of growth of GDP per capita		
	1960-1970	1970-1980	1980-1990
Developing countries	3.3	2.4	0.1
By regions:			
North Africa	8.2	1.2	−0.3
Sub-Saharan Africa	1.8	−0.4	−2.6
Western Asia	4.1	1.0	−4.3
South and East Asia	2.6	4.1	3.7
Latin America and the Caribbean	2.7	2.4	−1.1
Mediterranean	3.7	3.7	1.1

Source: United Nations, Department of International Economic and Social Affairs.
At 1980 dollars and exchange rates.

numbers understate the plight of debtor countries. They are being forced to live off their capital by underfinancing education and health programmes and postponing essential maintenance of their basic infrastructure, in effect, cannibalizing their economies. As early as 1984 the *World Development Report* reported:

"For Africa the 'debt crisis' had a different meaning . . . (with) one half to three fourths of the African population subsisting in absolute poverty where people are too poor to obtain a calorie-adequate diet."

According to the World Bank's conservative estimate, during the decade of the 1970s the number of those in this income group, "the absolutely poor," increased from 650 million to 730 million. In the 1980s, that number has increased to well over 1 billion, or one out of every four or five persons on this globe struggling to survive on less than $1 a day.

In 1973 the then President of the World Bank, Robert MacNamara, made a landmark speech in Nairobi. He spoke of "the bottom 40 per cent" of humankind that were unable to enjoy the improvements in income and welfare of modern science and technology. This was—and is still—the percentage unable to enjoy the most elemental necessities of life—food nutritionally adequate, housing, clothing, education and health care—in a phrase, "basic needs." In this category there should also be included the provision of those

Figure 5: *The Persistent Income Gap between Rich and Poor Nations,1965-1990*

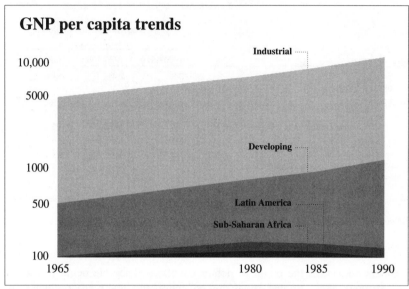

Source: Human Development Report, 1990 (UNDP)
and Social Indicators of Development, 1989 (World Bank Publication)

aspects of life that are subsumed under ''dignity,'' that is, aspects that pertain to useful employment, civil rights, and the like. If these factors were taken into account, the numbers of those in ''absolute poverty'' would be much higher, and the category might be more appropriately labelled ''the absolutely deprived.''

The direction of these trends were thus evident well before the 1980s and the acute phase of the debt crisis, but they were accentuated during the 1980s. Given the extremely unequal distribution of incomes and the greater ability of the rich to contend with adverse conditions, the plight of the poor is understated by national averages. To address this deficiency and provide a more meaningful measure of the concept of ''welfare'' or ''well-being,'' the UNDP has prepared a *Human Development Index*. This encompasses many factors other than income. In non-statistical terms, the human dimensions of the poverty status are well summed up in the 1990 issue of the *World Development Report* that is devoted to the theme of poverty:

Figure 6: *Debt Indicators in Developing Countries, 1979-1989.*

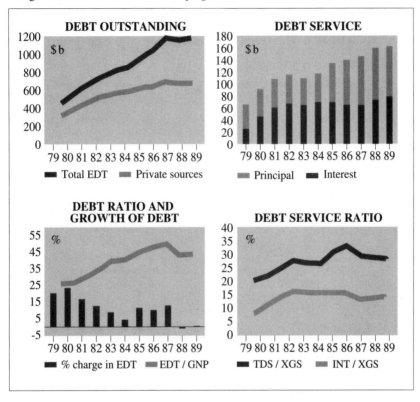

Table 5: Condition-of-life indicators for selected countries, 1985

Country group	Poverty		Social indicators		
	Percentage of poor in population (percentage)	Number of poor (in millions)	Under five mortality rate (Per 1,000)	Life expectancy (in years)	Net primary enrollment (percentage)
Sub-Saharan Africa	47	180	196	50	56
East Asia	20	280	96	67	96
China	(20)	(210)	(58)	(69)	(93)
South Asia	51	520	172	56	74
India	(55)	(420)	(199)	(57)	(81)
Eastern Europe	8	6	23	69	90
Middle East and North Africa	31	60	148	61	75
Latin America and the Caribbean	19	70	75	66	92
All developing countries	33	1116	121	62	83

Source: The World Bank, *World Development Report,* 1990

Figure 7: *Condition-of-life indicators for Industrial, Developing and Least Developed Countries*

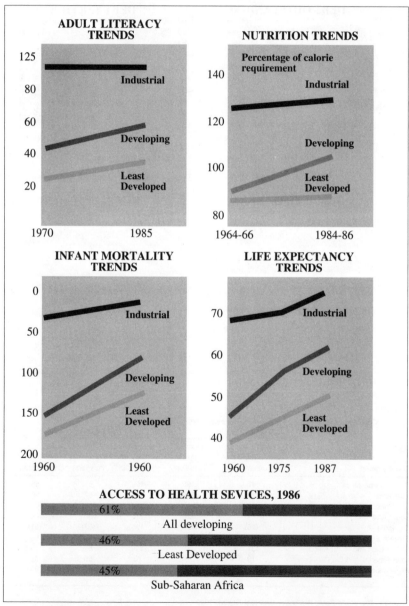

Source: Human Development Report 1990, UNDP

"Being poor means being unable to attain a minimal standard of living and having insufficient money to purchase adequate food, clothing, and housing. It also means low life expectancies, high death rates among infants and children and few opportunities to obtain even basic education."

In the poorest of the developing countries, on average, 4 out of 10 children under the age of five suffer from malnutrition, with 15 million dying each year. More than 500,000 women who might otherwise live through childbirth, die because of the lack of facilities and adequate nutrition. Almost two thirds of the deaths of the new born and infants result from causes that could easily be remedied: diarrhea, respiratory infections, measles and tetanus. And 100 million of those who live to the age when they would normally expect to be able to attend formal schools find they are denied any educational opportunities; hundreds of millions more must contend with inadequately equipped schools and poorly trained teachers. The result is rampant illiteracy. This has profound implications for the future "independence" of those countries, particularly with regard to their prospect of eventually escaping from a state of economic, cultural, political, technological and scientific dependency that is a form of peonage or colonialism.

To add to the despair, under such conditions there is a diminution of hope in another sense. When it is realized that the resources transferred to service the debts are roughly equivalent to the decline in investment it becomes clear that future growth is virtually foreclosed.[5] For the debtor countries as a group since 1982, the dramatic decline in gross capital formation as a percentage of GDP has had a devastating effect. Its magnitude is shown in Figure 8. A perusal of Table 6 and Figure 9 reveals the magnitude of the decline in investment as a percentage of GDP in several Latin American countries after 1982.

Third world leaders have been driven to declare openly that their people's needs for physical survival and for political stability must come ahead of paying the interest on their outstanding debts. With ever-greater frequency and vehemence, the political leadership of the hard-pressed debtor countries are questioning not only the sustainability but also the morality of the asymmetric impact of the process that puts the greater burden of adjustment on their shoulders, that, in effect, exacerbates a situation where the third world with over 80 per cent of the world's population enjoys barely 20 per cent of the global income, and where the average American enjoys an income more than 20 times greater than the average African or Asian.

From time to time, there has been a compassionate response to this situation, especially when the eyes of television cameras have revealed desperate

Figure 8: *Gross Capital Formation as a percentage of GDP, 1980-88*

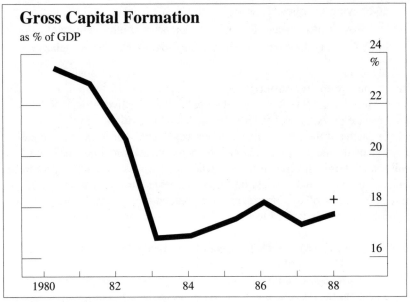

Source: The Economist

Table 6: The impact of the debt crisis on growth and investment
in selected Latin American countries, 1970-1987

	Cumulative change. output per capita (percentage)		Investment/GDP (percentage)	
	1982-87	1970-81	1982-87	1970-81
Latin America	−3.3	32.9	16.6	22.6
Argentina*	−14.5	9.5	12.7	20.8
Brazil*	3.9	81.5	16.3	23.3
Colombia	9.0	36.7	18.3	18.4
Costa Rica*	−9.7	29.2	18.2	22.5
Chile	−5.7	12.9	12.0	16.7
Ecuador*	−10.5	87.3	17.8	24.2
Mexico	−14.4	49.2	17.8	23.2
Peru	−5.7	13.5	21.2	23.4
Uruguay	−9.5	35.8	9.7	12.3
Venezuela	−13.1	5.7	19.0	25.9

* Because the debt crisis started earlier in some countries, ECLAC calculated the "crisis" period changes in those
countries from 1981 instead of 1982

Source: ECLAC. *Economic Panorama of Latin America, 1988. September 1988.*

Figure 9: *Net Inflow of Capital and Net Transfer of Resources in Latin America and the Carribean, 1977-89*

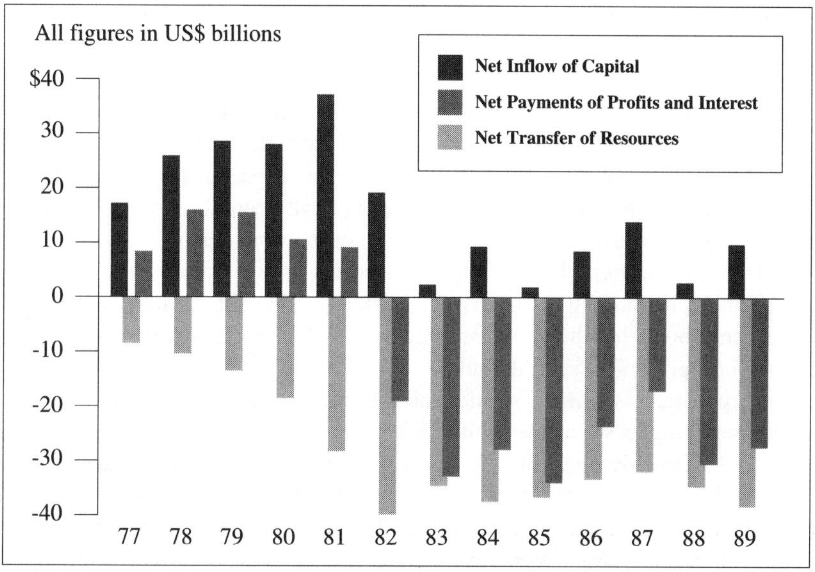

All figures in US$ billions

Net Inflow of Capital
Net Payments of Profits and Interest
Net Transfer of Resources

Source: ECLAC, on the basis of data from the IMF

famine conditions in graphic human terms for a wide audience. Some modest debt forgiveness for official debts has been provided by Governments recognizing that there are limits to the debtors' endurance—and that the debts will not, in any case, be serviced. But by and large, debt relief has been provided only to the degree deemed sufficient to keep the debtors "in the game."

Those who believe that this is an inadequate response point not only to the injustice of the prevailing process but, as importantly, to its implications for the global community in terms of the fragility and unsustainability indicated by the *dynamics* of the situation: the *continuing* growth of the debt that developing countries have to carry, the *continuing* high percentage of their export earnings that must be devoted to servicing their debts, and the continuing misery of hundreds of millions of people in the third world.

THE GROWING UNITED STATES FOREIGN DEBT: THE "SECOND DEBT CRISIS"

There are many who believe that even if present trends were to lead to a series of massive defaults by major debtor countries, the global financial system would be shaken but not felled. The main reason for this optimistic view is simply that since 1982 the creditors have been able to build up their reserves against such an eventuality. While the commercial banks have indeed used the time to strengthen their financial condition, the optimism would seem to be more in the nature of wishful thinking rather than a hard-headed assessment about the ability of the creditor community to weather a financial storm brought on by such defaults.

A realistic assessment would find the present global financial condition extremely fragile when the United States has been transformed in the span of less than one decade from the world's largest creditor nation to the world's largest debtor nation. If this were not enough, the United States banking and corporate sectors have been enfeebled by the excesses of the 1980s credit binge in lending for speculative real estate developments and junk bond financing for mergers and acquisitions. The two developments are symptomatic of a decade-long binge during which the United States paid for every $3 of imports with $2 of exports and $1 of IOUs.

The deterioration of the United States economic/financial condition has thus been aptly characterized as "the second global debt crisis." As early as 1985, referring to the large and growing foreign debt of the United States and to the related United States budget deficits, commentators began to talk not only of the second debt crisis but, as well, of "the triple debt crisis."[6] While third world debt stood at more than $1,300 billion at the outset of the 1990s the net foreign debt of the United States reached $675 billion. This was five times larger than Brazil's, the most indebted of the third world debtor nations, and larger than the combined debts of the group of 15 developing countries labelled "problem debtors." At present rates of increase, the United States foreign debt will reach $1 trillion by the end of 1992 and by 1995 will exceed the combined foreign debt of all third world countries.

This debtor status is further entrenched by the related development of foreigners owning more assets in the United States than the United States holds abroad. The continuing trade surpluses of Japan, Germany and other countries and the continuing United States trade deficits will assure a long-lasting transformation in international economic-financial relations, especially as Japan (with net foreign assets of over $300 billion as of 1991) and Germany (with $254 billion) and other countries enjoying mounting trade surpluses continue to buy up United States companies and real estate and establish plants in the United States.

A "debt explosion" phenomenon in the United States underlies these troubling trends. The other side of the debt coin, so to speak, is the decline in United States savings rates. During the 1980s, it fell from 7 per cent to 3 per cent. Part of the explanation for these trends of low savings and high household debt can be attributed to the increase in the real value of household assets, principally homes, which increased by over 37 per cent in real terms over the 1980s. This discouraged savings out of current income (less need to save for old age) and encouraged borrowing against the increased property values. The same phenomenon has been taking place in other industrialized countries. In Japan, the household effect is estimated to account for 3 per cent of the drop in the savings/GNP ratio. Indebtedness of business and government was also increasing at a rate that far exceeds the increase in their incomes. Counting household, business and governmental debts, Americans are now in debt to the tune of over $13 trillion, an amount that is about 2.5 times the United States GNP. This is a ratio not reached since the 1930s, the years of the Great Depression, when the United States economy was shrinking and when more than one of three Americans were unemployed.

Recession fears and the bursting of the junk bond bubble have slowed the credit binge dramatically. The 1990 drop of 8 per cent in the real valuation of the wealth of American households has reduced spending and raised savings, with a depressing effect on the economy, accentuating the speed and depth of the recession. Yet private credit has continued to rise at a 6 per cent rate, a rate that is still several times higher than the rate of increase of the country's GNP, which is forecast to be about 0.9 per cent in 1990 and 0.1 per cent in 1991. It seems that the "culture of credit" is very deep-seated and continues to be fostered and rationalized as a necessary condition to sustain the economy's momentum at rates that can provide sufficiently high levels of employment and avoid a lengthy and deep recession akin to the Great Depression of the 1930s.

As is evident from an examination of Figure 10, the United States rate of savings fell from 7 per cent of disposable income in 1980 to just over 3 per cent in 1987 and has remained at that low level. The likelihood of a substantial increase in the United States savings rate and a commensurate decrease in their consumption, and in the importation of capital that this spending and the growing budget deficit engenders, is not promising simply because deliberate policy initiatives to achieve this outcome would strengthen

Figure 10: *US Saving Rates as Percentage of Disposal Income, 1980-87*

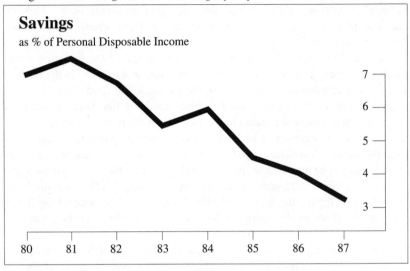

Source: Department of Commerce

the recessionary factors. As importantly, it is not likely because this pattern is deeply rooted in the prevailing cultural and political institutions. As Peter Passell noted in reviewing a study by Frank Levy and Richard Michel, The Economic Future of *American Families*,

> "no one really knows how to persuade Americans to save more or study harder. . . . (when) exhortations to fiscal virtue are not likely to work on a generation that still sneers about Gerry Ford's WIN button, Jimmy Carter's appeals to turn down the thermostats and Ronald Reagan's promise to raise revenue by cutting taxes."[7]

Turning this savings trend around is a herculean task.

The scope of the requisite measures would entail, therefore, systemic changes large enough to have an appreciable impact upon productivity rates and related consumption and investment patterns. The difficulty in making this change is evident when one identifies the trends that need to be reversed:

- during this period, when savings rates as a percentage of disposable income were declining, personal consumer spending per head was rising by over 3 per cent per year;

- during these years, credit card debt more than tripled, rising from $50 billion to $180 billion which represented 5 per cent of their user's income; consumer instalment credit doubled from $300 billion to over $600 billion—and all this while the per capita national output rose by barely more than 1 per cent.

By the end of the 1980s, through successive budget deficits, the government debt reached $2,900 billion and corporate and household debt reached $2,100 billion. During those years the debt of non-farm businesses in the United States increased from 45 to over 60 per cent of the country's GNP, raising the average cost of interest on corporate debt to a level almost double that of the 1970s and over three times higher than in the 1950s and 1960s.

In part this perilous situation can be attributed to the reduction of United States exports to debtor third world countries that once absorbed over 40 per cent of their exports. Those countries are now forced to drastically cutback on their imports as a means of coping with the servicing of their own debts, thereby reversing a trend that between 1973 and 1983 saw United States exports to these countries rise sixfold, providing one job in every six in United States industry.

Thus this shift from trade surplus to trade deficit is symptomatic of a profound, that is, systemic change that goes beyond the mere numbers. The most telling indication of the profound nature of this change is the fact that the adverse trade balance, for the first time in 30 years, now includes investment income in the trade deficit category. The United States has long had a deficit in its merchandise trade account. Until 1981, it was more than compensated by a surplus in the "services" trade category that incorporates the flow of investment earnings. Only in 1988 did the net earnings on overseas investments become negative and augmented rather than offset the merchandise trade deficit, thereby exacerbating the adverse trade balance. At the beginning of the 1980s, at about the time of the onset of the third world debt crisis, the United States had a net investment income of more than $30 billion from *net* foreign assets of about $150 billion. This has now been reversed: the inflow from these investments has been overtaken by the outflow. The trade deficit, which totaled only about $20 billion over the decade of the 1970s, exploded by 1987 into a deficit of more than $150 billion, an increase of 750 per cent.

The trade deficit declined to $137 billion in 1988 and to $92 billion in 1989, a change of direction that has been hailed by some as a turnaround reflecting an improvement in the competitive position of the United States in the global economy. A more realistic assessment of the trends would see this "improvement" as an exceptional occurrence.[8] The basis for the assessment of continuing historically high trade deficits as a longer-term phenomenon is simply that the gains made in reducing it from the astronomical heights do not appear to be sustainable.

This pessimistic view is based on a basic underlying trend that has characterized the United States economy for the past few decades, namely, the decline in the rate of productivity, a decline deeply-rooted in the savings, investing and consumption patterns. Productivity of the United States economy over the last century has averaged a rate of growth of about 2 per cent but fell to 1.3 per cent in the first half of the 1980s.[9] Table 7 indicates the trend in United States productivity rates over a span of 40 years. It should be noted that the performance of the United States manufacturing sector has been ''respectable'' as compared to the other industrialized countries it competes with—as shown in Table 9 and Figure 11. However, the manufacturing sector now contributes only about one fifth of the GNP, hardly enough to lift the average rate of growth of the nation's productivity. The United States GNP rate of increase is forecast at 0.9 per cent rate of growth in 1990 and 0.2 per cent in 1991.

Tracing the causes of this relatively poor performance leads us to an examination of the consumption/savings and investment factors. The nub of the problem is the low United States saving rate and the use of a great part of its savings for current consumption and ''unproductive investments,'' such as those for speculative financial wheeling-and-dealing and for military purposes. The factors underlying these trends are difficult to slow down and reverse, especially as a large part of this decline in productivity can be attributed to the changing structure of the American economy in which the more highly-productive manufacturing sector is contributing less and less as a percentage of the nation's output and employment.

This underlying low productivity factor is reflected in the trade deficit that has cumulatively brought the United States to the position where foreigners own more of America than Americans own abroad.[10] To keep the United

Table 7: United States annual productivity growth, 1947-1986 (percentage)

1947-1955	1955-1968	1968-1973	1973-1980	1980-1986
2.9	2.5	1.5	0.4	1.1

Source; United States. Economic Report of the President. 1987, table B-43.

Table 8: Changes in manufacturing productivity in the United States and its major competitors
(average annual percentage change)

		United States	Japan	Canada	France	Federal Republic of Germany	United Kingdom
	1981	2.2	3.7	4.8	3.1	2.2	5.1
	1982	2.2	6.1	−4.5	7.0	1.4	6.1
	1983	5.8	5.4	7.2	2.6	5.9	8.5
	1984	5.4	7.2	10.8	3.0	3.8	5.5
	1985	5.2	5.6	2.5	3.1	3.9	3.6
	1986	3.7	1.7	−0.3	2.4	1.7	2.8
	1987	2.8	4.1	1.8	3.7	1.3	6.9
Average.	1961-70	3.0	17.9	4.9	9.1	7.7	4.4
Average.	1971-75	3.0	7.1	3.4	5.4	5.3	3.6
Average.	1976-80	1.8	7.1	2.2	4.6	3.9	1.4
Average.	1981-87	3.9	4.8	3.2	3.6	2.9	5.5

Source: United States. Bureau of Labor Statistics. *Current Labor Statistics. Monthly Labor Review.* August 1988

States economy growing, it must rely on the inflow of capital from abroad or the savings of foreigners that are willing to purchase United States equities and Treasury bonds and the like. This dependence on the inflow of foreign capital has necessitated, in turn, the maintenance of a wide differential between interest rates in the United States and in the countries from which the capital has been coming. As that differential narrows—as it has since 1989 when both Japan and Germany began to raise their interest rates—the inflow has decreased: the inflow of foreign investment in long-term assets fell from $142 billion in 1989 to $40 billion in 1990. During this same period, there was an increase in United States investment abroad, so there was a net outflow of long-term capital of $22 billion. The implications of this shift are painfully evident in many sectors of the United States economy, particularly in the banking and corporate sectors with their high failure rates.

The weakened condition of the United States banking system

The troubled state of the United States banking and corporate sectors is also a key symptom of the debt malaise. There is the scandalous crisis of the savings and loans, the savings "thrifts" and non-financial companies in the banking or near-banking business. They require a rescue operation estimated

Figure 11: *U.S. Annual Productivity Growth (Decline) 1988-1990*

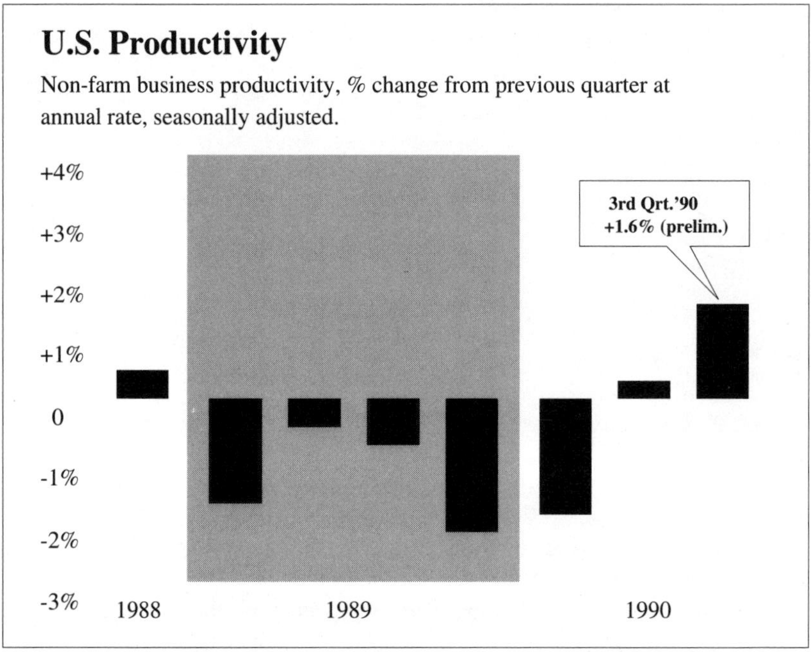
U.S. Productivity
Non-farm business productivity, % change from previous quarter at annual rate, seasonally adjusted.
+4%
+3%
+2%
+1%
0
-1%
-2%
-3%
1988
1989
1990
3rd Qrt.'90
+1.6% (prelim.)

Source: US Department of Labor

to cost about $500 million each year over 30 years. The banks are reputed to be in a healthier state: the largest 50 bank holding companies in the United States are estimated to have $110 billion in capital and $40 billion in reserves to cover $58 billion of "problem assets." Yet, as the 1990s begin, there are about 1000 banks on the "danger list" of the Federal Deposit Insurance Corporation (FDIC), a situation calling for bailouts amounting to $4 billion in 1991 and $5 billion in 1992, or $1 billion more than the FDIC has available unless and until there is an infusion of new capital either by the Government or by the banks themselves. They have unveiled a plan to go deeper into debt by establishing a fund to borrow $10 billion for that FDIC replenishment to be repaid over 20 years through a special assessment.

The list of "troubled" banks includes 134 banks. Forty of the 100 largest United States banks have lent the equivalent of more than 100 per cent of their equity for projects in a commercial real estate market that has gone into rapid decline. The 10,000-odd banks are estimated to have over $750 billion of "rubbish" on their books: real estate loans accounted for about 40 per cent of their lending in 1989, the year before the market began to drop, and the adjusted reserves of five of the largest banks are less than 16 per cent of their "risk assets."

It is thus hardly surprising that some of the largest United States banks have been downgraded in terms of credit rating, including Citicorp, the largest United States bank. Citicorp is considered by some to be the most under-capitalized, with $8.6 billion in equity capital and almost $10 billion in non-performing assets, against which it has set aside only a 33 per cent reserve, one of the lowest ratios among major banks that have a large amount of third world debt on their books. The general picture, therefore, is one where the financial claims of a significant proportion of the banking system far exceed the value of their underlying assets.

In trouble themselves, bankers are inclined to cancel credit lines to customers and to cut back on lending. The financial situation of the United States corporate sector more than justifies this cautious approach: United States corporations are now devoting about 60 per cent of their earnings just to pay interest on their debts, a proportion that is about double that of "normal times;" as a percentage of the total number of firms in business, failures are twice as numerous and as a percentage of the GNP, twice as costly as those during the 1981-1982 recession. This high rate of failure has, in turn, further worsened the financial plight of the banking sector that has already been weakened in the process of weathering the third world debt crisis, as is indicated by Table 9 which shows some of the write-offs of those debts that many of the major banks have had to make.

Table 9: Exposure and reserves for LDC debts of major United States banks
(in millions of United States dollars)

	Total foreign exposures	Total LDC reserves	Coverage of total exposures	Second quarter write-offs
Citibank	$10,471	$2,400	22.9%	$631
Bank of America	$5,400	$1,700	31.5%	$438
Chase Manhattan	$4,600	$1,730	37.6%	$546
J.P. Morgan	$2,800	$1,736	62.0%	$197
Chemical	$3,837	$1,187	30.9%	$268
Manufacturers Hanover	$5,500 (a)	$1,481	n.a.	$450
Bankers Trust	$2,640	$1,900	72.0%	$82

(a) Data represents estimates.

Source: Thompson *Bank*watch

There is another troubling development that worsens the United States banker's plight, namely, the fragility of the banking system in other countries because banking today is highly integrated. Japanese banks have over one third of the exposure of the global banking system. Thus any serious weakening of Japanese banks transmits an additional strain on the global banking system and on the economies affected by them. Japanese banks have not been immune to the adverse impact of third world difficulties in servicing their debts, but Japanese banks could take this in stride when their capital/lending ratios were flexible. Times have changed rapidly. The Bank for International Settlements has demanded stricter capital-adequacy ratios (8 per cent minimum capital-to-risk ratio by March 1993), and this comes at a time when the banks are being shaken by having highly-leveraged loans collateralized by real estate and stocks that are plummeting in value. The retrenchment in process will hit the United States economy hard and the United States financial system in particular.

The United States economy and its banking system are fragile, like the performer doing a high-wire act who counts on still winds. The danger lies in the fact that by virtue of United States indebtedness United States policymakers have little room to manoeuvre. Thus constrained, they cannot exercise the leadership that is called for, namely, radical changes tantamount to structural adjustment of the international system. They must first start with putting their own house in order.

The debt status of both the third world and of the United States is a reflection of massive global imbalances in trade and capital flows that have occurred and, *more significantly*, continue to persist. A realistic appreciation of the international debt crisis requires that the debts of both parties be viewed in their scope and dynamic as one big global crisis, with the element of debt symptomatic of a *systemic* malaise. When to this worrisome situation the environmental factor is introduced, the scope of the analysis and of the remedies must be broadened even wider. Lester Brown, President of the Washington-based Worldwatch Institute, has written in *State of the World 1990* that "if the world does not seize the opportunities offered by the promise of change, the continuing environmental degradation of the planet will eventually lead to economic decline." And by the same token, economic decline will eventually lead to continuing environmental degradation of the planet. The circle is vicious; the challenge is to make it virtuous.

CHAPTER 2

THE ENVIRONMENTAL CRISIS

Global environmental degradation aroused deeply-felt concern long before the debt crisis forced its way onto centre stage. For many years the "environmental issue" took many forms, none considered global in scope or characterized as being of a "crisis" nature. In any case, the politicians who were reluctant to take action could find solace in the historical record revealing that the phenomenon of "environmental consciousness" has had sporadically intense but short-lived popular support. In the early twentieth century in the United States this concern for the environment sparked and briefly sustained a politically powerful conservation movement. It campaigned against public alienation of vast tracts of forest and other public lands to rapacious commercial "lumber barons" and their cohorts seeking to preserve large regions as "conservancies", nature reserves and public parklands. However, with some important but limited successes to its credit, the movement soon flagged and lay virtually dormant for decades, though an underlying "wilderness culture" never seems to have died, in part thanks to the cultural legacy of writers such as Rousseau, Thoreau, London and others.

Beginning in the early 1950s, the popularity of the environmental cause once again came alive and this time took on a vastly expanded dimension in both its nature and its scope. This upsurge in popular concern and support for "the environmental cause" can be attributed in part to the media with its print and visual reportage of environmental horror stories involving large-scale accidents. Giant oil tanker spills and sudden tragic nuclear and poison gas emissions have made household names of the Torrey Canyon and the Exxon Valdez and of Three Mile Island, Chernobyl and Bhopal. In larger part this rising awareness is a response to the related fact that scientific understanding is revealing more and more about the global scope and dangers of environmental problems that are now understood to be cumulative and thus growing more serious.

The disturbing implications apply particularly to the phenomenon of ozone

35

layer depletion and "radiative trapping" or the "greenhouse effect" as a consequence of the increasing levels of emission of chlorofluorocarbons (CFCs) and carbon dioxide (CO_2) and other gases. All are believed to threaten significant climate change with consequences that might be injurious: raising sea levels, reducing water availability and soil moisture, and disturbing natural ecosystems. The greenhouse effect is attributable in large part to the man-made increase in carbon emission levels, most of which originates with the burning of fossil fuels, particularly coal and oil and, to a somewhat lesser extent, natural gas and deforestation.[1] There is, thus, a close and complex relationship between environment, energy and development that poses difficulties for policy-making at both the national and the international level of governance.

THE BUILD-UP TO THE LOOMING ENVIRONMENTAL CRISIS

Almost everyone, it seems, has now lined up on the side of "sustainable development" and against pollution, deforestation, global warming, ozone depletion, loss of biodiversity in flora and fauna and the like. The sentiment is reminiscent of the popular support in the United States in the early part of the century for the conservation movement which elicited enough enthusiasm and political pressure to prompt President Teddy Roosevelt to exclaim in exasperation, "everyone is for conservation, no matter what it means." The exasperation expressed by President Roosevelt probably reflected his sense of the limitations of his power to act as he felt he should on an issue where "the right thing" to do was quite clear. Establishing national parks and wilderness areas was within the purview of his nation-bound mandate and in terms of implementation, rather straight-forward. This cannot be said, however, about the task facing policy makers today with respect to changing the energy/development relationship to achieve environmental objectives.

The problem is global in many of its dimensions—as with radiative trapping or the greenhouse effect and with ozone depletion. These environmental issues pose an exceedingly complex challenge. Implementation calls for far-reaching measures to slow down and then reverse both the global historic trend of increasing energy use per capita and of population growth. The dimensions and dynamic of the trend are closely related to population and economic growth, and especially to the nature of such growth with indus-trialization and its production and transport attributes. As a perusal of Table 10 reveals, the trends over the last century indicate that there has been a four-fold increase in total energy use during the last four decades and almost a 14-fold increase over the last century.[2]

Historical trends are not easily reversible under the best of circumstances. They are especially difficult even to slow down when so many of the global community live in absolute or near poverty and aspire to higher living stan-dards, with what this implies with respect to increasing energy use and in-creasing carbon emissions. This dilemma has given rise to *academic* consideration of draconian measures that would slow or stop global growth *as a matter of deliberate policy.* Needless to say, such a policy would meet with fierce resistance in both the richer industrialized countries and the poorer developing countries. From a global perspective a difficulty arises simply from the fact that their resistance has different sources and takes different forms.

In the case of the industrialized countries, the phenomenon of ''growth-mania'' is a key cultural/political attribute of all the prevailing economic systems. A foretaste of the reaction to the prospect of a slow growth or a no-growth future is provided by the heated controversies of the early 1970s on the theme of ''a zero-growth society.''[3] There have been many approaches put forward to address this problem. All of them suggest that we can have both more growth and more or rather sufficient energy if energy is used

Table 10: Growth in income and energy use, 1890–1990

	1890	1950	1990
World population (billions)	1.49	2.51	5.32
Industrial energy use, p.c. (Kw)	0.32	1.03	2.30
World energy use (terawatts)	1.00	3.26	13.73
Cumulative industrial energy use since 1850 (terawatt-years)	10	97	393

Source: John Holdren, *"Energy in transition." Scientific American Special Issue: Energy for Planet Earth, September 1990. p. 160.* A terawatt is equal to a billion tons of coal or 5 billion barrels of oil per year. The data were compiled by Professor Holdren.

differently and in different forms and therefore derived from different sources. Amory Lovins and others have been tireless in pointing the way to "the soft energy path" that is technologically possible. The tough nut to crack is the social engineering to achieve that difference or to make the changes necessary to bring the available/desirable energy-producing and energy-using technologies into wide use. This is a task that involves radical changes in energy-related systems of production, transport and living patterns.

Past experience indicates the difficulty of changing the fossil energy-GNP ratio. As we know now, despite the oil shock of the 1970s that raised fossil fuel prices 10-fold, the days of "oil as king" are by no means numbered. The market-cum-regulatory/financial approach has fallen far short of achieving the desired shift in the global energy mix, and of doing so in a "reasonable" time. Reliance on the price elasticity of demand for oil and other conventional forms of energy to dampen their consumption has been effective only in the short term and in a limited way. When viewed over a longer term and in relation to the minimum target that environmental considerations call for, the verdict is a failing grade: the demand for fossil fuels has continued to grow in absolute terms. And even more importantly, since the mid-1980s the fossil fuel consumption-GNP ratio has ceased to improve significantly.

These trends are clearly evident from a perusal of the latest Worldwatch Institute's annual report, *State of the World 1990*. It reveals that the 1973 and 1979 oil shocks had a strong impact initially, but the effect was relatively short-lived. From 1950 to 1973 the average annual global rate of increase in carbon emissions was "a remarkably steady 4.7 per cent." Then for a decade from 1973 to 1983 that average rate fell to 1 per cent, with improved energy efficiency accounting for about a third of this drop; however, since 1983 the annual average growth rate has shot up to 2.8 per cent, with 1988 showing the highest annual rate of increase, 3.7 per cent.[4] Thus, despite the favourable trend of a fall in the ratio of carbon emissions per unit of GNP, the net effect has been a doubling of the volume of carbon emissions over the last quarter century.

Evidently prevailing policies are not working to achieve the desired environmental effect, particularly in the United States where the reliance on the market has been strongest and where regulations are the weakest among the industrialized countries. This outcome should not be surprising. History reveals that major shifts in the global energy mix have taken a long time to achieve. *A priori* reasoning indicates that this is so because the changes in the energy mix are both a causal factor and an indicator of structural change in the economies that use the energy. This is evident from a review of the past patterns of movement from peak use of coal to peak use of oil, a shift that took over three generations and was concurrent with a major transformation of the global economy.

In the case of the developing countries, the hunger for the tantalizing fruits of growth—and of energy—is palpable. This group of countries has over three quarters of the world's population but only about one fifth of the world's electric supply. Their demand is projected to grow to about a third of global demand by the year 2000, implying that they will account for about 60 per cent of the increased global demand. With the electric power demand expected to grow by as much as 7 per cent per year and with each kilowatt of capacity costing at least $2000, the developing countries will need about $125 billion per year. This would more than double the present rate of investment that these countries would have to allocate to expanding their electric power supply.[5] There will be, admittedly, a severe constraint on the demand side in light of the difficulty in obtaining the requisite amount of capital to build new power plants or expand existing ones, but even the most financially constrained programme has profound implications with regard to the increase in the use of fossil fuels as these countries pursue a programme of energy development as a precondition for industrializing and for providing the amenities of convenient electrical energy for heating and cooking.

The heavy reliance on fossil fuels will not be substantially reduced even when these countries shift the emphasis of their energy policy away from building new capacity—a shift forced on them by their inability to borrow enough—to investing in measures to achieve greater energy efficiency which, in any case, shows a very much higher return. The third world is replete with case histories where generating costs could be cut substantially by small investments to improve power plant efficiency by measures such as fitting capacitors to power cable to reduce transmission losses, installing variable speed controls on electric motors, improving load management and designing for co-generation.[6]

At best, given their stage of development with its emphasis on expanding their energy-consuming industrial sector, the 1.4 per cent of electricity needed to expand GDP by 1 per cent may be reduced to 0.9 per cent by the year 2010. If this increase is achieved with a greater reliance on hydropower generation, there also might be a more favourable environmental impact as this would slow the rate of increase of dependence on fossil fuels in these countries. But given their developmental objectives and their limited capacity to buy and adapt more energy-efficient and environmentally-benign technologies, and the consequent substantial increase in their demand for all forms of energy, it would not be prudent to count on a significant environmental bonus from this quarter.

China provides an example. With its exceptionally heavy reliance on coal, and coal of a type and a quality that is especially environmentally damaging, the global warming impact from that country alone could more than counterbalance the carbon emission reduction from the energy-efficiency and energy-switching efforts promoted by energy/environmental programmes in much of the rest of the world. *The ability of countries such as China to make this switch is limited* by the host of factors that contribute to the institutional rigidities so closely associated with poverty and underdevelopment. The constraints facing such countries stem not only from the limited pool of skilled experienced professionals and workers in this field, but from the limited capital available as well. This is particularly so when such countries are at a capital-intensive phase of development and are, at the same time, under intense pressure to service their foreign debts, exacerbating their difficulties in diverting scarce capital for achieving an environmental objective that at best will pay off only in the longer term.

Some progress has been made in slowing environmental degradation in its myriad forms and innumerable sources; but, with few exceptions, both the legislative record and the committed resources have fallen far short of what might have been expected in light of the public's avowed concern about the seriousness of the environmental *problematique* as a life-threatening issue of global proportions.

THE ELUSIVE CONCEPT OF "SUSTAINABILITY"

Part of the explanation lies in the operational vacuity of the banners under which the environmental movement marches, such as the seeming oxymoron, "sustainable development," and the questionable slogan, "small is beautiful." Seeking to enlist or at least not antagonize those who aspire to a better life in terms of higher incomes and all that goes with it, the message is not only that there is not, nor need there be, a conflict between the maintenance of environmental quality and economic growth, but rather that they are mutually reinforcing.[7]

This faith in a "sustainable development" approach is credible only on the daunting assumption that new patterns of growth can be attained. The challenge then revolves around the definition or specifications of "newness" and what this would imply in terms of the nature and degree of change:

- On the one side, there are many who believe that only modest institutional changes are needed, that is, that the existing economic systems

need only minor modification in the form of special regulatory constraints and incentive systems to force or cajole decision makers to
"do the right things" environmentally;

- On the other side, there are those who suggest that concern for the
  long-term calls for a development process radically different in terms
  of the volume and the forms of energy that are an integral part of the
  conventional development or growth process, and that this, in turn,
  calls for radically different institutions or a substantially different economic system in terms of who make the key investment decisions and
  by what criteria.

The first school of thought would largely rely on "market forces," albeit
modified by taxes and subsidies that would "internalize" the relevant "externalities" and by the imposition of a regulatory framework. As we shall
see when discussing the "market approach" in Chapter 8, this approach has
its limitations. But it might suffice to note that these limitations are central
to the position taken by those in the second group who are skeptical about
the efficacy—as well as the equity—of a market-driven environmental policy
within the present institutional system. Their doubts are based on the conviction that this approach will not suffice if the economic/financial system
operates with its overwhelming reliance on "business" decisions driven by
"the bottom line" measured at short-term annual intervals and in financial
rather than socio/economic terms. The present system of private decision-
making is simply not capable of factoring into its calculus those conceptual
costs and benefits that cannot be counted in any investor's cash register and
call for "shadow pricing."[8] How does a businessman count societal benefits
when damages are avoided, say by flood prevention measures or preservation
of aesthetic beauty or serenity? The institutional implications of this fact are
profound at the level of national and international decision-making. There are
many obstacles to giving environment its due weight in the scheme of things.
These are discussed in Chapter 6, but only after considering, in Part II (Chapters 3 to 5), the necessary conditions for resolving or substantially easing
both the debt and the environmental crises.

PART TWO

THE NECESSARY
CONDITIONS
FOR RESOLVING
THE TWO CRISES

"If the late 1980s was a period of impressive public speech about the global environment, the 1990s will test whether political leaders around the world are prepared to move beyond words to action. . . . Here, on the cusp of the 1990s, we must launch in earnest a decade of action against world poverty and environmental degradation."

—*Gus Speth, President of the World Resources Institute*[3]

CHAPTER 3

THE KEY FACTORS: CREATING CONGENIAL INTERNATIONAL CONDITIONS

THE DEBT FACET OF THE GLOBAL CRISIS

Over the last few years the focus of concern has been the danger of breakdown of the financial/economic system precipitated by massive defaults of the third world debtors. Thus the proposals for easing or removing the likelihood of such a cataclysmic *denouement* of the debt crisis have largely been based on various assumptions as to the minimal necessary conditions for achieving this limited objective. To assess the desirability as well as the feasibility of the proposals in terms of the limited objective of breakdown-avoidance, their proponents have had to construct models. These models contain a host of assumptions about the relationships between myriad factors such as the rates of growth of the industrialized countries and of the developing countries, the form and pace of structural changes in these economies, the changing volume and patterns of international trade and capital flows in the form of lending/borrowing, investment and official development assistance (ODA).[1] Few have striven for determining the minimal conditions sufficient for the resolution of the crisis in both avoiding such a breakdown and achieving a state of affairs where there is not only continuing improvement in the social and economic welfare of all of humankind in employment and income but also greater equity, and all this within the constraints of maintaining environmental quality. After all, the first order of business is to avoid breakdown and return to a normal state of affairs where the debtors can achieve "creditworthiness." But even in terms of this self-imposed constraint, an examination of the most widely respected of these modeling exercises should give cause for worry.

This assessment is evident from a consideration of five key conditions that have been identified as necessary for the sustained servicing of third world debts:

1. a *rate of growth* of the major industrialized countries of between 3 per cent and 4 per cent, accompanied by a diminution of *trade barriers*, or at least no increase in these barriers;

2. a recovery of the *prices of the primary commodities* that are the mainstay exports of the debtor developing countries—and a concurrent improvement in their *terms of trade*;

3. a lowering of the level of *real interest rates* to its historic range of between 1 and 2 per cent;

4. a reversal of the present direction of capital flows and a significant increase in the *flow of new funds to* the debtor countries.

In addition, as a fifth necessary condition we should add that each of the recipient countries "get their house in order." This calls for policies and institutional changes to address issues such as rapid population growth, corruption, inadequate technical and managerial standards of competence, extreme income disparities and "unrealistic" official rates of exchange. If we focus on the first four it is simply because these pertain to the creation of an international milieu that is congenial for all to grow and prosper. Without that milieu only a few of those developing nations that do "the right thing" in terms of national policies can make the transition from debtor to creditworthy nation.

Each of these key assumptions underlying the modelling exercises need to be examined to illuminate the difficulties on the path ahead and to assess the probabilities of achieving the desired objectives.

THE GROWTH/TRADE NEXUS AND THE ROLE OF PROTECTIONISM

Current modelling exercises differ quite widely with regard to the weighted average rate of growth in the industrialized countries required to enable the debtor nations to raise their foreign exchange earnings to both service their debts and to attain minimally "acceptable" (politically sustainable) annual rates of growth, say 2 per cent per capita. These estimates range from 2.5 to 4 per cent, which implies—since the United States has normally absorbed about 70 per cent of third world exports and almost 90 per cent of Latin America's—a United States growth rate of about 5 per cent, or about twice the United States' historical rate of productivity growth.

Despite an exceptional performance in 1988 that attained a 4 per cent increase in the GNP of the industrialized countries and a 9 per cent increase in the volume of world trade, the overall *average* growth rate in the industrialized countries over the last five years has been far short of that minimum. Nor is the outlook bright for bettering that target rate in light of the dismal performance of the United States economy of less than 1 per cent in 1990. As Table 11 shows, the World Bank's forecast of the annual average growth in the high-income OECD countries for the first half of the 1990s is in the range of 2.4 to 2.6 per cent, a projection roughly in line with those of the OECD, the IMF and other institutions.[2] Subsequent developments have given grounds for a more pessimistic forecast of less than 1.8 per cent for the OECD countries in 1991 and 1.5 to 2 per cent for the medium-term.[3]

The implications of the possible range of forecasts are especially dire for the third world debtors. The prospects for the expansion of markets for their

Table 11: GDP growth and interest rates for high income and other countries—
with high growth and low scenarios

Country group	1980 GDP (billions of dollars)	Average annual growth of GDP (percentage)					
		1965-73	1973-80	1980-86	1987	1988	1989
Low-income economies	784	6.0	4.6	6.1	6.1	8.9	4.3
Middle-income economies	1,622	6.9	4.9	2.5	3.5	3.0	2.8
Sub-Saharan Africa	213	5.9	2.7	0.3	−1.1	2.5	3.5
Latin America and the Caribbean	716	6.5	5.1	0.9	3.0	1.2	1.5
Severely indebted middle-income economies	791	5.4	5.2	1.0	2.5	1.8	1.4
High-income economies	7,914	4.6	3.0	2.5	3.4	4.3	3.6

High-income economies	Trend for 1965–87	Recent experience 1980–88	Scenario for 1988-95	
			Adjustment with growth	Low
Inflation (local currency)	6.4	5.6	4.2	4.1
Nominal rate of interest (a)	8.8	10.2	6.6	4.5
Real rate of interest (a) (b)	3.0	5.5	3.0	4.0

(a) Average six-month rate on Eurodollar deposits
(b) Nominal interest rate deflated by the GDP deflator for the United States

Sources: The World Bank *World Development Report 1989.*
          The World Bank *World Development Report 1990.*

exports, and thus of their foreign exchange earnings, are dismal enough without being compounded by the growing likelihood that capital will be diverted for the Gulf War aftermath and for the reconstruction programme for the region and for Eastern Europe. To compound the problems, the markets of the industrialized countries are likely to be harder to penetrate because of recession-induced protectionist pressures so that tariff and non-tariff barriers in the industrialized creditor nations will likely rise, or, at best, not improve in the near to medium-term. Disguised as "fairer trade" and trade under "voluntary export restraints" (VERs), for the last decade there has been an appreciable rise in the percentage of trade affected by non-tariff barriers. This trend has made it more and more difficult for third world exporters to expand their sales in United States and European markets. Over the last decade the trade affected by VERs has almost doubled. About 21 per cent of the manufactured exports from third world countries to the United States and the European Economic Community face such non-tariff barriers as compared to 14 per cent of such exports from other industrial countries.

In these industrialized countries, including Japan, one of the barriers takes the form of subsidy programmes for their domestic producers. This applies to sugar, dairy products, rice and other primary commodities that are in direct competition with third world exports. These subsidies to farmers in the industrialized countries of the OECD amount annually to over $300 billion.[4] It is estimated that liberalizing the trade in farm products world wide by the elimination of such subsidies and related tariffs would result in an expansion of global trade by as much as $100 billion, of which the third world would be, of course, one of the beneficiaries.

The protectionist measures, together with VERs and other forms of non-tariff barriers, have had the effect of constraining about one third of the developing countries' agricultural exports and about one fifth of their manufactured goods in seeking to gain entry to the United States market alone.

Nor are the trends propitious. Since 1981, through quotas on sugar and other commodities and increased anti-dumping actions against imports from these countries, the United States has increased its non-tariff barriers from less than 1 per cent of imports from the highly-indebted third world countries to more than 4 per cent. Over these years the European Economic Community and Japan have hardly been more receptive to third world imports. The result is that, whereas 20 years ago about 30 per cent of food imports had to contend with these barriers, the percentage has more than tripled to 90 per cent.[5] Since the pressure to make these barriers even higher has not abated under more favourable conditions, the slowing of growth in the industrialized countries will not be conducive to a reversal of this trend.

Despite their rhetoric espousing "free trade," politicians have continued to be receptive to the protectionist appeals of their constituents—as Table 12 demonstrates in providing a capsule picture of these trade barriers and their rise from 1965 to 1986.

The impact of these trade barriers, according to some estimates, has been to reduce the annual output of the developing countries by as much as 3 per cent. The ironic aspect is that this is roughly equivalent to 0.6 per cent of the collective GNP of the industrialized countries, or twice the value of official development aid (ODA). Former World Bank President, Barber Conable, aptly observed that such policies and practices are a ''poor trade indeed (when) developed countries are taking away with one hand twice what they are giving with the other.''

Although there has been a 9 per cent increase in the annual volume of global trade since 1983, third world countries have hardly benefited commensurately since their percentage of this total global trade has slipped badly. Latin America's share fell from well over 12 per cent in 1950 to less than 5 per cent today, and the non-oil exporting developing countries, as a group, have managed since 1983 to achieve an increase that is only about one third their prior annual average rate. Thus very few of the debtor countries have been able to rise on the figurative trade tide that is supposed to float all boats, and few of the heavily indebted countries can count on this happening in the near future. The failure of the GATT negotiations under the Uruguay Round has provided a confirmation of that dismal prospect.

Table 12: Percentage of major imports facing non-tariff barriers in selected countries, 1965-1986

	Food		Manufactures		Agricultural raw materials		All commodities	
	1965	1986	1965	1986	1965	1986	1965	1986
All countries	36%	89%	5%	51%	2%	51%	17%	54%
EEC (total)	38	96	2	56	2	51	15	58
Belgium-Luxembourg	40	96	35	58	3	49	19	61
Denmark	45	96	1	52	3	43	11	54
France	46	98	3	64	6	55	17	66
Federal Republic of Germany	46	96	4	58	3	50	16	60
Greece	na	94	na	48	na	36	na	49
Ireland	na	91	1	45	na	33	na	47
Italy	39	98	2	62	—	53	13	62
Netherlands	33	94	3	56	—	58	19	59
United Kingdom	19	94	3	47	2	48	10	52
Japan	51	99	11	41	2	69	34	50
United States	17	57	27	59	5	46	27	57

Source: The World Bank's International Economics Department

There are other reasons to question the basic hypothesis that relies on the relationship between changes in the GNP growth rates of the industrialized countries and changes in the amount of foreign exchange that would become available to debtor countries through exports, direct investment and official aid. The difficulty of projecting the likely relationships between growth and other key variables stems from the substantial indeterminacy of several critical factors. Among them are the lack of knowledge about the price and income elasticities of demand and of supply for the exportable goods and services of a very diverse group of developing countries. This indeterminacy arises in turn from the rapid and erratic changes in global economic conditions that make past relationships a questionable guide to future behaviour. Thus the rigour of the modelling exercises gets rather flabby.[6]

This indeterminate quality of the modelling exercises applies with particular relevance to developing countries. By virtue of stage of development, size and other factors, they vary greatly in their dependence on foreign funds and technical know-how and have different capacities to respond to export and import-substitution opportunities. It is also especially difficult to factor-in the impact of transnational corporations (TNCs) on developing country exports when (1) their activities account for a high percentage of the host country's exports, particularly industrial and service exports, and (2) these firms shift their investments towards service rather than manufacturing industries and enter into joint ventures and franchising arrangements that have no standardized pattern. The degree of dependence of third world countries on foreign-owned TNCs for their industrial output and for export earnings of manufactured goods and tourist-related services can run very high; for example, 70 per cent in the case of Zambia and over 30 per cent in the case of Argentina.[7]

If no modelling exercise can provide solid footing at a time when the universe is changing rapidly in fundamental ways and when the characteristics and rates of change differ so greatly among nations, there would seem good reason to be skeptical about computations that show what rate of growth in the industrial world can be counted upon to provide commensurate growth in income *and export earnings* in the third world. This skepticism is reinforced by the difficulty of forecasting what will likely happen both to the movement of those commodity prices on which the developing countries largely depend for their export earnings and to the movement of interest rates and the terms of trade.

All of these factors have a direct impact on the debt burden the third world countries are being expected or pressured to carry. Their plight has been rendered even more desperate by the trade patterns that have evolved. International initiatives, such as the GATT talks, hold little promise of significant change. As a result, their frustration, fueled by a sense of an even greater degree of powerlessness, has been rising to a point where they are more than ever questioning the efficiency and equity of the trading system of the current "international economic order."

Commodity prices and the terms of trade

On this score the outlook is just as gloomy. The developing countries account for one half of the world's primary commodity output, and primary commodities have always been the mainstay of their exports. At the onset of the 1980s their prices dropped precipitously to levels not experienced since the Great Depression. Together with the related deterioration in the terms of trade, this has been one of the main contributing factors transforming the problem of debt servicing from the business-as-usual basis to one of crisis proportions.

The crisis nature of the situation has not been eased by subsequent developments with respect to commodity prices and the terms of trade, though in the last few years there has been an impressive increase in the value of world trade and a rise in *The Economist's* commodity price index. It rose by 46.5 per cent during 1988 alone, leading that journal in its issue of 2 July 1988 to headline the story with the sensational caption, "Commodity prices in orbit." By mid-1988, the indicators registered a rise in the *average* price of *all* raw materials to reach its highest level in 15 years. But this reflected a resurgence of *some* commodity prices: during that year the food prices index had risen by over 30 per cent, wheat prices surged in one month by about 20 per cent, while the prices of such commodities as maize and soybeans rose about 75 per cent; the metals price index doubled.

All this was not as helpful as the numbers might appear because the greatest price rise occurred in temperate zone products and in such metals as nickel and zinc that are produced mainly in the industrialized countries. In any case, the 1987 base is misleading since the index had fallen to its lowest level by 1987, one third below the 1980-84 average. The trend is dramatically illustrated in Figure 12 which traces real commodity prices from 1870 to 1990.

As of early 1991 commodity prices (with the exception of fuels) have fallen in real terms by 50 per cent below the 1988 peak according to *The Economist* index, and by more according to the IMF. Using different weights, the IMF index reveals that a steep decline in real terms has occurred during

Figure 12: *Real Commodity Prices (1870-1990)*

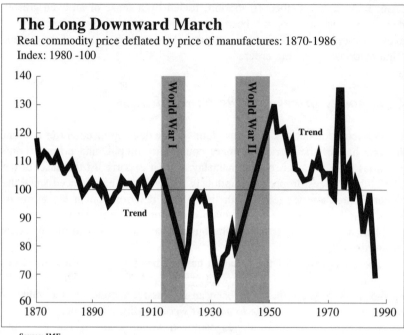

The Long Downward March
Real commodity price deflated by price of manufactures: 1870-1986
Index: 1980 -100

Source: IMF

the past two decades. This has meant a slip in the export earnings of the developing countries of one third from what they would have been had prices maintained their average real levels of the 1970s and 1980s. This blow is worsened by the grim prospects that the prices of the commodities they rely upon for export earnings are not likely to recover. This is due above all to structural and technological changes that have forever reduced the demand for most of these commodities: compared to the demand per unit of GNP growth 20 years ago, copper by 25 per cent, iron ore by 40 per cent, and tin by 50 per cent.

The debtors' condition has been exacerbated by changes in the terms of trade reflecting, on the one side, the falling commodity prices, and on the other, the rising prices of the manufactured goods. *The Economist* has estimated that in 1986 alone the developing world as a whole incurred a national loss in income from the deterioration in their terms of trade of about $65 billion, the African developing countries accounting for about $19 billion.

The situation has improved only marginally, hardly relieving the pressure on the economies of primary commodity exporting countries. Over the last decade the adverse trend, as shown in Table 13, has exacted an exceptionally heavy toll.

It has been a process analogous to trying to run up an escalator that is going down. With a desperate need for foreign exchange, the policy makers of the debt-laden developing countries have been opting for those measures that would enable them to *rapidly* raise their export earnings. They are under pressure, therefore, to settle for sales at almost any price, even below cost. Since they depend on a narrow range of exportable commodities, this further depresses prices. It also has the effect of downgrading the importance of any adverse environmental impacts that are felt only in the longer term. Thus there is little or no compunction about extending cultivation to lands that are submarginal, thereby exploiting their resources in a manner that may be damaging the ecological base of the economy.

Table 13: Change in export prices and terms of trade, 1965-1988
(average annual percentage change)

Country group	1965-73	1973–80	1980–86	1986	1987	1988
Export Prices						
Low- and middle-income economies	6.2	14.7	−4.9	−10.6	11.0	6.1
Manufactures	6.4	8.2	−2.2	9.4	8.6	8.9
Food	5.9	8.6	−2.7	7.6	−7.0	14.4
Nonfood	4.6	10.2	−4.8	−1.1	21.7	2.8
Metals and minerals	2.5	4.7	−4.4	−4.8	11.4	28.2
Fuels	8.3	26.0	−10.1	−46.7	22.0	−15.0
High-income OECD members						
Total	4.8	10.3	−1.4	12.2	11.4	8.3
Manufactures	4.5	10.9	−0.3	19.0	13.7	7.0
Terms of trade						
Low- and middle-income economies	0.1	2.8	−2.7	−10.9	2.3	−0.2
Low-income economies	−4.9	4.1	−3.0	−16.0	4.3	−1.1
Middle-income economies	1.8	1.9	−2.7	−9.1	1.8	0.1
Sub-Saharan Africa	−8.5	4.8	−4.0	−21.5	2.9	−1.4
East Asia	−0.6	1.2	−1.3	−6.1	0.5	1.1
South Asia	3.7	−3.4	1.5	3.1	1.0	2.0
Europe Middle East and North Africa	−	−	−	−	−	−
Latin America and the Caribbean	3.8	2.3	3.3	−14.0	−2.3	1.7
Severely indebted middle-income economies	4.3	1.7	−2.2	−11.4	1.6	0.2
High-income economies	−1.2	−2.1	0.5	7.0	0.2	0.5
OECD members	−1.0	−3.3	1.1	10.6	−0.5	0.7
Oil exporters	0.3	11.5	−7.3	−40.8	11.7	−16.5

Source: The World Bank *World Development Report 1990.*

As an added depressant, recent scientific and technological developments have been occurring on a scale that is playing havoc with the market for many primary commodities. Over the longer term, it is likely to be increasingly difficult for the producers of these primary commodities to recapture their traditional markets once they are lost. The pattern has already become evident. In the 1970s higher prices stimulated the users of these primary commodities to greater efficiency and to turn to substitutes. Copper provides a good example. The amount of copper used per unit of GNP in the industrialized countries fell by 20 per cent between 1973 and 1986. This can be attributed not only to technological improvements involving laser technology, but also to the fact that the traditional users of copper have been induced by the higher prices to resort to fibre optics. The same pattern is evident with regard to substitutes for sugar such as aspartame and saccharine. Furthermore, as might be expected, the producers of primary commodities in the industrialized countries have had a greater capability to take the steps required to increase their share of that shrinking primary commodity market, thus leaving the developing country exports to bear the main brunt of the changed technological and market conditions.

It is not surprising, therefore, to find the IMF forecasting that in real terms commodity prices can be expected to remain at present levels until 1992 despite the growth in incomes and population over the intervening years. After 1992, the prospects are equally dismal. Thus it would be the most irresponsible form of wishful-thinking to count on the prices of most of the tradeable commodities exported by the third world to break out of the deep cellar into which they have slumped.

The level of real interest rates

This factor, as well, provides no grounds for optimism. The prevailing rates are inordinately high by historical standards and, more importantly, in light of what is sustainable, that is a level in the range of 1 to 2 per cent. That happens also to be the level that has prevailed historically. The movement of interest rates was pushed upward to unprecedented heights in the early years of the 1980s. This was the intended result of the so-called Volcker shock that boosted interest rates in the United States to over 20 per cent. It was a primary factor in precipitating the actions of Mexico and Brazil that brought on the debt crisis panic of 1982. By the mid 1980s there was a slight decline from the stratospheric heights, but the rates soon moved upward again to the unsustainably high levels. This increased the transfer from the debtor poor to the creditor rich nations since every point rise in interest rates increases

the annual payments on the debts of the 17 highly indebted countries by
approximately $8 billion, and much more when all third world debtors are
included. It is not surprising, therefore, that the debt burden continues to
grow and arrears continue to mount, as Figure 13 illustrates.

The need to lower interest rates is a common thread running through
almost all current proposals for resolving the debt crisis in a manner that
would facilitate third world development.[8] As early as 1969 the authors of
the Pearson Report, *Partners in Development*, observed that a debt crisis
would loom within a decade:

"The future depends on the course of future lending and whether the
relative role of hard and soft lending will change. If the flow of new

Figure 13: *Net Disbursements, Debt Service, and Net Transfer (1982-88)*

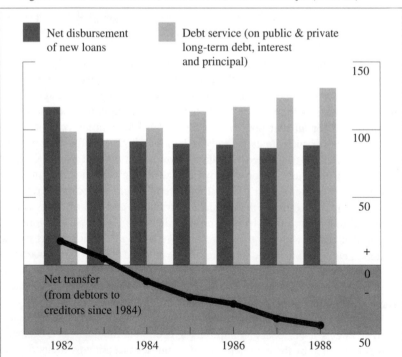

lending were to remain at the level of 1965-67 with no change in its composition, the projection shows that by 1977 debt service would considerably exceed new lending, except in South Asia and the Middle East where they should be about equal. . . . Over-all there would be a large net transfer (after deduction of debt service) arising from lending and going from developing regions to the industrialized countries.''[9]

This prognosis was based on trends in the volume and terms of lending in 1968 when rates and maturities were far more favourable and the total international debt outstanding of developing countries was less than $50 billion. Though the numbers have changed, the analysis and its conclusions apply with even more force today. The level of *real* interest rates not only needs to be lower, it needs to be very much lower than the 6.8 per cent average level which has been the average of the past five years. One key question is, how much lower? The simple answer is enough to reach the historical average level of real interest rates, that is, between 1 and 2 per cent.[10]

The basis for setting the target as low as 1 to 2 per cent is simply that borrowed funds for development purposes cannot be expected to earn a higher rate *in financial terms.*

This low financial rate of return on borrowed funds for development purposes reflects the fact that there is a long gestation period from initial investment to the time of the financial pay-off for funds allocated to the building of basic infrastructure from roads to research, education and health facilities and for all that goes into making a viable community. The social rate of return for such funds is likely to be much higher if, for example, the reduction of crime is counted as a short term benefit derived from the use of more capital to education or employment—creating activities that may not be financially attractive but have a high rate of return in societal terms. To illustrate with an example: the criminal distribution and sale of drugs is now estimated to syphon off $110 billion per year in the United States alone and double that world wide. If this were to be reduced a significant part of that reduction could be attributed to a programme devoted to improving education, health and hope. The returns would be high but not measurable. In any case, they are not entered into the financial calculus of conventional appraisals. The broader concept of development does or should count them.

But this return can only be achieved over a long period of time. A low interest rate is a necessary condition for economic-financial advancement. This is illustrated by the experience of all countries that are now industrialized but borrowed in their early stages of development at real rates of interest below 2 per cent. When they were compelled to pay more or were rash enough to commit themselves to pay a higher rate, defaults usually followed. In effect, this reduced the rate paid.

Internationally, the lowering of real interest rates hinges on the United States by virtue of the importance of the United States economy in world trade and capital flows. The range of responsibility must be widened to take in other players such as Japan and the European Economic Community. Their policies now have significant impact on trade, capital flows and exchange rate changes. Thus the United States could not act on this matter alone. Their decision to change interest rates might be offset or nullified by the actions of other countries that choose not to follow suit or cooperate in following the United States lead. This interdependence has prompted calls for coordinated leadership by the United States, Germany and Japan, and, by extension, calls for the establishment of "rules of the game" for trade and capital flows akin to the Bretton Woods agreement that operated from 1945 to 1970.[11]

Necessity will, over time, undoubtedly force changes that will bring real interest rates back to their historically lower levels. The big question is whether the "necessity" is forced by cataclysmic events or is made by deliberate steps to make the landing a soft one.

The factor of financial flows to meet the minimal objective

The critical question is whether the financial gap that debtors face is "bridge-able" under any reasonable scenario that can be envisaged. A positive or hopeful answer can be given only if certain conditions are fulfilled. These conditions call for substantial changes on both the donor and the recipient sides of the flow equation. As a first step, the donors must arrest the decline in world savings. They fell in aggregative terms from 26 per cent (as a ratio to GNP) in the early 1970s to about 20 per cent by the end of the 1980s, and threaten to decline still further as Japan and Germany, once the largest savers, join the trend.[12]

The developing countries must do the same, having experienced an even larger drop of 8 per cent over this period, a trend that is a reversal of the substantial rise in savings rates in these countries before the 1973 oil price shock. Deeply-rooted factors account for these trends. In the case of the industrialized countries, it was the inflationary psychology and the "wealth effect," and in the case of the oil-importing developing countries, the deterioration of the international trade climate and the debt servicing pressures.

As a second step, the United States must reduce its dependence on foreign-generated savings that had been running at well over $100 billion per year during the 1980s. This would at one and the same time reduce the price of capital (real interest rates) but also make more of the global pool of capital available for third world countries. There is a further reduction possible when capital flow is channeled at below-market rates through aid programmes, both bilateral and multilateral.

With this Official Development Assistance (ODA) there is of course an obligation on the recipient side of the equation that is labeled "conditionality." The third world countries receiving ODA receive subsidized funds on condition they make substantial changes in institutions and policies and practises to provide some assurance that both their own and borrowed capital would be utilized more effectively. The conditionality attached to ODA is designed to assure this "improvement," though, as we shall see later (in the section of Chapter 13 entitled, "The international financial institutions as structural adjustors"), the donor's concept of how the desired efficiency is to be achieved must be questioned.

How much capital do the third world countries "need?" There are too many factors to consider in modelling exercises designed to generate estimates of capital requirements to give a definitive answer. These factors differ in their qualitative attributes and in their relationships one to the other from country to country, making it difficult to even group them by some key common characteristics. There is also the "soft" aspect pertaining to the choice of the growth rate targets and, from the environmental perspective, the choice of the patterns of growth that also must be part of the targeted objective. All this complexity and ambiguity stimulate a great many questions about models churning out rather precise numbers.

However, even after allowing for these conceptual, methodological and statistical difficulties and those pertaining to the reliability and availability of the data that is to be inputted, the modelling exercises could be instructive, if used with caution. They have provided a range of estimates of the net capital required annually to achieve a stipulated annual rate of growth in per capita incomes, estimates that are useful as points of reference even when we abstract from the underlying assumptions as to rates of population increase, environmental "costs," structural changes and the like.

Some of the earliest estimates, vintage 1983 to 1985, placed the minimal net inflow of borrowed funds, investment and aid necessary to achieve an annual 2 per cent rise above present levels in per capita incomes at a figure as low as $60 billion and as high as $120 billion for all developing countries.[13] To achieve the same targeted rate of growth for the 17 highly-indebted countries, the World Bank estimated the additional requirement at $10 to $15 billion each year until 1995. Therefore, the Organization of African Unity and the United Nations Advisory Group on Financial Flows to Africa calculated Africa's additional annual requirements to be in the range of $5 to $10 billion; the Economic Commission for Latin America and the Caribbean estimated that, at a minimum, the additional "public resources commitment" would have to be about $60 billion annually. The orders of magnitude indicate a four-fold increase above present levels just to meet the lower end of the range of the estimated capital requirements from 1990 onwards.

And all these estimates, it should be noted, take little account of the estimated capital requirements if environmental considerations are factored into the calculation, particularly if achieving environmentally benign growth calls for an additional price with all that implies in terms of extra costs for programmes such as research on new energy technologies and for their development and diffusion.

MEETING ENVIRONMENTAL OBJECTIVES

The necessary conditions for heading off the global environmental threat and for addressing a host of other environmental problems are simple to state but difficult to implement. It was long the conventional wisdom that the necessary conditions for reconciling growth and environmental objectives involve a trade-off between the pursuit of economic growth and the attainment of a "satisfactory" standard of environmental quality. So long as the maintenance of an acceptable environmental quality is assumed to be a goal attainable only at the expense of higher incomes and improved levels of "welfare," the environment was bound to lose out to growth. The concept of this issue as a "zero-sum" proposition began to fade in the early 1970s when the idea took hold—albeit tentatively—that the development process was not only compatible with environmental quality but could be enhanced by environmental protection measures. During the last two decades this view of a mutually reinforcing relationship between environment and growth has itself become the conventional wisdom. The phrase "sustainable development" has become the favoured cliché.

However, virtually all global model-builders agree that with rising income levels and rising population, the use of energy will continue to grow; the main conventional sources—oil, gas, coal, hydro and nuclear energy—will continue to play a large role even 50 years into the future with resultant high rates of carbon emission.[14] The conundrum facing policy makers at both the national and global levels of governance is to reduce the rate of increase of the use of fossil fuels in all its forms—and to do so *without sacrificing growth.* Therein lies the dilemma and the seeds of an environmental crisis: how can the debtor countries grow to service their debts and, at the same time, provide for "the better life" that comes with "development" in the broadest sense of that concept?

Environmental activists have ranged in their answers from reliance on modest modification of "market forces" as they operate (or ostensibly could be made to operate) with minor institutional change, to reliance on far-reaching institutional changes that both reflect and reinforce that concern for environmental quality. For the latter school of thought, the key to the resolution of this seeming conflict between growth and environment is found in a phrase: "*new* patterns of growth," with all that that implies.

This view has been clearly articulated by Maurice Strong, the Chairmanof the 1971 United Nations Conference on Environment and of the forthcoming 1992 United Nations World Conference on Environment and Development. He has called for two basic steps as necessary to establish these patterns:

1.   "On the national level, a major transition to a less physical kind of growth, relatively less demanding of energy and raw materials and,

2.   "On the global level, a revamping of the present international system of arrangements and institutions to better serve the interests and aspirations of the developing world."[15]

More than a decade later, in 1989, Jim MacNeill, former Secretary-General of the United Nations World Commission on Environment and Development (the Bruntland Commission), framed the issue in essentially the same terms:

"After three years of work, *The World Commission on Environment and Development* gave its answer to the 'sustainability question': a heavily conditioned 'yes'. . . . The needs and aspirations of today could be reconciled with those of tomorrow providing there are *fundamental* changes in the way nations manage the world's economy . . . . a world with new realities, realities that have not yet been reflected in human behaviour, economics, politics or institutions of government.'' (emphasis added)[16]

Taking these words at face value, if the threat of global environmental degradation is to be addressed on the appropriate scale and with the appropriate speed, it is necessary that institutional changes be forged at all levels of governance, from local to global. Shifting towards alternative energy sources and towards alternative life-styles that reduce the need for energy per unit of growth calls for profound cultural, social and political changes, in addition to the economic. Some degree of success can be achieved by policies that rely heavily on market forces, but given the nature and magnitude of the environmental challenge, a market-based approach will clearly not suffice.

Much of the rhetoric in support of environmental causes evades the question of systemic change by positing little or no conflict between development and environmental goals and then proposing policies and programmes that are hardly new or fundamental. Many of those marching under the banner of "sustainable development" believe either that growth is a questionable goal or that measures for the protection of the environment are growth-promoting. Few are aware of the substantial financial costs in the short-run, and fewer still are prepared to weigh the benefits against the costs. Slogans advocating simplistic solutions devoid of operational content are likely to be counter-productive: in so far as they are misleading, they foster false hopes followed by discouragement and cynicism. Thus, beyond widespread public awareness there is a need for *understanding* as to the goals tempered by costs and as to the modalities that include political as well as economic and cultural dimensions. This caution applies particularly to the global aspects of the environmental issue that must be addressed at several levels of governance, including the international.

The basic conundrum revolves around the complex symbiotic environment/energy/development relationship: what, if anything, has to be given up with respect to energy and development to achieve environmental quality objectives? How are the decisions to be made? By whom? By what processes? Public arousal—though not necessarily commensurate with an understanding of the ramifications—opens a window of opportunity, but that opportunity needs to be seized by spelling out *feasible actionable programmes*, bearing in mind the costs, benefits and uncertainties and the institutional changes.

The political dimensions of the struggle on the environmental front must address the issue of who pays and who benefits. For global-wide environmental problems that call for greatly expanded programmes of scientific/

technological and policy-oriented research and follow-through measures, there can be an agreement in principle that the funding should be shared internationally since its scope is world wide, indeed, planet-wide, and its benefits are humanity's, those present and those yet to be born. There is, therefore, both an *inter*-generational as well as an *intra*-generational dimension that needs to be addressed.

With regard to the intra-generational aspect, that is, pertaining to those now living, the necessary condition to emphasize is simply that while all should enjoy the benefits of a qualitatively acceptable environment, the means of contributing to achieving this state of affairs is uneven. Those living in the developing world aspire to reach a much improved living standard and all that constitutes "the good life." This is an understandable aspiration that cannot be compromised by concerns for the environment when growth and environmental quality are in conflict. One key assumption of any environmental action programme must recognize, therefore, that poor countries are not in a position to adopt new patterns of development called for on environmental grounds that are costly and provide uncertain and longer-term benefits. They have neither the funds nor the skills to themselves design or buy the technologies and the programmes that are "appropriate" on environmental grounds, nor to wait until they are available when they are under intense pressure merely to survive.

Aid in the form of new capital and technical assistance and —in the case of debt-burdened developing countries—of debt relief to staunch the eviscerating drainage of capital is, therefore, a necessary condition to meet this aspect of the environmental *problematique*. Some of this aid should take the form of prioritizing environmental research on "alternative" energy. The third world countries are desperately in need of simple and cheap technologies that can enable them to utilize the environmentally preferable sources of energy, particularly "stand-alone" forms, that is, those outside the grid energy networks such as solar, biomass, wind and shallow gas.[17] All of these energy sources would respond to their particular needs, especially the needs of the most desperately poor, the rural poor.

A successful precedent for internationally-funded research targeted on third world needs is the Consultative Group on International Agricultural Research (CGIAR). This is a programme of global cooperation at the level of global governance with the World Bank taking on the responsibilities as the secretariat. The 1981 United Nations Conference on New and Renewable Sources of Energy included an analogous programme. It highlighted the need for accelerating research on more environmentally preferable sources of energy so as to reduce the dependence on fuelwood in the third world, thereby reducing the ecological damage that this dependency engenders.[18]

Aid in the form of providing relief to third world countries from the pressures of servicing their debts is a necessary condition for their cooperation in global environmental programmes. Without such debt relief they can not be expected to have a willingness or a capability to place a priority on environmental goals. Under the pressures of the debt overhang, they may give lip service to the cause, even make token gestures, but they will then go on as before. Environmental considerations will take a back seat to the present imperatives of surviving in an international context that is not yet congenial enough for them to indulge the luxury of maintaining environmental quality. This is especially true for the programmes with benefits that are global or regional and for which they are expected to bear all or almost all of the costs, including the costs of foregoing some activities. The issue of the Brazilian tropical rain forest is a case in point.

In the industrialized countries, environmental programmes are constrained when investment decisions are made on the basis of the short term and the criterion of those in business who look to the financial "bottom line" or those in political life who seek fast payoffs that can win them re-election within their brief electoral mandate. Until the influence of this narrow temporal perspective is broadened, the requisite environmental actions will continue to be made in only a token way. Breaking this pattern is a necessary condition for meaningful action on the scale commensurate with the magnitude and urgency of the environmental problems. Although in response to public pressure there has been some movement to reach international agreements that set environmental targets such as those already achieved for chlorofluorocarbon and CO_2 emissions, the progress in operationalizing has been slow and the achievement is still meager. But the prospect of attaining even the modest goals of these agreements is not bright especially when they have heavy costs and the benefits are uncertain and diffused. Even the Governments of the richer industrialized countries are balking at the costs for global environmental programmes that are estimated to run into the hundreds of billions annually to fill gaps in key areas of scientific, financial and socio-economic knowledge and to implement and monitor programmes on the basis of this knowledge. Probabilities must be calculated so that policies can be made in the light of better knowledge. Only then can funds on the requisite scale be expected.

This raises a key question that has already been posed in connection with the resolution of the debt crisis: where is the money to come from, and on what terms and conditions?

CHAPTER 4

FINANCIAL ASSISTANCE: POTENTIAL AND LIMITATIONS

The developing countries, with few exceptions, are basically reliant on their own internally-generated capital for investments, whether for private or public purposes. However, like the United States, Canada, Australia and a host of other countries in the early phases of their development, capital inflow through borrowing or foreign investment was exceptionally helpful and welcomed. Though there were frequent defaults and some instances of voluntary debt forgiveness (as cited in the section on debt cancellation, Chapter 9 (c)), these countries over several decades increased their productive capacity to a point where they were able to pay back these loans and even become net suppliers of capital to third world countries at their early stage of development. The pattern is historically one of capital flowing from richer to poorer countries, or to war-devastated countries, as after the Second World War under the Marshall Plan and loans made under the aegis of the World Bank.[1]

In the 1980s, the traditional pattern of capital flows reversed; it is now flowing from the poor to the richer countries. Private lending, private foreign investments and official development assistance (ODA) have all fallen off drastically. It is essential, therefore, that the flow of capital be reversed to once again assume its historically traditional pattern of flowing to the poorer countries—and on terms that are not onerous either financially or in conditionality that further erode their already shredded pride and semblance of sovereignty. Not since the conquistadores plundered Latin America has the world experienced a flow in the direction we see today. The estimated capital required for a global economy to grow in an environmentally sustainable manner and with greater equity has been as high as $3,000 billion over the next 20 years.

OFFICIAL DEVELOPMENT ASSISTANCE (ODA): CAN IT BE A BASIS FOR HOPE?

For developing countries, the sheer magnitude of the increase in required financial flow is overwhelming. The main burden must rest on the shoulders of each Government supplemented by official development assistance (ODA) under either bilateral or multilateral programmes. As Table 14 indicates, the ODA flows have been shrinking rather than expanding during the 1980s. In 1989 their aid to the developing world fell by 2 per cent in real terms (after taking account of changes in prices and exchange rates) and to less than one third of 1 per cent of their collective GNP, the lowest percentage level since 1977. ODA has since risen in real terms, largely thanks to the increased contributions of a few countries, with Japan expanding its ODA in 1990 to over $11 billion, surpassing the United States in absolute terms.

Hopes for achieving a significant increase in ODA must take account of the fact that the Japanese contribution to global capital flows (amounting to $600 billion for 1985-90) dropped by 50 per cent in 1990, and that Germany has become a net importer of capital. The 1990s will see a further retrenchment from the levels of the 1980s, which with its vaunted aura of prosperity was not a bonanza decade for assistance and the fact that this would involve reversing the prevailing trends. The key item is United States aid. It fell in absolute terms between 1988 and 1989 from $10.1 billion to $7.7 billion, and in relative terms to 0.15 per cent of its GNP or almost half of the 0.27 per cent that it contributed in 1980. This has placed the United States at the bottom of the ranking in the ODA's list of 21 donor countries: its ODA as a ratio to GNP is less than half of Japan's (0.32 per cent) and a sixth of that of the Scandinavian countries that have consistently contributed more than 1 per cent of their GNP. With increases in ODA by Japan, Italy and a few other countries, not including the United States and Canada, the total of ODA flows is no longer on a downward *real* trend. In light of the reflows for debt servicing, however, there is a long way to go to reach a point where the *net* capital flow is moving *towards* the developing countries rather than away from them. Hope that ODA flows might yet accelerate over the next few years must take into account factors such as the need for capital for Eastern European and Middle East reconstruction, not to mention the capital required in the United States, Europe and Japan to bring their infrastructure up to minimal standards of safety and adequacy. Symbolically, this diversion can be seen in the case of Italy. It has pledged an increase in ODA to reach the

Table 14: Official development assistance, 1981-88

All developing countries:	Current $ billion							
	1981	1982	1983	1984	1985	1986	1987	1988
1. Official development assistance (ODA)	36.8	33.9	33.9	35.0	37.3	44.4	48.3	51.7
of which: Bilateral disbursements	28.9	26.3	26.3	27.2	28.8	34.9	38.2	40.3
Multilateral disbursements	7.9	7.6	7.6	7.8	8.5	9.6	10.1	11.4

Source: Organization of Economic Cooperation and Development (OECD)

1 per cent of GNP target by 1993: only half of that will be allocated to the third world, the remainder being shared by Eastern Europe (43 per cent) and low-income Mediterranean countries (7 per cent). With a pledge of $38 billion for Eastern Europe made by 24 European countries and calls for $30 billion per year for the next five years, the trend in terms of sharing the ODA flows is being set. Without a much greater allocation of the global GNP to aid, the third world cannot expect to see a substantial change in the present depressing trends of slow *nominal* growth in ODA and stagnant or falling ODA in real terms.

The role of the Bretton Woods institutions, the IMF and the World Bank, reflects the depressing state of affairs with regard to the volume of aid flows from multilateral agencies. The IMF is now receiving reflows that exceed its lending—despite arrears that now amount to about $5 billion. The World Bank has become the main lending agency among multilateral institutions. In fiscal 1990 it lent $15.2 billion plus $5.5 billion in IDA credits. As Table 15 reveals, while its net disbursements in 1990 for both categories of lending totalled $9.3 billion, it too has been taking in more from the most highly indebted countries than it disbursed. This can be seen from an examination of Table 16.

With the 1990 approval of a General Capital Increase (GCI) authorizing a $74.8 billion addition to the World Bank's presently authorized capital of $96.6 billion to be phased in over six years, the sustainable lending level can rise above $20 billion per year during the early 1990s. This increase will permit its net disbursements to the highly indebted countries to become positive within the next few years. In light of the net outflow from the most desperately stressed debtor countries, particularly in sub-Saharan Africa, and the problem of mounting arrears that this has posed, special initiatives have been launched to assist them.

To achieve this extra financial flow for these countries, the "soft lending" or concessional arm of the Bank, IDA or the International Development

Table 15: World bank lending and net disbursements. 1986-1990

	1986	1987	1988	1989	1990
Commitments (a)	13,179	14,188	14,762	16,433	15,180
Disbursements (a)	8,263	11,383	11,636	11,310	13,859
Net disbursements (a)	4,432	5,656	3,428	1,921	5,717
IDA (b)					
Commitments	3,140	3,486	4,459	4,943	5,522
Disbursements	3,154	3,088	3,397	3,597	3,845
Net disbursements	3,021	2,940	3,241	3,404	3,628

(a) Excludes loans to the IFC.
(b) IDA excludes the Specialty Facility for Sub-Saharan Africa, includes special fund amounts.

Source: The World Bank.

Association, has been enlarged. A Special Programme of Assistance for Africa has been established for expanded cofinancing with bilateral donor agencies, and the African Development Fund has been replenished. The contributions to the Bank's "soft window", the International Development Association (IDA) and to its special "facilities" for Africa, are part of the ODA contribution which, in total, has not been increased, as yet. Over the next three years, in addition, the IMF can be expected to lend roughly $40 billion through increasing the IMF quota by about $15 billion, the General Agreement to Borrow (GAB) by about $12 billion (which, for the first time, has been made eligible for developing countries) and the Enhanced Special Adjustment Facility (ESAF).

Table 16: World Bank lending and net disbursements to highly indebted countries, 1986-1989
(Millions of US dollars; fiscal years)

Item	1986	1987	1988	1989
IBRD and IDA commitments	6,071	6,719	6,483	8,021
Gross disbursements	4,213	6,132	5,406	4,740
Repayments and interest charges	3,894	5,356	6,673	6,666
Net transfer	319	776	−1,267	−1,926

Source: The World Bank, *World Bank Annual Report, 1989*

Notwithstanding this extra effort by both the World Bank and the IMF to provide emergency assistance, the volume of lending by both institutions and by other multilateral development banks is not likely to be especially significant in relation to the size of the debt overhang with which these third world debtors must contend.

STRUCTURAL ADJUSTMENT LENDING: CAN IT PROVIDE AN ANSWER?

As the debtors have become more desperate in their struggle to service their debts and avoid outright default, and as the creditors have sought to assure that the debtors had sufficient resources to cope with this process—albeit with considerable slippage and traumatic confrontations—there has seemed to be a mutual interest of both the donor and the debtor communities in endorsing a policy whereby the World Bank and the other IFIs would speed up the preparation, approval and disbursement of loans. The response of the World Bank to the donors' endorsement of this idea was to shift some of its lending from its traditional project orientation to a quick-disbursement type of lending loans.

In the main, this took the form of "structural adjustment loans"(SALs) and "sectoral adjustment loans" (SECALs). The "project cycle" for such programme loans was thereby shortened from the average of two years (counting the time from inception of the identification mission to Board approval) to a few weeks. From 1980, when the first SAL was made by the World Bank, until 1989, more than 50 countries have received one or more SALs or SECALs. A dozen countries have had repeated dosages of the same medicine, in some cases up to three times. This approach has been rationalized as bitter medicine that the condition of the patient requires:

> "Adjustment lending has become a major part of the Bank's development assistance programme. . . (to) allow the Bank to play an active role in helping developing countries overcome the structural weaknesses that have hindered balanced and rapid development. . . . The Bank had to help Governments introduce reforms under extraordinary pressure due to the rapidly weakening external environment."[2]

Initiated modestly and tentatively in 1980, this type of lending now accounts for about one quarter of the World Bank's lending programme, as shown in Figure 14. By 1989, the total disbursements had exceeded $11 billion ($6.4 for SALs and $4.6 for SECALs).

Adjustment lending incorporates a qualitatively new element, a different and more severe type and degree of conditionality than normal project loans. Apart from the speed of disbursements, the feature of SALs and SECALs that has made this shift especially appealing for the creditors has been the greater leverage they can thereby exercise because the conditionality clauses enable the "advice" of the lending agencies to influence *more directly* and *more intrusively* the main instruments of policy and the key institutions of the debtors.

The structural elements, in the words of a World Bank official, involve "policies to alter incentives, improve efficiency and strengthen institutional

Figure 14: *Distribution of IBRD/IDA Commitments by Lending Instrument (1987-92)*

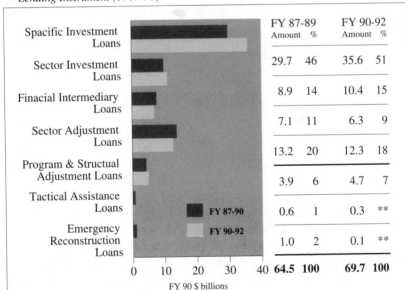

	FY 87-89		FY 90-92	
	Amount	%	Amount	%
Spacific Investment Loans	29.7	46	35.6	51
Sector Investment Loans	8.9	14	10.4	15
Finacial Intermediary Loans	7.1	11	6.3	9
Sector Adjustment Loans	13.2	20	12.3	18
Program & Structual Adjustment Loans	3.9	6	4.7	7
Tactical Assistance Loans	0.6	1	0.3	**
Emergency Reconstruction Loans	1.0	2	0.1	**
	64.5	**100**	**69.7**	**100**

FY 90 $ billions

FY 87-90
FY 90-92

Note: Amounts and percentages may not add to totals due to rounding
** Indicates less than 0.5%
Source: World Bank

capacity."[3] The policy and institutional package is standard for all debtors with only marginal deviations as to the degree and timing of their application. There is a uniformity, however, in the key assumptions underlying this pre-scriptive package. Namely, that the pathway to salvation lies in devaluation of their currencies, deregulation of markets, privatization of public entities, budgetary cutbacks involving reduction of subsidies, loosening of import barriers and the like.

Sufficient time has elapsed to arrive at an assessment of this approach, especially with respect to the key policy items in this SAL package, the exchange rate adjustment that involves a devaluation of the debtor country's currency and the reduction or removal of subsidies. Over the course of the 1980s, the average real exchange rate (trade-weighted and inflation-adjusted) of more than 80 developing countries fell by about 40 per cent. The drop was less than that recommended by the IMF and the World Bank as conditions for their lending. This devaluation has had an inflationary impact by making imports more expensive, and has often reduced investment and output because of its depressive effect on incomes.

Even in terms of strictly economic/financial criteria as reflected in the balance of payments, a study undertaken by the World Bank has concluded this devaluation has not proven successful for those developing countries dependent on the export of primary commodities, which is to say, most of them.[4] Reviewing that study, *The Economist* observed that the devaluations were not only rationalized on faulty assumptions, but in any case were "much bigger than were strictly required by a country's need to finance its current account."[5]

The cold statistics of the balance of payments effects hardly reflect the full negative impact. To do so, the scope of the assessment would have to be broadened to include the social and political implications. Under the terms of the conditionality clauses common to SALs, the social and political con-siderations have been generally subordinated to a policy of belt-tightening through devaluation and a host of complementary measures. It was believed that the debtors, in due course, would be able to return to a condition char-acterized as "creditworthy." The broader-based assessment has lead to an even greater measure of disenchantment with "structural adjustment" both as a concept and as an operational guideline. The World Bank's chief econ-omist for Africa put the matter succinctly: "We did not think," he said, "that the human costs of these programmes could be so great, and the economic gains so slow in coming."

None the less, the World Bank's public position is that the process is working reasonably well.[6] In a review of its SAL operations, a World Bank report notes that there has been an exceptionally high degree of compliance with the conditions set down in the loan agreements with respect to exchange rates, pricing policies and subsidy programmes, institutional changes and so forth. There is also an acknowledgment that there has been a consequent worsening of the maldistribution of incomes. For this adverse fallout corrective measures are being promised within the framework of the structural adjustment process.[7]

Underlying this treatment of the equity aspect is the view that in countries that have been traditionally ruled by elites, where the distribution of incomes are highly skewed, the outside advisory/lending agency faces a limited range of options, especially as the negotiations are undertaken with the elite group who know how to look after their own interests and can be counted upon to do so. Though often relegated to the side-lines as a secondary issue after efficiency, the aspect of "equity" is an equal contender for primacy of place.

The equity aspect revolves around the question as to what group speaks or negotiates for the recipient countries, and whether they are serving their own group interests or that of the nation as a whole. Though the matter is often raised, for the sake of doing business, the donors seldom persist in pressing for greater equitable sharing of the benefits or for greater concern for the environmental impacts in the face of opposition from the ruling elites. These aspects seldom are sources of irreconcilable contention between the donors and those who negotiate for the recipient countries. Brazil provides a case in point: using the criterion of the Geni coefficient that measures the degree of income equality, or the Lorenz Curve which illustrates the deviation from an equal distribution of income, Brazil ranks as the world's third worst, with the bottom 20 per cent of the population enjoying only about 2 per cent of the nation's income. Yet it is one of the biggest of the World Bank's borrowers. If the SAL should exacerbate that maldistribution of income, the issue is hardly academic.

The rationale usually given for treating the distributional aspect as secondary is simply that the "second-best" is all that can be hoped for and that "the best can be the enemy of the good." The donors could, however, send a powerful signal about their concern for equity (who benefits and who pays from its loans or grants?) by not lending to countries where the loans are likely to intensify the maldistribution of income. This might be evident from such factors as the unequal distribution of land holdings (in the case, for example, of livestock agricultural sector loans). The donors could also insist on specific features that ensure a compensating benefit for the disadvantaged through special subsidies or other means. Or they could insist on constraints with respect to the operation of market forces that would otherwise favour the better-off segment of the recipient country's population.

In 1974, Robert MacNamara, as President of the World Bank made a speech in Nairobi that focused on the plight of "the bottom 40 per cent," the proportion of humanity that had not been sharing in the unprecedented global growth of the previous three decades and were still living in conditions of "absolute poverty." With this seminal theme there was an explicit shift of focus. The World Bank broadened its concern for growth to include other facets of development. This was reflected in operations, and in a series of policy papers devoted to issues such as land reform, nutrition, health, education, population and "integrated rural development." A "special projects" division was established in the World Bank in 1975 to deal with these distributional aspects through identifying and preparing different types of projects. This division was abolished a few years later, a move symptomatic of a waning operational focus on the "poverty issue."

The recent spate of papers on the social impact of SALs and the *World Development Report* of 1990 devoted to the poverty theme reveal a renewed concern. Unfortunately, the figurative wheel has to be reinvented when the institutional memory is destroyed through staff changes and when staff are rewarded on the basis of financial through-put rather than on the basis of other indicators having to do with success in dealing with the difficult politically sensitive issue of income distribution. Helping the poor is difficult, and in terms of career advancement, dangerous. When this is so, operational realities tend to deviate from rhetoric.[8]

There was considerable attention directed to the global systemic aspects in the annual *World Development Reports* and other publications. But little of the concern about the systemic biases and instabilities was translated into operationally significant initiatives beyond what could be done on a project-by-project basis. Even from the IMF, the agency that is reputed to be more hard-headed and hard-hearted, there were expressions of doubt, not only about the social fall-out but also with respect to the economic aspects of the policy package incorporated in the structural adjustment lending programme. The authors of a 1988 IMF study that is part of a series, *World Economic and Financial Surveys*, observed:

"(there is) a growing realization that the earlier tendency to give a very large weight to export promotion was not in the debtor countries' best interests, and certainly not in the interest of the (lending) agencies. Moreover, it is becoming apparent that such an approach was also not even in the long-run interests of industrial country exporters who would be best served by stable, growing markets in the developing world."[9]

On the debtor side, doubts soon surfaced as it became evident that, for most of them, the results were disappointing in terms of the enhancement of their capacity to service their debts and grow at the same time. When account was taken of the social/political fallout, they realized that an exceptionally high price had to be paid for staying the course under the prevailing rules, to which they had to adjust. The rising chorus of criticism has led to a questioning of the rules themselves, and in particular to questioning the SAL concept as applied to individual countries: how are debtor countries expected to "adjust" to meet their debt and the other obligations to their citizens when the global system is not congenial and when the policy makers of the major industrialized nations are resistant to themselves undertaking a programme of "structural adjustment" within their own countries?

The issue of protectionist barriers, for example, raises the question: How can developing countries realistically be expected to export their way out of the debt trap when essentially the same advice is given to all of them regarding measures to enhance their export capacity? This is especially so when there is no assurance that the necessary market for these exports will be open, both through lowering protectionist barriers and reducing competing subsidies to their own primary producers. Their skepticism has been deepened by the growing realization that the donor community, through the SALs and SE-CALs, has been able to exert exceptionally great leverage to achieve massive changes in the key policies and institutions of the developing debtor countries without being cooperative and bearing the attendant risks that these imposed adjustment policies entailed.

This line of questioning has given rise to calls for *structural adjustment of the global framework* which would entail commensurate obligations on the industrialized countries to make the necessary changes. Broadening the scope of the structural adjustment concept is given further support when account is taken of the serious adverse environmental fall-out of the SALs. The damage stems from the biased orientation of SALs towards the short term and the financial pay-offs and a disregard or downplaying of the longer-term ecological considerations. The basic source of contention arises because of the philosophy and substantive content of a conditionality package that give the creditors a powerful leverage that is not only intrusive but intrusive with respect to key elements of national policy-making, namely, the macro aspects of development policy. This would be tolerable, even if disagreeable, if it held reasonable promise of being successful. However, the intrusion is vexing in the extreme when the "advice" rests on the questionable assumptions that (1) the donors know better what needs to be done than the Governments of the recipient countries, and (2) the borrowers in the debt rescheduling have to be bribed to do what is in "their" own best interests, whomever "they" might be who have the power to govern and can be expected to do so in their own interests.

These points raise issues that go beyond the aspect of income distribution and who benefits from and who pays for the loans; it touches directly on the concept of "sovereignty." This sovereignty issue, in former times associated with the stigma of colonialism and imperialism, has become a source of friction between the donor agencies and the borrowers. The SAL type of lending involves foreign private bankers and a variety of experts from the international financial institutions becoming deeply involved in making decisions related to questions such as the *desirable* path of development, its speed and distributional characteristics, the degree of dependency on foreign trade, the mix of government sector/private sector roles and others. These are the issues that give the concept of sovereignty its very meaning and its value.

Because of the intrusiveness of this type of aid and its high risks, there will likely be greater resistance by the debtors with the passage of time. It is this resistance, plus the rate of failure—even in *limited* objectives of avoiding defaults, arrears and such—and the potential damage this type of lending might do to the creditworthiness of the lending institutions as arrears mount, that will constrain further expansion of SALs and SECALs. The ratio of quick-disbursement lending will likely plateau at its present level of about 25 per cent of the World Bank's lending programme and then decline. As SAL-type lending falls as a percentage of World Bank lending, it appears that the financial resources will be committed to the support of the guarantee role that the World Bank is being pressed to assume in response to current United States policy initiatives. Providing such guarantees diverts more World Bank resources to the major debtors, putting off the day when the World Bank could once again be a major *net* contributor of capital for the whole of the third world community of nations.

OTHER OFFICIAL SOURCES OF CAPITAL: WHAT POSSIBILITIES?

If net capital flows to the developing countries, particularly to the heavily-indebted and African ones, will not likely increase in volume and on terms commensurate with even the minimum estimates of the need for additional capital, it becomes necessary to consider some extraordinary measures to achieve a rapid and large increase in the flow of capital to the poorer nations on a sustained basis. The measures could take several forms:

- Special Drawing Rights (SDRs). From time to time the issuance of SDRs has become a hot topic; consideration has been given to a massive issuance in a manner that would involve a break from the conventional allocation by quotas so as to make the developing countries the main recipients and by "delinking" their issuance from Congressional or Parliamentary approval. These proposals have never been acceptable to the major shareholders in the IMF, and there is as yet little prospect of change in their policy position;

- Diversion of the "savings" from reduced arms expenditures to augmenting ODA programmes; currently, the United States contributes about 0.15 per cent of its GNP to aid. This is the lowest percentage of the donor community, but the argument is repeatedly advanced in self-justification that when its military expenditure is included, its contribution is above 6 per cent of its GNP, the highest of the industrialized countries. The prospects of a change of attitude are not bright given the United States budgetary position;

- Exacting royalties and taxes from users of "the global commons" —the oceans, outer space and Antarctica—for the benefit of the developing countries; the income from such taxation and royalties would yield tens of billions of dollars, from the seabed mining royalties alone, an estimated $6 billion annually.[10] There is a long way to go on that politically bumpy road, as demonstrated by the prolonged seven-year negotiations on the *United Nations Convention on the Law of the Sea*, an agreement that has, as yet, not been ratified by the United States. In any case, the necessary institutional arrangements would take considerable time to establish and make operational.

Other ideas have been advanced, such as, for example, those of Professor Paul Streeten. He advocates establishment of some key institutions of a "new international order" such as an international central bank, an international investment trust and an agency to collect an international income tax.[11] It is not clear, however, (1) where the money is to come from, (2) whether many of these functions are already within the mandate of an international agency but not operational for reasons having to do with the difficulties of getting agreement by the major economic powers, and (3) if these difficulties do exist, how they are to be overcome.

Meantime, there has been little progress on any of these suggested initiatives for providing the trade and capital flow conditions necessary for resolving the debt crisis. Despite the dim prospects for achieving these conditions, an aura of complacency has emerged in the creditor's camp. The underlying basis for this attitude lies in the confidence reposed in the private sector as lenders and as investors in the third world, a confidence which underlies the United States initiatives of the Baker Plan and then the Brady Plan. Both plans have relied upon bankers *voluntarily* to agree—on the basis of certain inducements—to write off part of the third world debts on their books and pass the benefits of the write-down or discount directly to the debtor nations, and to grant temporary waivers on the repayment of interest and principal for a stipulated period.

Private bankers: could they—would they—come to the rescue?

For the last few years some developments have raised the hope that private capital flows to the debtor third world countries can be substantially increased if there are sufficient market-based incentives for lenders and investors and if these are underwritten by guarantees to reduce the risks, at least in the short term. John Williamson, a fellow of the Institute for International Economics, has suggested that the World Bank could augment the flow of private capital through offering guarantees in co-financing arrangements, these guarantees being phased out as the Bank raises its lending levels and is in need of the newly authorized capital.[12] This approach still depends on voluntary flows of private capital. The issue as to what kind of guarantees will induce them to once again return to normal lending and investing can only be tested over time.

   The "normal" role of the private commercial banks in lending to the third world for long-term programmes and projects has not been historically impressive. In retrospect the 1970s can be seen to have been exceptional in terms of both the volume of private bank lending and the criteria for the decisions to lend and to borrow. Private capital flows were facilitated by profound institutional changes in the international financial system, principally the establishment and rapid maturation of the Eurodollar market as an offshore financial arrangement to develop the syndication phenomenon. That was the means by which commercial banks could share the risks in recycling the unprecedented volume of funds called "petrodollars."

In this process the counterpart players to the bankers have been the zealous borrowers who responded too willingly to the loan-pushing lenders. They were tempted by the conditions that have been described as a "debtors' paradise," with low or negative real interest rates and the expectation of rising commodity prices and of favourable terms of trade for primary producers continuing indefinitely. This expectation was buttressed by an old theme dating back almost two centuries that became fashionable in the late 1970s and early 1980s; namely, the neo-Malthusian limits-to-growth hypothesis that stressed the finiteness and therefore the likely shortages and ever-rising prices of the globe's limited natural resources in the face of rising population and incomes. The popular resurgence of the Malthusian illusion occurred with the first oil shock in 1973. It continued to be reinforced by the fact that for the subsequent six years there seemed little cause for worry about declining commodity prices and deteriorating terms of trade—and, therefore, about mounting debts.

The policy makers who encouraged this development were apparently not disturbed by any collective memory of previous financial crashes. Dire warnings of the 1960s from the authors of the 1969 Pearson Commission Report, *Partners in Development*, and by others were conveniently forgotten or ignored. Even at a time when the absolute and relative size of the debt of third world countries was miniscule relative to today and real interest rates were much lower, the author of the Pearson Commission Report had pointed out that there was no way of avoiding a debt crisis within a decade unless the gross flow of capital transfers continued to accelerate by at least 8 per cent per year and/or the proportion of the aid flow on *softer* terms was increasing commensurately. The warnings were based simply on the inexorable logic of compounding and exponentiality. Unless some significant exogenous factor intervened, the only question about a breakdown in this process was when and how it would occur.

The tragic outcome envisaged by the authors of the Pearson Commission Report was put off for several years by the OPEC price hikes of 1973 and 1979 and the consequent petrodollar recycling. The rate of capital transfer increased for a time by more than the stipulated 8 per cent per year. The phenomenon of capital flight brought the day of reckoning closer, as did wasteful non-productive use of the borrowed capital, but even careful well-planned and executed deployment of the capital would not have been sufficient to do more than put off that day *when the real interest rates charged for the borrowed capital exceeded the rate of increase in productivity of the borrowed capital.* The writing was on the wall but few cared to read the warnings. Both lenders and borrowers indulged the illusions of gamblers, but then many play the odds in casinos hoping to come out ahead. The player-participants of this global casino on both the lending and borrowing sides were in for a rude shock when Paul Volcker escalated interest rates in 1979 as a key element of a strategy to slow inflation.

Private lending and private investment flows fell precipitously at the beginning of the 1980s. The decline accelerated almost immediately following the Mexican and Brazilian suspension of payments on their loans in the summer of 1982 with a 23 per cent reduction of bank lending and private investment from the $74 billion level of 1981. This can be seen from a perusal of Table 17 showing net private resource flows to the developing countries as a group and to the low-income countries as a special case. By 1986 it was down to about one third of the 1981 level, with bank lending down to about one eighth.

Bank lending has increased slightly from its low point in 1988 when it amounted to less than $6 billion, almost all of it involuntary. While private investment has gone up somewhat, returning to the levels of the late 1970s, the prospects for *significant* and *adequate* increases in total private capital flows to the third world debtor countries does not seem promising so long as three conditions prevail: (1) the debt overhang continues to grow, dampening expectations that the debtor countries will make a sufficient recovery and thereby reduce the risks of instability and default; (2) large amounts of capital continue to be committed to the Eastern European countries, and soon to the

Table 17: Net private resource flows, 1981-89

All developing countries	Current $ billion									Percentage of total(s)		
	1981	1982	1983	1984	1985	1986	1987	1988	1989	1981	1985	1989
PRIVATE FLOWS	74.3	58.2	47.9	31.7	21.4	28.2	34.4	38.7	40.7	54.1	37.2	37.3
1. Direct investment (OECD)	17.2	12.8	9.3	12.3	6.6	11.3	20.9	23.4	22.0	12.5	7.8	20.2
2. International bank lending (b)	52.3	37.9	35.0	17.2	15.2	7.0	7.0	5.8	8.5	38.1	18.0	7.8
3. Total bond lending	1.3	4.8	1.0	0.3	5.4	2.7	0.5	0.4	1.0	0.9	6.4	0.9
4. Other private	1.5	0.4	0.3	0.3	1.3	3.9	2.5	4.9	5.0	1.1	1.5	4.6
5. Grants by non-governmental organizations	2.0	2.3	2.3	2.6	2.9	3.3	3.5	4.2	4.2	1.5	3.4	3.9

Low-income countries	1981	1982	1983	1984	1985	1986	1987	1988	1989	1981	1985	1989
PRIVATE FLOWS	10.1	9.6	9.0	6.6	10.6	11.9	13.2	13.8	9.9	26.0	26.6	23.8
1. Direct investment (OAC)	4.2	2.4	1.7	1.8	1.5	2.0	2.8	3.0	na	10.8	3.8	5.2
2. International bank lending	4.7	5.5	5.4	3.1	6.0	4.8	6.0	5.8	na	12.1	15.1	10.0
3. Total bond lending	x	0.2	0.4	0.1	1.1	1.8	0.9	0.9	na	x	2.8	1.6
4. Other private	x	0.1	0.1	x	0.3	1.3	1.4	1.6	na	x	0.8	2.8
5. Grants by non-governmental organizations	1.2	1.4	1.4	1.6	1.7	2.0	2.1	2.5	na	3.1	4.3	4.3

(a) Percentage of total represents the percentage of total net resource flows; official development finance + total export credits + private flows
(b) Excludes Taiwan, Province of China.

Source: OECD

Middle East when recovery programmes get underway following the Gulf War; and (3) the debtor countries suffer from a lack of the requisite infrastructure, including educational, research and health facilities, and from a lack of qualified technical, scientific and managerial personnel and of the extraordinary entrepreneurial talent needed to operate in an environment characterized by lax enforcement of laws and of the other attributes that could militate against corruption and arbitrary political interference.

Initiatives have been proposed by the World Bank Group to attract more of the global pool of available investable capital to the third world. An example is the billion-dollar Multilateral Investment Guarantee Agency (MIGA) that is designed to reduce the political risks for private investors. Another is the Emerging Markets Growth Fund (EMGF). It has been set up by the International Finance Corporation to facilitate private capital flows by offering diversified portfolios of investment opportunities in third world enterprises. Although helpful, these initiatives are modest: MIGA may contribute to a slight resurgence of foreign private investment flows to the developing countries; the EMGF is targeted to raise $50 million, a miniscule amount in relation to the need. Little prospect exists for a substantial capital flow breakthrough as a result of either of these initiatives.

There is a tantalizing pool of capital to tap, however, if the conditions can be created to induce the return of a substantial portion of "flight capital" estimated to amount to several hundred billion dollars.[13] There is, as well, an enormous pool of capital in the portfolios of pension funds, mutual funds, insurance companies, and credit unions in the industrialized countries. The Japanese banks alone hold over $700 billion in short-term foreign securities. A great deal of the optimistic expectation derives from this huge potential that exists in Japanese private financial institutions, but there are clouds on that horizon of hope.

The Japanese will first have to contend with the collapse of what has been described as "the biggest speculative bubble seen this century." The prospect is rather ominous:

"Some moneymen working in Tokyo are starting to take an apocalyptic view. Phrases like financial crisis and debt deflation are increasingly being heard. . . . Such fears are well-founded, and have been for some time. Japan is indeed in the early stages of financial trauma, the consequences of which will be felt the world over."[14]

In any event, in the case of those debtors paralyzed by poverty and with an already weak infrastructural base in need of serious repair, not to speak of modernization. It does not appear realistic to expect much from any of these quarters. Just to restore per capita income levels in Africa and Latin America to pre-1980 levels, let alone to enable the citizens of the indebted countries to hope for positive rates of growth, the orders of magnitude are far beyond what can be tapped from the private sources. This is especially so given the reluctance of private bankers to venture once again into the minefield of lending to third world countries.

Through their umbrella organization, the Institute for International Finance, the private bankers have declared categorically that they will opt out of such long-term lending as a *matter of policy*. Their statements and their behaviour have given eloquent confirmation to the seriousness of this stance. They have responded sluggishly to pleas and inducements, as is evident from the reduced flow of net commercial long-term lending to the highly-indebted countries. The flows of bank lending that were attained during the 1970s were exceptional and, *ex post*, can be seen as unlikely to be repeated whatever pleas, inducements and guarantees are offered. "Once bitten, twice shy" seems to be the operative slogan.

Even the exotic items of the "menu approach" of innovative financial instruments holds little promise of attracting bankers into the game again. Given their appreciation of how perilously thin is the ice they are invited to skate on, few are prepared to participate. None the less, there has been some activity with bankers trading their dubious assets for bonds and for hard assets in the developing countries through "debt-for-equity" swaps, "debt-for-nature" swaps and other variants such as "debt-for-scholarship" swaps, "debt-for-good works" swaps and "debt-for-dignity swaps."[15]

All of these initiatives—as we shall see when the concept and application of swaps is discussed more fully in Chapter 7—have helped to slightly reduce the debt owed by some third world countries. But overall, as is evident from the *continuing rise* in the total debt owed by the third world countries, this has served only to slow the rate of increase and not to reduce the debt overhang. These initiatives are clearly not enough.

It is wishful thinking to envisage a quick return to voluntary lending and a substantial rise in foreign private investment in the third world debtor countries. It is not even clear that private bankers should be expected to meet long-term capital requirements since their traditional role has been limited to the provision of suppliers' credit and project financing for ventures with quick financial returns. At any rate, new money will not be forthcoming from the bankers whose views are probably well reflected in the statement of Willard Butcher, Chairman of Chase Manhattan Bank, that "debt forgiveness and new money are incompatible."[16]

If initiatives to provide new money on the requisite scale will not be forthcoming from the private sector, even with guarantees, the ball is then in the court of the major third world debtors who have an option of taking unilateral initiatives, and/or in the court of the major industrialized countries who must then exercise leadership. This places the heaviest responsibility on the world's largest economy, the United States. Leadership—exercised in a cooperative manner—is one of the key necessary conditions for resolving the debt crisis and doing so in a manner that also addresses the threat of the global environmental crisis.

CHAPTER 5

LEADERSHIP: CONTENDING WITH THE "SECOND DEBT CRISIS" AND SUMMITRY

In 1985, Mario Henrique Simonsen, the former Brazilian Minister of Finance, raised a provocative question: "Who is to be held responsible for the debt crisis: commercial banks that behaved as imprudent lenders, or debtor developing countries that misused the borrowed external funds? This is the fashionable question in witch-hunting circles, where every crisis provides a unique opportunity to practise their favourite sport. The debate reflects nothing but poor logic...A plausible explanation for the debt crisis must rely on either some external factor or the inadequacy of the recycling system, or both."[1] In answering this question, most analysts point the accusing finger at the external factor of the 1973 oil shock that increased the price of oil four-fold. This action was destabilizing in adding an estimated $250 billion to the import bills of oil-importing developing countries and adding several times that amount to the reserves of the oil exporters. Thus begat the "petrodollar recycling" phenomenon, the incubation period for the crisis that broke in the summer of 1982. It is pertinent to ask: why did the process of recycling take the form it did with its lack of control and the attendant danger?

Answers to this question indicate that the spotlight should not be on the petrodollar phenomenon per se but on the manner in which it was handled, that is, on the institutional context or system wherein this process took place. The decision makers on both the lending and borrowing sides could well be characterized as persons having "an attitude of fiscal laxity, a nonchalance about fiscal deficits" a description that Jacques de Larosière, former Managing Director of the IMF, applied to policy makers both in the United States and in the debtor countries. However, the consequences of their actions cannot be adequately explained with reference to their policy mistakes and motivations. The search for explanations must turn to the objective factor that Simonsen refers to, namely, the "inadequacy of the system" and particularly in this case, the inadequacy of leadership.

Every system—and the global economic/financial system is no exception—operates by explicit or implicit rules, hopefully for the maintenance and promotion of the "common good." In any case, they operate for the provision of the "rule of law" to set parameters for the conduct of everyday affairs. In today's global international economic/financial condition with its crisis tensions, there is a clearly recognized need for arrangements designed to provide what has been called an "international public good," that is, the establishment and maintenance of a global milieu characterized by the rule of law, acceptable modes of behaviour in commerce and everyday activities and other attributes of a desirable world in terms of stability, fairness and openness.[2]

THE UNITED STATES: A LEADER BETWEEN A ROCK AND A HARD PLACE

Leadership has a critically important role in providing and assuring the array of services or conditions that make up this public good at every level of governance. In the international arena, low real interest rates are a vital public good that is especially important for the resolution of the global debt crisis. Leadership is clearly essential to achieve the cooperation or coherence necessary to lower global real interest rates.

The root cause of the phenomenon of high real interest rates can be found in two salient facts: (1) for the past decade the United States economy has been absorbing well over half of the global supply of available capital and contributing little or nothing to that supply; (2) meantime, from the mid-1970s to the mid-1980s, there has been a global decline in the rate of investable savings as reflected in the fall of the savings/GNP ratio in industrialized countries by 5 per cent (from 25 to 20 per cent) and in the developing countries by 8 per cent.

Vital as it is to correct these trends, the lack of success thus far should not be surprising. The nature and degree of the adjustment required to bring the situation into balance poses a formidable challenge. In the absence of bold effective policies, it might well require a depression on a global scale to achieve the required adjustment that would bring real interest rates down to their historic levels. The real source of danger implicit in the international debt crisis might be said to arise, therefore, from the side of the United States as a debtor as well as an incapacitated leader. Under the current circumstances, *it is the constraints on the ability of the United States to exercise the requisite degree of leadership in concert with other of the major nations that makes the prevailing debt crisis situation exceptionally fragile.*

There is a Panglossian view, however, that the United States still remains capable of playing the requisite leadership role despite the level of its indebtedness and despite continuing budget deficits and the continuing increase (albeit at a slower pace) in household and business indebtedness. Those who see the rosy side of the picture point to key ratios, noting that the United States current account trade deficits peaked in the mid-1980s at 3.3 per cent and thereafter declined to average during all the years of the 1980s a manageable level of about 2.5 per cent of its GNP.

This reassuring statistic, however, hardly takes account of some critical changes in the structure of the United States economy over the last two decades, changes that accelerated during the 1980s and have immeasurably weakened the United States economic/financial hegemonic power:

- The increased dependence of the United States economy on exports as the percentage of GNP attributable to net exports rose from 4 per cent of GNP in 1960 to over 8 per cent by 1990, and *by 1990 is estimated to have accounted for 90 per cent of the economy's growth;*

- The growing percentage of manufacturing that has moved off-shore and will likely continue to do so in light of the cheaper costs of production, a trend that probably will accelerate with respect to Latin America as "free trade" agreements are negotiated to take advantage of low-cost labour in countries like Mexico, as is evident with the rapid growth of the *maquiladoras*;

- The productivity of the United States economy has been rising exceptionally slowly both in absolute terms and relative to its principal competitors, Japan and Germany. Both are still running record high surpluses in trade with the United States, Germany having passed the United States as the world's largest exporter in 1990;

- The decline in the quality of the United States infrastructure affecting not only urban transport and housing stock, but also the educational and health facilities and services available to the United States population. The deterioration is reflected in educational and health standards that are at crisis levels and in the rise in the number of those living in dire poverty with its culture of broken families, crime and drug addiction.

The most damaging impact stems from the fact that the level of private spending and government expenditures on *current* consumption has been at the expense of direct productive investment and its support systems in research, education, health and infrastructure, further depressing the rate of increase in productivity. These trends have exacerbated the sclerotic condition of the United States economy that began in the mid-1960s with the beginning of the decline in productivity growth from the 3 to 4 per cent level of the 1940-1970 period. There was a dramatic drop in the rate of productivity growth in the late-1970s after the oil shock made its impact, dropping the growth to a level well below the historic average of about 2 per cent. The era of the 1980s with its philosophy and style of leadership accentuated the downward trend.[3]

Remedying this condition by drastically slowing the rate of increase in consumption and redirecting the savings to productive investment is not a sufficient nor politically feasible answer to this deep-seated malaise. Such measures would help precipitate a *major recession*. In the short term, United States policy makers are thus between the proverbial rock and hard place. Even when it comes to the longer term, United States policy makers are ideologically constrained from making the structural or system changes that are necessary for their own resurgence and, thereby, for the long-term resolution of the global debt crisis. It is this aspect of the current situation, compounded by the global environmental crisis, that makes it premature to indulge in a complacent assessment that the worst is over or that structural adjustments by debtor countries and modest measures of debt relief will see us through.

Wide-ranging changes in policies and in institutional arrangements are required, in short, structural adjustment that will enable a substantial rise in the United States savings/taxation rate and in investments that lead to a higher rate of productivity from investments in plant, in infrastructure, in research, in education, in health and the like. Without this bold approach, there can be no expectation that they will escape the consequences of having become a debtor nation on so great a scale and in so short a time.

Under the best of circumstances it would be difficult to slow and then to reverse these trends in a reasonable span of time. But it is clearly impossible when the current United States Administration resists raising taxes for the affluent rich and altering its spending priorities to provide the majority of its population the necessary education, health research, and basic infrastructure, and when many American households are attracted to the "culture of consumerism" that is continually being reinforced by advertising. Greed has been the credo of the 1980s, and though book publishers find that "greed is out, environment is in," there still is a long way to go.[4] Perhaps the most graphic illustration of one important facet of the nature of the 1980s is revealed by noting the patterns of expenditure and incomes changes over this period: the top 5 per cent of income earners in the United States increased their real incomes by 50 per cent and benefitted from a 20 per cent cut in income taxes, while the bottom 20 per cent of income-earners suffered a 15 per cent drop in real incomes and had their taxes raised over the same period. This, in turn, might help explain the shifting pattern of expenditures with spending on staples declining as a percentage of disposable income while luxury cars doubled as a share of the total car market, and the share of expenditure doubled for cut flowers, boats and foreign travel.

Professor Benjamin Friedman has aptly characterized the prevailing condition of the United States economy—and by extension the global economic/financial situation—as "systemic bankruptcy:"

> "The consequence of growing federal indebtedness is a slow, gradual erosion of the foundations of the ability of the United States to be effective in international competition, as well as in its role as a global political leader; (the consequences of the growing corporate indebtedness has) rendered the United States economy fragile (with) danger of potential defaults, disruption of the financial system, and . . . (in a phrase, suffering from) a systemic bankruptcy."[5]

The overwhelming international significance of the present state of the United States economy, symbolized by its status as the world's largest debtor, is that *United States policy makers are severely constrained from taking the necessary corrective steps with respect to both the Third World debt and the environmental crisis.*

THE OTHER LEGS OF THE TRIPOLAR LEADERSHIP: HOW STRONGLY CAN THEY BE EXPECTED TO PULL?

Clearly, the requisite leadership cannot be provided by the United States alone. As the world's largest economy by a factor of 2, and as the major buyer of the available global pool of capital, the United States must, indeed, be the key player. To a lesser extent, starring roles must be given to Japan and Germany. As the major trade surplus countries, they are fated to be the principal suppliers of the necessary capital. Significant differences exist, however, between the major economies in their rates of savings, in their ratios of investment to GNP and in their rates of productivity increase. Though there have been many admonitions, warnings and declarations of intent to bring these rates into greater harmony, thereby to reduce the levels of real interest rates, realign and dampen the volatility of exchange rates, the ad hoc efforts to achieve coordination through the meetings of the finance ministers, have not been able to do much about these phenomena.

Apparently it is difficult to reach agreement among the leading industrialized nations as to the nature, timing and speed of change,[6] but none the less, a tripolar leadership has been emerging. There is general agreement among them about the desirable direction and the acceptable limits of such change in policies designed to reduce real interest rates, stabilize exchange rates, and lower barriers to trade and capital movements and establish a more "open" global system. But there is little agreement on how vaguely-defined objectives are to be accomplished, and on how conflicting priorities are to be reconciled.

They can agree about the desirability of lowering interest rates but meanwhile both Japan and Germany are raising their rates in response to immediate pressures. Germany, for example, will be devoting a large part of its available financial resources to Eastern European rehabilitation. The new investments in east Germany are expected to be as high as $40 billion in 1991 alone. Twenty-four of the OECD countries have already pledged about $38 billion over the next five years, but the major contribution will be coming from Germany for economic and geo-political reasons. Its other commitments to lower interest rates and increase its ODA to address the concerns of the global community-at-large, therefore, will likely be modest. This puts the major onus on the Japanese, the other country with a large trading surplus and commensurate foreign exchange.

Several years ago, The New York Times columnist, Flora Lewis, was able to write in a column datelined, Tokyo:

"Ideas (related to spending) butt up against deeply ingrained Japanese traditions which they feel strongly define their specific identity. . . . A cultural, philosophical, even moral transformation, is involved as great as the change brought about by America's Commodore Perry who battered open Fortress Japan or by General MacArthur's occupation regime. It won't happen overnight. . . . (As for aid), the obvious answer when riches become a burden is to give them away, but the Christian tradition of charity is not a part of the Confucian order. Japan will have to learn about giving, as well as earning."[7]

Much has happened since to indicate that the glacier is moving, and given the factors to which Ms. Lewis alluded, moving faster than might be expected. Japan has become the leading contributor to the flow of official development assistance (ODA), surpassing the United States aid levels in absolute terms before the decade of the 1990s had even begun. With an output valued at about 12 per cent of the world's GNP, Japan has responded with a contribution (albeit much of it in the form of "tied aid") greater than that of the United States with its global GNP share of 25 per cent. How long this will continue, however, is a moot question.

The Japanese will be constrained in their efforts to assist with third world problems, even though their own banks are heavily involved as creditors, and they have a great deal at stake. First, much of their financial surplus will be spent domestically on costly public works and home building to bring their living conditions closer to American and European standards. The process has already started in earnest with a planned allocation for public works projects of Y430 trillion ($3,200 billion) over the next 10 years, an amount that will raise expenditure on public works alone to more than 7 per cent of Japan's GNP. Secondly, through a well-established investing pattern Japanese capital is flowing to the United States to sustain that economy's continued importation of Japanese products and to slow the depreciation of the dollar (or its converse, the appreciation of the yen). Thus it will prove more difficult than it appears to direct a much larger part of their financial resources to the third world, whether directly or indirectly through the transnational agencies.

Thirdly, and perhaps most decisively, trouble is brewing at the source of this cornucopia: the Japanese economic miracle is beginning to flag. The Nikkei index of stockmarket prices has fallen from astronomical heights. A spectacular drop of 48 per cent during the first 10 months of 1990 erased "paper wealth" amounting to Y300 trillion, or almost double the third world's outstanding debt; the land bubble has also burst, with a 20 per cent drop in 1990. A further fall of 30 per cent is expected during 1991 to "bring down to earth" the inflated values that have priced Japan's total stock of property at a theoretical Y2,000 trillion, equivalent to about half of Japan's GNP or to about four times the value of the total stock of property in America.

The threat to the Japanese banking system comes not only from the collapsing credit pyramid with its shaky foundation built on the speculatively inflated value of these stocks and property assets as collateral; in addition, they must now contend with problems posed by rising interest rates and tougher international standards for capital-adequacy.

The talk, therefore, is of Japan being in the early stages of financial trauma, a situation well described by Christopher Wood in *The Economist* in an issue that surveyed the Japanese financial/economic scene:

> ". . . (with) the bursting of the biggest speculative bubble seen this century, some moneymen working in Tokyo are starting to take an apocalyptic view. . . . Yesterday's collective euphoria can too easily degenerate into tomorrow's collective panic. . . . Sadly, much of that hard-won wealth could now be destroyed far more quickly than it ever was created. . . . In a consensus society (such as Japan's) the longer the suspension of reality lasts the greater the potential for panic when everyone changes their minds simultaneously . . . Even Japanese pragmatism has its limits."[8]

Under these circumstances, especially if the worst case scenario comes to pass, the Japanese leadership would be severely constrained. Japanese funds provide a major underpinning for the global asset markets, so the fallout would be felt worldwide.

Coordination: frayed on trade

The stresses have been compounded by and have contributed to the fraying of the global cooperative framework. This is most dramatically illustrated by the 1990 *denouement* of the Uruguay Round of the General Agreement on Tariffs and Trade (GATT). The negotiations became a virtual battlefield between members of the industrialized countries that form the Group of Seven club and between them and the developing countries. The Japanese stood on the sidelines, but they would have had to be brought kicking and screaming into any possible agreement on agriculture export subsidies and other trade barriers. The flagrant example is provided by the protection afforded their rice farmers, a level of support through tariffs and non-tariff barriers that enables them to sell their product on the domestic market at a price several times higher than imported rice.

The other evidence of the retreat from global co-operation can be found in the regionalization of trade agreements. Like the Europeans, the United States has already embarked on a policy of promoting a regional trading bloc with the countries of the American continent, both to the north and south, under the banner of what it euphemistically calls a "free trade agreement."[9] The Japanese appear to be doing the same with countries of the South-East Asia region. With such leadership, it is not surprising that global cooperation in trade is still a long way off, a prospect that darkens the horizon of hope for the third world debtors that face high non-tariff barriers and that are expected, none the less, to trade their way out of their debt trap.

The matter goes deeper than a will to cooperate based on a recognition of mutual interest. The underlying source of difficulty is the daunting challenge of bringing the productivity of the major economies into line through adjustments in trading patterns and living standards. The changes required are sweeping for all concerned.

The consultation *cum* coordination process becomes more difficult to resolve when it is conceived as being a "zero-sum" situation, that is, where what one party gains is matched by what the other party loses. The real difficulty arises when coordination requires applying pressure for policy changes that are so fundamental as to be tantamount to calling for transformations in long-standing cultural patterns related to seemingly innocuous economic activities such as consumption, savings and investment. The investment aspect takes on special significance in light of the importance of transnational corporations in international trade and capital movements. The likelihood is that their private financial interests will be in conflict with national Governments, yet be so financially powerful as to be beyond their control. This has prompted economists such as Fred Bergsten and Robert Reich to advocate a "GATT for Investment" that in the words of Bergsten "would round out a three-pronged agenda for the '90s that the new tripolar management must address to maintain a stable world economy in the 21st century."[10]

The ability to forge a coherent set of policies in these fields of trade, monetary policy and investment will prove very difficult. What is required —as we shall discuss in Chapters 10 and 11—is "global structural adjustment." "Structural adjustment" has long been applied to the third world by multilateral institutions as part of their lending operations. "Structural adjustment lending" (SAL) has been a means of imposing conditions on borrowing countries. For industrialized nations, the adjustments required are no less urgent and no less sweeping, though given their greater wealth and incomes, the adjustments would appear easier for them to achieve, and achieving them is an essential condition if these countries are to play the leadership role required to guide the world's economy out of the crisis danger zone.

This entails recognition of and adjustment to a hegemonic shift. A leadership vacuum for tackling *both* the debt and the environmental crises would be dangerous. Both these crises must be addressed *at the same time* if the deteriorating trends with respect to each of them is not to become too difficult to correct before the adjustment is made for us abruptly and painfully. The crises are mutually reinforcing:

- If the debt crisis continues in its present form and magnitude, it will exacerbate environmental damage, most particularly in the third world, and impede the funding for policies, programmes and projects that are environmentally corrective;
- If the environmental trends continue on their present trajectory, they will worsen the ability of the debtor countries to service their debts as productivity declines due to the damaging impact of the neglected or inadequately treated environmental factors.

Breaking this vicious cycle calls for leadership through international cooperative arrangements that see the issues as symbiotically related. If we are to find our way out of the state of global disequilibrium or debt and onto the path to recovery characterized by greater equity and an environmentally sustainable future, the roots of the present crisis must be understood as deep-seated. It is also essential that we recognize the institutional obstacles that need to be overcome in assessing the many proposals put forward.

We turn to consideration of these obstacles, therefore, before tackling the proposals.

PART THREE

OVERCOMING THE INSTITUTIONAL OBSTACLES TO CHANGE

"In the three years since *Our Common Future* appeared we have gone through an explosion of conferences and meetings on sustainable development around the world. We have gone through a change of rhetoric, but so far we have seen very little action. Action is not only urgent, it's long overdue. All of the indicators are moving in the wrong direction. Hopefully, this will turn around within the next decade."

—Jim MacNeill, former Secretary-General of the World Commission on Environment and Development (the Brundtland Commission)[1]

CHAPTER 6

THREE BARRIERS

There appears to be so much public support for the resolution of the debt and the environmental crises and so much appears to be at stake, yet somber assessment indicates that the rhetoric is running far ahead of the action. This conundrum gives rise to the question: In light of such support, why is it so difficult to do "the right thing?" There are barriers that need to be identified and understood *in context*, the better to overcome them.

These barriers can most helpfully be considered under three headings:

1. *Inertia* with its related sources and attributes: ignorance, skepticism, fatalism, alienation and such;

2. *The aversion to risk-taking* exacerbated by the exceptional degree of uncertainty about environmental processes and their implications, and about the associated costs and benefits;

3. The resistance to change by those having a *vested interest* in the *status quo* and unwilling to countenance anything more than slight but not sufficient modifications thereof, and fearful of the costs in financial and other terms.

All of these are related and sometimes mutually reinforcing, but it is useful to distinguish them as a guide to policy-making and institutional change at the national as well as the international levels of governance.

THE INERTIA FACTOR AS A BARRIER TO CHANGE: INNATE HUMAN CHARACTERISTIC OR SYSTEM-CONDITIONED?

The inertia factor embraces two concepts, the concept of *perception* and of the *response* to perception.

The *perceptual* aspect refers to the tendency to see things only in ways that are familiar and acceptable. This is a generally prevalent societal characteristic that is a concomitant of ignorance, indifference, lack of imagination and parochialism. Ignorance and indifference are often fostered: the political ploy of placing great reliance on "bread and circuses" is an all-too familiar one. It is a classic diversionary tactic in defence of the *status quo* in the face of a growing realization that the appropriate responsive action to a crisis calls for *new* ways of doing things. The inertia rooted in parochialism is also a powerful force limiting both awareness and concern for national or global pressures, unless and until these pressures make a strong direct impact on day-to-day living conditions.

The *response* aspect refers to the tendency in almost all societies, whether democratic or authoritarian, to accept the continuation of past and prevailing conditions with their supportive institutions, even when this acceptance is seen as likely to lead to unacceptable outcomes. Conditions have to become exceptionally uncomfortable not only because of physical hardship, but also in terms of the intensity of anxiety before the aversion to the risks of change tip in favour of some form of action. In its most extreme form, this is sometimes referred to as "the dinosaur syndrome," illustrated by the analogy of the frog in boiling water: if dropped into boiling water the frog will jump out, unharmed; if left in cool water gradually heated to come to a boil, the frog will not move—alas!

Social behaviour, it seems, is influenced only slowly over time by its history; people tend to respond to situations in a manner based on past or learned experience. It is rare for a society to respond to predicted events, unless they threaten to be catastrophic and there is a societal memory of such occurrences within the lifetime of the past generation or two. One could ascribe this characteristic to an innate behavioural attribute of *homo sapiens* when acting as a group or collectivity.

The rationalization for this passivity or high level of tolerance often manifests itself as skepticism, cynicism or alienation carried to a point of fatalism, especially when reinforced by fear under coercive regimes. But in most cases, acquiescence is secured by cultural conditioning that induces widely shared views that accept the key features of the prevailing order. Leaders of every society, if they are to remain leaders, have to inculcate attitudes that reinforce the established system. A central element of this defensive strategy is mythology in the form of theoretic underpinning that can rationalize the *status quo* in its essential features *as a system*. Just as Karl Marx stood as an icon for those who extolled command-economy structures and processes in so-called communist countries, there has long been a virtual deification of Adam

Smith and of the beneficence of "the invisible hand" or "impersonal market forces" in so-called capitalistic societies. This process has ascribed to the ideological icons a set of views about the *morality* and *efficacy* of their respective systems, in one case, planning and the operations of a command economy, and in the other case, competition and the operations of a free market. The inculcated popular views are caricatures of their writings, but for the powers-that-be that serves the purpose all the better.

Thus in the creditor communities a great deal of faith is being placed in so-called market forces or the market system as the main institutional arrangement to achieve the daunting objectives of overcoming both the international debt and the global environmental crisis. In large measure this view of the power and beneficence of the market processes is based on the inertia principle of opting for the minimum amount of change necessary to realize any given objective—or its converse, *opting for a downgrading of the objective to conform to a minimal degree of necessary change.* For those with this ideological outlook, neither the debt nor the environmental crises provide a sufficiently compelling reason to get off the inertial pathway of reliance on the prevailing market-based system. The system is slightly modified, of course, to take account of "externalities," that is, the societal costs and the benefits not entered into the calculus of the private decision maker as investor or as consumer.

With respect to the debt issue, this market-based approach is essentially one of coping rather than curing. It takes the form of advocating as *sufficient* a case-by-case treatment of the problem that has been characterized as "muddling-through" and as "the menu approach." The latter, as we shall see in Chapter 7, relies on faith in the benevolent power of so-called "market forces." Leaving to one side the issues of the nature and extent of the external economies and diseconomies and how close the market conforms to the idealized competitive conditions, two further questions should be posed:

- Do the proponents of reliance on the market forces give adequate recognition to the implications of the unequal power of the parties in the market place and the asymmetric impacts of the market outcomes, both *intra*-generationally (the equity or distributional aspect) and *inter*-generationally (the aspects of the long-term sustainability of income growth and the maintenance or improvement of the environmental quality-of-life)?

- How do these proponents give adequate weight to structural changes that are required if the *denouement* is to be a global economic system that grows with much greater sharing and much greater sensitivity to environmental quality?

With regard to the environmental aspect, there is unanimous recognition that the prevailing economic system thrives upon and therefore fosters a "consciousness of unsustainability." Accordingly, the scope of the changes required is daunting. Despite that recognition of an elephantine problem, the proffered solutions can be characterized as mousy variants of a market approach. This confidence in market forces may well be the product of wishful thinking based on the experience of a crisis of recent memory, the so-called oil shocks of the early and late 1970s that seem to have been weathered in a successful fashion.

True, there has been no cataclysmic breakdown, as the panic mongers of the time seemed to fear; but this favourable assessment of the power of the market system to handle such a shock conveniently forgets or dismisses the aftermath of the oil crisis: radical changes in the patterns of global trade and capital movements, unprecedented foreign exchange disequilibria and levels of debt and the dire consequences that flowed from this manner of resolving that crisis. The method of "resolving" that problem can be said to have given birth to others, including the global debt crisis with its incalculable human costs, and to have weakened the world community's response to the looming environmental crisis with its ecological and social/economic costs—and dangers.

RISK AVERSION AS A BARRIER TO ACTION

The concepts of hazard, risk and uncertainty are critically important in the process of policy-making. A danger always emanates from the phenomenon of "hazard," which is an inherent attribute of all systems with the potential for the occurrence of an incident or series of events leading to a catastrophic outcome. The risk is the chance of such an undesirable event or progression of events happening in a certain time, but it can be defined to reflect the likelihood of the unwanted events and their consequences occurring. The occurrence can be in relation to routine operating conditions—such as excessive or abnormal levels of emissions into the environment—or in relation to exceptional happenings such as accidents like Bhopal or Chernobyl that emitted massive amounts of dangerous substances.

Uncertainty is inherent in risks, but the routine operations of a system—

such as those that apply to trends in trade and capital movements and in the use of energy in the development of economies—provide a basis for assessing the probability and consequences of risks. The degree and scope of risk can be changed, after all, by altering policies and programmes, and if the alteration is significant enough, by making changes in the prevailing institutional arrangements or systems.

The Hamlet principle could be neatly summed up in a phrase, "when uncertain, refrain." Governments have had an understandable tendency to act like the Prince, moving very cautiously, if at all, in response to the urgings of those who advocate bold measures. This is true whether with regard to the debt burden of the third world or with regard to environmental degradation with its dangers of irreversible damage from phenomena such as global warming due to radiation-trapping and skin cancer enhancement due to ozone depletion. Given the stakes involved and the uncertainties of both the cost and benefit sides, the sluggish response can be attributed to the factor of risk aversion in the calculus of those governing by Hamletian rules.

There are several approaches to handling this factor of risk:

- Risk minimalization with respect to the outcome by taking bold and prompt action early; in effect, this "plays it safe" *at almost any cost* on the grounds that great danger exists in *not* acting boldly when delay is likely to be incalculably costly. This applies particularly to the threat of irreversible environmental damage, in which case the benefits of avoiding the feared outcome of delay are beyond measure. Accordingly, there is no need to count the cost. This take-no-chances view can be characterized as essentially an insurance or "no regrets" approach. In the case of the debt crisis, the threat is one of damage that can be reversed (except for those who die or are irreparably injured, as in the case of brain damage for infants and children from nutritional deficiencies) until the strain goes beyond the tolerance leading to social breakdown that would take years to repair. The ambiguity of this borderline, being social and not scientific, makes the "no regrets" rationale much weaker than in the case of the environment threat.

- Risk minimalization with regard to what has to be done now, that is, counting the costs and the benefits *before* taking that leap into a costly "no regrets" prevention programme for which both the need-urgency and the outcome are uncertain.

In either case, the key elements of risk assessment centre on the degree of uncertainty with respect to available information (scientific, economic-financial and socio/cultural/political), and the costs and benefits that go beyond financial aspects to include the negative and positive impacts of adjustment in terms of inconvenience-convenience, discomfort-comfort and pain-enjoyment.

Focusing on the issue of debt, the kind of information needed relates to such things as the social/cultural/political costs. With regard to the economic aspects, it relates to the costs of production and the market conditions for the debtor country's exportable goods and services. This depends in turn on the price and income elasticities on both the supply and the demand sides that are affected in turn by existing and prospective tariff and non-tariff barriers, the amounts and terms of credit available, the efficiency with which the borrowed or invested funds are used and the like.

With respect to the environmental issue, to take only the facet of climate change, a great deal of information is essential for policy-making, information that can provide answers to questions such as the following:

- Has there been any climatic change at all?
- If so, can such changes in temperature ranges be attributed to specific causal factors?
- If so, to what degree can the changes be attributed to the use of the various fossil fuels?
- What might be the physical consequences to life on earth of various ranges of temperature changes?
- What are the likely financial and non-financial costs of various degrees of prevention?
- What are the likely costs of adjusting to the temperature changes, as calibrated by the various degrees of prevention?
- What are the relationships of costs and benefits in these various scenarios for both industrialized countries and developing countries?
- In any global agreement, what cost-sharing formula would be equitable (assuming the cost-benefit aspects were to be the basis for the criteria) and feasible (having in mind comparative financial and other resources and capabilities both technical and political)?

In dealing with issues so complex in nature and so global in scope as debt and environment, both separately and in their interrelationship, policy makers have to contend with unknowns, immeasurables and non-commensurables and attempt to assess the trade-offs that are the very essence of policy-making.

In both issues the trade-offs are between the *short term* costs or sacrifices that are rather certain in terms of financial and other resources that need to be committed and the *long-term* gains that are uncertain, especially for those categories of benefits measured by the avoidance of damages through actions taken before such damages occur. How can the benefit of peace of mind be put on the scale in making the trade-offs that are the essence of policy-making? *The benefit of avoiding possible catastrophic* outcomes is impossible to "count" even under the best of circumstances, and thus rather difficult to factor into decision-making. The costs and benefits include, therefore, factors that go beyond the financial, economic and social.

Enormous stakes are involved in the costs and benefits. To achieve environmentally *significant* measures, we are dealing with high costs for programmes to stabilize and then reduce CO_2 emissions. This one programme has been estimated to require an additional annual expenditure ranging from $100 billion to $300 billion, the spread in estimates depending on the emission reduction targets and a host of other factors.[2]

A Trilateral Task Force Report in 1991 has ventured to suggest that

"if a Grand Bargain on global warming were negotiated an aggregate flow of funds of about $20 to $30 billion a year would be needed assuming the lowest cost measures available..and if United States data were to be applied worldwide, the total cost of reducing CO_2 emissions by 40 per cent in an efficient global programme will amount to less than $100 billion at the 1989 level of world economic activity."[3]

Two other items should be added: the cost of programmes to cut the emissions in terms of the impact on the growth rate of global GNP, the estimates of which range from 0.1 to 0.3 per cent reduction annually; and the costs of other programmes on the environmental agenda, such as, for example, environmental clean-up costs. For the United States alone, this has an estimated price tag in excess of $300 billion per year according to the United States Environmental Protection Agency.[4] These are rough numbers, but the ball-park figures have understandably given policy makers reason to pause before taking the plunge.

Before money of this magnitude will be forthcoming, policy makers must answer some specific and concrete questions. Since every increment of insurance against the worst case scenarios entails a given expenditure of financial and other resources—assuming a calibration can be made to establish the costs for each increment of improvement—the budget controllers would want to have answers to the following questions àpropos the debt relief and environmental improvement programmes:

- Assuming the degree of a debtor's misery can be calibrated, what is the tolerable limit before they opt out of the process—and with what consequences for the creditors and for the quality of the global environment?
- What degree of climate change is "acceptable?" Or what is the tolerable limit of environmental damage before the point of no return is reached, with catastrophic consequences for the future?
- How does the answer to the last question influence the answer to the earlier ones?

Additional problems add to the uncertainty and the risk having to do with the implications for the competitive position of any one country that undertakes an expensive initiative if the others do not follow.

- In explaining their resistance to international environmental initiatives, United States policy makers have expressed their fear that if they step out too far in the lead (and they claim leadership with an annual expenditure of over $30 billion including the funding for research to improve the relevant technologies) they risk suffering a cost disadvantage. This is especially so if acting as pioneers in applying costly environmentally desirable technologies and programmes proves to be ineffectual, a possibility that would make such policies and their programmes even more expensive. The risk poses a formidable barrier that can be overcome only by global cooperation that spreads the risks on the research side as well as in its application.

This reluctance to gamble is likely to be greater when those who bear the costs and those who reap the benefits are not within the same region or nation, or where there are quite separate groups on the cost and benefit sides. This asymmetry between geographic areas or political jurisdictions or between different generational and income groups is an aspect of this policy dilemma pertaining to risk that is of special significance for the developing countries.

Where the scope is global, the impacts on the cost and benefit sides are bound to be different between industrialized and developing countries. This is clearly seen in the available scientific knowledge that calculates the likely range of climate change and related physical effects, such as rising ocean

levels and cropping patterns and productivity. The effects of these are estimated to have the potential of redoing the national incomes of the industrialized countries by less than 1 per cent over the next half-century, but would
likely have a much more harmful impact on developing countries.[5]

When the benefits are notional in terms of damage-avoidance or prevention
and asymmetrical, with the major part accruing to the parties bearing the
lesser part of the costs, there is an understandable reluctance to undertake the
programme, especially when the costs are large and governments are struggling with tight budgets. The governments and the business leaders in the
industrialized countries have been busy counting the heavy financial costs of
living up to the various promises of achieving and maintaining an acceptable
global environment where they are expected to incur a part of the costs that
is disproportionate to their benefit. As these estimates and the associated
uncertainties of the cost and benefits have been toted up, the degree of enthusiasm for the programmes has noticeably waned.

Indeed, counter-attacks are being launched by the vested interests that
would be immediately effected by environmental programmes. In the case of
the carbon emmissions reduction programme, the oil industry is in the forefront of the battle, as one would expect, waving the self-serving banner of
patriotism with security of supply but hardly daring to launch a frontal attack
on the environmental issue. The business community's battle is being waged
with all weapons including public relations advertisements that stress the need
for adequate energy and economic growth and argues, as Mobil does in its
advertisements, for "contributions from each of the coal, petroleum and
nuclear options that can make a difference in the strength of the American
economy."[6]

Which brings us to the third barrier to change, vested interests.

THE SYSTEMIC NATURE OF VESTED INTERESTS AS A BARRIER TO ACTION

Special interests pressures

The factor of vested interests is probably the most powerful barrier militating
against change. We should expect opposition from those who stand to lose
the most from proposed changes, and those who expect to be called upon to
assume the major part of the costs for policies and programmes to implement

the changes without any expectation of enjoying a proportionate benefit. This opposition manifests itself in many ways.

In connection with the debt crisis, the major creditors have been the larger banks that collectively constitute a powerful lobbying force in their respective countries. With few exceptions, they have shown a fierce resistance to any proposals that would force them to provide debt relief and force them to reduce the book value of their accounts receivable from third world countries to the values placed on them in the secondary market for these questionable assets. They have also fought for tax concessions for any write-down of the value of these assets.

This hard-nosed position is cloaked under a rationale that might be labelled ''moral rectitude,'' a posture by creditors *vis à vis* third world debtors that lessons have to be taught to debtors as an incentive for them to be on better behaviour in the future. This view is clearly expressed by the former chairman of the Federal Reserve Board, Paul Volcker, who gave testimony before a United States congressional committee that was considering measures of debt relief:

> ''The debt burden,'' he said, ''is the result of poorly thought out economic policies in many third world countries and the proper solution is fundamental policy adjustments (on their part). Writing down or writing off such debts would encourage the debtor Governments to weaken in their efforts to pursue the austerity policies which are necessary.''

In his testimony he was undoubtedly reflecting the policy of the United States Administration and of most of the other supporters of the muddling-through approach.

The reasons for this posture are not difficult to fathom. As Professor Paul Klugman has astutely noted, ''for creditors as a group, the current debt strategy has been a pretty good bargain even in the short run.''[7] Bankers and creditor Governments can be expected to defend their own narrow interests by supporting an approach that places the greater strains on the debtor side of the process. With time the banks have had the opportunity to build up substantial reserves against the anticipated losses from bad sovereign debts. But weakened as they are now with collapsing real estate loans and junk bonds for speculative ventures that have gone sour, they are even less willing and able to be accommodating to third world debtors. In the case of Japanese banks, the issue is one of protecting their financial bottom line to weather a stockmarket and real estate crash; in the United States, the very viability of the major banks is at stake with their credit ratings being downgraded and many already in receivership and in need of a governmental bailout. Trying times and desperate circumstances breed hard-headed bargaining positions.

In connection with the environmental issue, there is of course a wide array of interested parties that find it to their advantage, at least in financial terms and in the short-run (and for many that is all that counts), to maintain the *status quo*. Under the prevailing circumstances, they would agree to making the suggested changes in their practices only if forced by regulations or enticed by some market-incentive scheme. Though many studies have shown that for any given impact regulatory constraints are more cost effective, most environmentalists put a great deal of faith in price changes to redirect consumption patterns and to induce cooperative behaviour by polluting firms.

Ordinarily consumers have a vested interest in the convenience of their present lifestyles that is reflected in the sales trends favouring goods such as disposable diapers, hair sprays, air-conditioners and large air-conditioned cars. This applies to many who describe themselves as environmentalists who might like to do the right thing but find the choices rather limited, especially when their bank accounts are rather limited. John Sawhill, the President of the Washington-based organization, Nature Conservancy, has made a troubling observation: "One wonders what will happen to popular support for the environment—which is said to include three out of four Americans polled on the issue—when the price of unleaded gas goes above $2 or $3 a gallon."

The answer often advanced in support of price hikes to dampen demand for environmentally-damaging products or services is the experience of the post-1973 years after the first oil shock that raised the price of oil several-fold. The immediate impact of the oil price shocks of 1973 and 1979 was a rapidly slowing rate of increase in the consumption of fossil fuels. In the United States the rate of increase dropped from almost 5 per cent per year to about 1 per cent, as consumers opted for smaller and more fuel-efficient cars and other measures. Transportation is especially important because almost three quarters of oil consumption in the United States is for the automotive sector. Although only 4 per cent of the world's population, the American public uses about 40 per cent of the world's output.[8] But from 1983 onward, the percentage has climbed until it is almost back to the original rate of increase. The ratio of oil consumption to GNP has slightly improved in absolute terms, but the picture over the longer term is less encouraging: between 1977 and 1983 United States oil consumption fell by 28 per cent, from 18.8 to 15.2 million barrels a day; today it is about 20 million.

There is a mutual dependence between the producers of fossil fuels and the industries and utilities with heavy investments in the technologies adapted to the use of these carbon-emitting fossil fuels. Both have a vested interest in the prevailing consumer culture, and they reinforce it by advertising. It is clearly not enough to depend on the price elasticity of demand to achieve a long-range change in consumer preferences when virtually free rein is given to those who promote products and services on the basis of an appeal to non-price factors, and when, in fact, their advertising and public relations efforts are subsidized by allowing the costs of such activities to be deducted in calculating their taxes. These deductions mean, in effect, that the public is paying part of the cost for the employment of lobbies for these vested interests to maintain this right to countervail public policy initiatives.

The culture of consumerism or of unsustainability will prevail until some changes are made that go beyond price movements. This is especially so in our information age, when price is only one of many factors in a culture heavily influenced by advertising that is designed to sell on the basis of brand rather than price. The insidious aspect in this market-distortion pertains to the promotion of brand names which enable these vested interests to make the non-price factors a key influence in consumer behaviour, thereby enabling them to capture what economists refer to as "economic rent." Its capitalized value is reflected in the asset called "goodwill" on the books of these companies, an asset often greater than that of their physical plant and their other assets combined. The resistance of the vested interests to changes that might be brought about by the price factor and competitive market forces is thus understandable. They prefer so-called "market forces" that are weighted and distorted by the exercise of vested interests seeking short-term financial gain without weighing the social costs into their profit and loss calculations.

But to their arsenal these vested interests also bring direct and indirect political pressure to stop or slow down the enactment of regulatory constraints and/or fiscal measures of taxes and rebates that will induce the desired changes towards more environmentally acceptable technologies, *when these are available*. Often they have no incentive to make the alternatives available, and if they do, their powerful position enables them to do so as and when it suits their financial interests. Funding for environmentally benign alternatives is a key element in any effective strategy. When this aspect of an environmental policy is considered, it is evident that the actions being taken are working at cross purposes.

This should not be surprising. A great deal of justifiable notoriety is attached to the vested interest group loosely characterized as "big oil" but which extends across the whole power supply spectrum from oil to coal to natural gas to hydro and nuclear power segments of the energy industry. All have become skillful and powerful practitioners of the art of protecting their vested interests and, together, their vested interest in the conventional sources of power as against those of alternative energy sources.

This bias is reflected in the disproportionate support given to research on conventional sources of energy as compared with research on alternate forms of energy. One has only to look at the direct budgetary outlays by Governments and the private sector for energy-related research to appreciate where the priorities are actually being placed. And to look beyond that at both the combination of incentives and disincentives, tax credits and penalties that affect the rate of transition towards environmentally-benign energy technologies, and the weight given to factors such as durability, life-cycle costs and social-environmental costs and benefits.[9]

Despite this resistance by the private sector to environmental regulatory constraints on grounds of the additional costs and the greater complexities, progress is being made with the control of emissions, effluents and other deleterious by-products of industry. But it is a slow process, and the report cards for all industrialized countries still show failing grades. The spate of internationally and nationally legislated and proposed actions is impressive —until one looks more closely at the procedural and the substantive aspects in terms of their target-setting and the funding for their implementation and enforcement.[10]

Beyond these rather straightforward strategies and tactics in the exercise of the power of vested interests, a broader, more subtle but no less important interpretation of vested interests should be considered, namely, the forces that work to maintain the stability of the prevailing system on the basis of their own special advantage. These groups, in the exercise of their power in influencing policies, can be relied upon to constrain the political policy makers from making radical changes, that is, those changes that in scale and scope have ramifications that are *systemic*. Since these problems are of a scale and scope that might well call for measures that address *systemic* weaknesses or failures, the actions taken are likely to be much more modest than the rhetoric would suggest.

There are several systemic features that can be identified as contributing to this state of affairs.

- *In the case of politicians*, a myopic condition prevails; incumbents facing near-term re-election are pressured to give little weight to the longer-term future that is beyond their term in office, and to give little weight to those national or international perspectives that are beyond the *immediate* concerns of the electorate in their respective constituencies. Even were they to have the best of intentions with regard to the long-term future, the politicians and their policy advisers must face the problem of factoring in the greater risks on the costs and benefit sides given the greater uncertainty and greater gaps in the scientific and other types of information that are needed to make a judgement;

- *In the case of management in the private sector*, the time-horizon is hardly longer when the investment decisions are made on the basis of quarterly returns or the annual "bottom line," that is, on the basis of a high discount rate that gives little weight to the long-term. This practice is even more common in the face of uncertainty, especially when environmental regulations will oblige them to internalize the "external diseconomies" of environmental damage from their operations. Thus policy making in the public and private sectors tends to be constrained by both a short-term and a parochial perspective.

SYSTEMIC PRESSURES: POVERTY IS THE GREATEST POLLUTER

The *systemic* aspect of vested interests manifests itself most dramatically in the situation where the parties to an agreement are unequally balanced. The chairperson of the *World Commission on Environment and Development*, Gro Harlem Brundtland, made this point well when she stated,

> "The gross mismanagement of our planet has much to do with an inequitable distribution of the benefits of development (leaving) close to a billion to live in poverty and squalor, a situation that leaves them little choice but to go on undermining the conditions of life itself, the environment and the natural resource base."[11]

The environmental damage that can ensue from the existence of poverty is most evident in the case of the developing countries burdened with severe debt servicing obligations and dependent on a narrow range of exports to earn the foreign exchange to meet these obligations. Their pressured circumstances incline policy makers to take less account of environmental consequences that can be felt only over the longer-term. Examples are deterioration of a watershed by clearing forest cover and continued dependence on fuelwood which the rural populace relies upon, in many cases for as much as 90 per cent of their energy requirements for cooking and heating. This pressure is increased by the fact that the Governments of developing countries have collectively about one hundredth of the capacity of the industrialized countries to undertake research on more environmentally desirable energy technologies.

Furthermore, the policy makers of the poorer indebted countries find it extremely difficult, to diversify and thus break away from a pattern of trade involving the export of those primary commodities whose cultivation has an adverse environmental impact.[12] These struggling countries may welcome foreign investors even when such investments are lured by the promise of environmental standards that are less stringent and that can be financially justified only on the basis of the export of pollution-intensive products. The temptation to apply lax environmental regulatory standards is greater when the prices of their exported commodities fall, as they have during the decade of the 1980s. Then there is a corresponding need to increase the volumes exported merely to maintain the level of foreign exchange earnings, whatever the consequences for the environment.[13]

Since the onset of the international debt crisis in 1982, the debtor countries have been pressed to commit themselves to undertake structural adjustment as a condition for the creditors agreeing to add the unpaid interest to the outstanding debt and, on occasion, coming forth with some additional loans. One unintended result of the usual conditionality associated with these Structural Adjustment Loans (SALs) is a reduction in the budgetary allocations to programmes such as research, health, education services and related infrastructure. The reductions apply as well to programmes involving the environment such as waste disposal, water and air pollution control and other environmental protective measures. All sectors that can not show a quick payoff in terms of improving the foreign trade balance become, under these circumstances, low priority candidates for the scarce financial and other resources. This process with its intense quality of stress and neglect for the environment undoubtedly prompted Mrs. Indira Ghandi to once describe poverty as "the greatest polluter."

Addressing the poverty issue from the perspective of the debt and the environmental crises calls for approaches that are systemic and global in their scope. Proposals have come forward in great profusion. But given their more limited time-frame and limited objectives, these proposals are almost all ameliorative rather than corrective and are rather modest in their institutional implications. Some proposals are more sweeping in as much as they address the common systemic sources of both the debt and environmental crises and are accordingly more radical in the institutional implications especially with respect to action at the global level of governance.

We turn now to these proposals.

PART FOUR

PROPOSALS: COPING OR CURING?

".... the bewildered tourist encountered a hungry lion in the treeless desert.

'What did you do?' asked his friend.

'I climbed a tree,' said the tourist.

'But there were no trees around,' observed the friend.

'But what would you have done?' replied the tourist.''

—A Norwegian parable[1]

"It is now becoming clear that after a debt crisis of the magnitude experienced in the 1980s, a new approach for the 1990s is needed to break this debilitating pattern. . . . With the original goal of debt strategy still far out of reach, we should revise our goal for the immediate years ahead, concentrating instead on the return to sustained economic growth in the debtor countries.''

—Stanley Fischer and Ishrat Husain, World Bank economists[2]

CHAPTER 7

MARKET-BASED PROPOSALS — THE DEBT CRISIS

Problems attract proposals; by 1985, three years after the global debt issue became a "hot" topic, the Bank of England had compiled a list of more than 150 proposals that purported to deal with the situation, either to ease the strain or to provide a cure. Since then there have been many additional entries contributing to what the Ottawa-based North/South Institute in its *Review '88-Outlook '89* described as "a whole supermarket of ideas and schemes available for attacking these (debt crisis) problems."

Few of these proposals, however, are placed in the context of the *mega* transition or transformation of the contemporary global economy that is reflected in the occurrence and persistence of the double-headed global debt-environmental crisis. By and large the proponents of these proposals accept the key elements of the existing institutional framework and address the issues as "problems" rather than as "crises," and, therefore, as transitory phenomena. Thus the "cure" is a package of measures that would return the global economy to the *status quo ante* even though the "normal" operations of the global economy, as a *system*, gave rise to the troublesome crises.

"MUDDLING-THROUGH," OR THE DEBT WORKOUT PROCESS VIA THE "MENU APPROACH"

Proposals for a market-based approach to resolving the debt crisis have been the most common. Despite the greater variations in detail, most have a common assumption, namely, that the debt crisis is basically a temporary liquidity problem. Those who hold this view regard the current situation as stressful but not dangerous. They believe that it was brought on by an unfortunate conjuncture of events, principally a sharp and steep drop in capital inflows and reactive measures which intensified the problem—and continues to do so. This assumes that when the crisis is eased and eventually "resolved," it is not likely to recur. Thus the problem is regarded as transitional, and all that is required is a course of action that can be labelled "crisis management" or "muddling-through." This approach is reactive and limited in its objectives and scope to avoiding default and hastening the return to conditions where the debtors will once again be deemed to be creditworthy.

Recognizing that adjustment fatigue has been mounting and poses the threat of a breakdown of the process, a new wave of suggestions have involved innovative financing schemes to ease the strain. These proposals place the reliance for change on market-driven measures designed to entice creditors to accept conversion of debts owed them into other assets. It has been dubbed, therefore, from the outset "the menu approach" and "euphemisms for fancy packaging of a lemon."[4]

In 1982 when panic was in the air with talk of a global debt crisis, there were, at one extreme, those who felt that the appropriate course would be to let market forces guide the adjustment process and allocate between the debtors and creditors the costs and the benefits of mistaken imprudent decisions and of wise or lucky decisions. In their schema the creditor bankers would have to face the fact that the sovereign debts on their books, labelled "accounts-receivable," were assets not worth their face value, and they would accordingly have to write them down to the value reflected in the so-called "secondary market" for such loan sales.

Today by this market's valuation, this would mean discounting them on average by more than 60 per cent of their face value, and for some by more than 90 per cent. Thus the power of the market place would force the debtor-creditor relationship to conform to the changing realities of international economic relations.

A small minority, most notably Professors Milton Friedman and Allan Meltzer, have decried governmental involvement and would let the market process work to make the parties involved on both the creditor and debtor sides pay for their mistakes. This quick and dirty resolution would provide rough justice, in their view, and be less costly for the global community-at-large. Few share the judgement of these "pure market" advocates as to either the justice or the costs. This is regarded as the remedy without illusions or the "procrustean-bed solution:" creditors and debtors made the bed they must now lie on.

The draconian implications of this market-driven form of adjustment have been tempered by offering both debtors and creditors a veritable *smorgasbord* of choices from currency switching options to repurchase of discounted debt, plus a variety of conversion techniques such as debt-equity swaps and such jargony-exotics as "exchange offers with debt defeasance through collateralization." The more mundane items on the menu include the following: new money instruments such as new money bonds and commodity-linked bonds, interest retiming agreements, interest capitalization, facilities for trade, contingency and bridge financing, interest and currency switching options and securitization and currency switching techniques.[5]

The hope is that with such a range of choices both the creditors and debtors can, *if they wish*, convert the debts into bonds or into shares or into some other form of productive assets of the debtor countries. The resultant discount would be absorbed on the basis of negotiations between the debtors and the creditors. This process changes not only the *value* of the claims held by creditors but also the *attributes* and the *ownership* of these claims. Since such international transactions are complex and invariably incorporate elements of risk and concessionality, these market-based transactions call for third party involvement, that is, Governments or governmental agencies brought into the process to bear some of the adjustment costs and/or some of the risk and, in rare cases, to apply regulatory control. But the "market-based plus governmental involvement" proposals are generally modest in terms of their institutional implications. On that account, they might well be characterized as coping techniques, that is, ways to prevent a breakdown by reducing the stress of servicing debt without making *significant* changes in the prevailing global financial system.

Multi-year rescheduling agreements (MYRAs) were the conventional mode of the "debt workout" process in the early post-1982 phase. Through the negotiations involving one debtor and a group of creditor banks, MYRAs resulted in lower interest spread charges and a stretched-out schedule of repayments which had the effect of lowering the *present value* of the debt. In negotiating, the debtors and creditors were aware of the declining discounted valuations of the third world's debts on the so-called secondary market for third world loans. In effect, the market forces were operating to bring about a measure of *de facto* debt relief, but rarely debt forgiveness.

The contentious issues revolved around the degree of debt relief that the creditors were willing to give and what they asked from the debtors in return for the "voluntary" lending of *new* funds. The capitalization of unpaid interests invariably included in the negotiated debt rescheduling agreements had the effect of increasing the amount of total debt. For both parties the process was open-ended as unpaid interest and new money raised the debt rather than lowering it. However, the volume of new money being lent to third world debtor countries and the degree of concessionality or softening of the terms has not been enough to brighten the sordid picture except in a few exceptional cases. But so far it has been enough to keep the debt workout process from breaking down. Despite long and acrimonious stand-offs in the rescheduling negotiations and increasing arrears no serious defaults have, as yet, occurred.

The qualitatively *new* element added to this process through the menu items is the guarantee feature: more private capital is expected to flow once again to the debtor developing countries when creditor Governments and multilateral institutions assume the role of guarantors. In effect this would transfer much of the risk from the private banks to the public via obligations assumed by the public institutions. The World Bank was most often singled out as the appropriate agency to play this role, especially since its willing-and-eager declaration that it ''seeks to play an important *catalytic* role in the search for market-oriented, negotiated solutions (through) opening doors for more innovation with respect to alternative, consensual forms of debt relief.''[6] That guarantor role has now been assumed by the World Bank at the behest of the United States and Japan.

The application of the risk-transfer proposal generally takes two forms:

1. Reducing interest rates through various forms of subsidization by the conversion of the debts into guaranteed longer-term financial obligations, and

2. Converting debt into ownership of equities and other assets in the debtor country.

Both merit consideration.

Reducing interest rates on outstanding loans through transferring risk and conversions

The need to lower interest rates is a common thread running through almost all current proposals for resolving the debt crisis. As early as 1969 the authors of the Pearson Report, *Partners in Development*, observed that a debt crisis would loom within a decade if the real rate of interest at which developing countries borrowed remained above 2 per cent. This prognosis was based on trends in the volume and terms of lending in 1968. The total outstanding international debt of developing countries was then less than $50 billion, with rates and maturities far more favourable:

"If the flow of new lending were to remain at the level of 1965-67 with no change in its composition, the projection shows that by 1977 debt service would considerably exceed new lending, except in South Asia and the Middle East where they should be about equal. . . . *Overall there would be a large net transfer (after deduction of debt service) arising from lending and going from developing regions to the industrialized countries.* . . . The future depends on the course of future lending and whether the relative role of hard and soft lending will change."[7]

The analysis and its conclusions apply with even more force today.

The critical element is the real rate of interest on loans in relation to the contribution that the borrowed capital can make both to the growth in income of the borrowing countries and, more importantly in the present context, to the rate of increase in foreign exchange earnings with which to service their debts. Every percentage point decrease in interest rates would lower the cost of servicing their debts, in some cases significantly, for all the debtors by as much as $10 billion; for the group of highly indebted, middle-income countries, by as much as $5 to $6 billion annually, and would lower their debt service ratio by as much as 4 to 5 per cent. But under prevailing conditions, there is little prospect that real interest rates would be brought down to that level, i.e., between 1 and 2 per cent.[8]

There has been an understandable emphasis on the interest rate side of the equation rather than on the productivity of the borrowed capital because the rate of interest is more amenable to change in the short term. This emphasis on lowering the level of real interest rates reflects the fact that it is more quickly achievable than raising productivity. One way to lower real interest rates would be to reduce the risk premium built into the rate by the transfer of risk from the shoulders of the creditors to Governments or governmental agencies. The main rationale for an intermediating agency and the guarantee feature is that it would tempt the creditors to accept the lower valuation of the debt to a level roughly reflected in the valuation set by the secondary market, thereby in effect lowering the interest rate paid on the borrowed capital.

The key question is: Would the reduction be sufficient, that is, to a level at which the cost of capital and its productivity would be brought into a sustainable long-term relationship? The main appeal of the guarantee as inducement would seem to rest on the impact it would have on reducing the rate of interest at which lenders and borrowers can strike a bargain. Although it is not likely to reduce the cost of capital to borrowers and despite its questionable impact on capital movement, the idea of lowering the interest rate through guarantees has a long history.

As early as 1983, Minos Zombanakis, a London banker, and Lord Harold Lever, former financial adviser to Labour Governments in the United Kingdom, advanced the idea of a guarantee arrangement being provided by the IMF or the World Bank. This had been envisaged for the World Bank when it was founded, and indeed was one the the main rationales for its establishment. For various reasons, it remained largely still-born as the institution evolved along other lines.[9]

Over the course of the last few years many names could be added to the list of proponents of basically similar proposals. Among them are many third world economists who had held high positions in the economic planning and financial portfolios of their respective Governments (Mahbub ul Haq, Paulo Nogueira Batista, Aldo Ferrer, Celso Furtado, Pedro-Pablo Kuczynski and Mario Henrique Simonsen), investment bankers (Felix Rohatyn, James Robinson, Eugene Rotberg and George Soros), academics (Professor Peter B. Kenen, Percy Mistry, Jeremy Bulow, Kenneth Rogoff and Jeffrey Sachs) and others (C. Fred Bergsten, William Cline and John Williamson).

Their proposals differ mainly in the techniques for their implementation, in the choice of the intermediating institution, and in some cases in the linkage with debt rescheduling and the attendant conditionality. The list of suggested intermediating institutions have included the following: the World Bank, the IMF, an affiliate of one or other of these institutions, and some form of independent entity, such as the International Debt Discount Corporation (Peter Kenen of Princeton University), the International Lending Agency (financier George Soros), the Debt Refinancing Facility (Mahbub ul Haq, formerly Pakistan's Minister of Finance and Planning) and the International Citizenship Fund (Jeremy Bulow and Kenneth Rogoff of Stanford and California Universities), and others with labels such as the International Solidarity Bank and the Debt Reconstruction Facility. (See Annex E for a detailed elaboration of these proposals.)

All proponents recognize that there are contentious issues related to how the risk transfer costs are to be shared and how the political-ethical fall-out of socializing the private risks is to be handled. The core idea of the Brady Plan put forward by United States Treasury Secretary, Nicholas Brady, embodies the principle of the guarantee and the intermediating role of the World Bank and the IMF. This is a bold step towards assuming the risks for mistakes of private banks if they will share the cost, that is, accept a *de facto* low rate on the money they lent. Ethics aside, the proposal is fatally flawed by its voluntary feature. Both on grounds of effectiveness and of equity (the so-cializing of private risk and "free rider" issue), the Plan is a feeble and misguided approach.

The record is not impressive and appears to vindicate the critics. The process of lowering the debt by collateralizing the new debt and by buybacks has succeeded only in modestly reducing debt servicing costs. Very little of the desperately needed *new* money has been forthcoming, and the costs to the debtors have been high. By the end of 1990 all the Brady Plan initiatives (in Mexico, the Philippines, Costa Rica, Bolivia and Venezuela) had succeeded in reducing their commercial bank debt by less than $16 billion. At the same time, the financing of the buybacks and the collateralization of the restructured debt has required a depletion of their hard currency reserves of about $7 billion and, as well, reliance on multilateral and bilateral aid and on bridge loans amounting to over $6 billion. On balance these transactions can thus be regarded as rather one-sided: on one side, a minor gain for the debtors but, on the other side, a substantial one for the creditors who have been able to convert some of the loans that should have been —or already were—largely written off as bad debts into secured bonds.

Further grounds exist for challenging the array of supporters of the in-termediating/guarantee arrangement. Professor Eaton, for one, has pointed out that the benefits are bound to be minor because such a facility acting as intermediator would not, in his words, "confront the features of the inter-national capital markets that led to the crisis in the first place." Professors Bulow and Rogoff, who advocate a facility that they would label the Inter-national Citizenship Fund (ICF), object to a facility that links its services as guarantor to debt repayment-relief arrangements. They prefer instead that the linkage be to obligations by the debtors to undertake "good deeds of global citizenship," deeds such as those related to lowering carbon emissions, drug eradication programmes, population control programmes and others that have significant externalities for the international community.

In sum, the main objections rest on the grounds of ineffectiveness, political unacceptability, and inequity as the resultant debt reduction (usually with little or no new money) keeps the debtors under unrelenting pressure to service the rest of their debts. Thereby it diverts scarce resources from worthwhile programmes and projects in their own country that could be of benefit to its citizens and/or to a global community concerned about environmental deg-radation, population growth and such in the debtor countries.[10]

The common assumption of those who support the establishment of an intermediating facility for debt relief objectives is that there would be a significant reduction of the debt overhang and that this would enable debtors to recover. This response has to be tested in the real world, not on *a priori* grounds because the responsiveness of the creditors cannot be assured. There are bound to be many "free riders" in any *voluntary* scheme. There is insistence, therefore, on the need to establish an *involuntary* arrangement. In the words of Professor Sachs, this would achieve "the *concerted* participation of the banks. . . . in reducing interest rates to sub-market levels on existing debt." Like many who advocate an intermediating facility, he believes that the desired results of a significant reduction in the *present value* of the third world's debt

> "could best be accomplished in the context of an international debt facility (IDF). . . . that would, in essence act as a kind of bankruptcy court in charge of guiding a comprehensive settlement. . . . (since) debt reduction, like bankruptcy, needs an institutional setting to bring it about to overcome an inherent free-rider problem."[11]

DEBT RELIEF INITIATIVES PUT TO THE TEST: MEXICO AND THE BRADY PLAN

The verdict as to the feasibility and desirability of governmental involvement in the proposed manner cannot be decided without testing. The first such test on an ambitious scale was undertaken in February 1988 when the Mexican Government launched a debt-for-bonds exchange auction with the collaboration and advice of a major private American financial institution and with the endorsement and cooperation of the United States Government. The principal was secured by Mexico's purchase of an equivalent amount of United States Treasury bonds, so the bidders were given some guarantee with regard to principal while Mexico assumed the risks. The results of the auction proved disappointing, with Mexico able to reduce its $100 billion debt by only $1.1 billion.[12]

Japan's Finance Minister, Kiichi Miyazawa, presented a variant of the Mexican auction idea at the summit meeting in Toronto in June 1988. Given the substantial financial support that Japanese sponsorship would make possible, the Miyazawa proposal could transform third world debt into securities on a larger scale and on a more regularized basis than the sporadic auction schemes. *At the time, on hearing of the proposal, the United States Treasury*

Secretary, Nicholas Brady, objected to the transference of risks from private lenders to governments or international agencies. The United States Administration objection was based *ostensibly* on the fear of a political backlash to any scheme involving guarantees that in effect take the private bankers off the hook with public money either from their treasury or from any of the international financial institutions.

The United States stone-walling of the Japanese proposal to offer guarantees to private bankers, with Japan making a major financial contribution to substantially increase the allocation of SDRs backed by a basket of currencies, was soon softened and then reversed. The reasons can easily be inferred.

In the early months of 1989, the new Administration of President Bush let it be known that the United States would look favourably on guarantees to encourage commercial bank creditors to pass on the discounts on their third world debts to the debtors as a form of debt relief, but with the proviso that the bankers undertake *renewed* lending to the third world debtor countries, without specifying either the amounts or other "hard" details. Pedro-Pablo Kuczinski, Chairman of First Boston International, is reported to have dismissed the news as "more smoke than substance." At the same time, Horst Schumann, managing director of the umbrella organization financed by commercial banks, the Institute for International Finance (IIF), is reported to have responded favourably, indicating that many bankers that are members of the IIF "might accept a 30 per cent reduction or so in their Latin American debt portfolios *in return for guarantees*." The guarantees, he pointed out, should not be regarded as "bailing out" the banks but as "bailing them in" so as to enable them to play a more active role in providing the funds urgently needed by the third world.

The guarantees had the expected effect of changing the terms of the discounts involved in the conversions. Thus when Mexico had a second go at its guaranteed auction scheme, the event was more successful than the first one. Negotiations under the aegis of the Brady Plan reduced Mexico's debt to $92 billion in early 1990, thereby cutting its $12 billion annual debt-servicing obligations to commercial bank creditors by a "disappointing" $4 billion, *but providing little of the hoped-for new money* that is desperately needed in light of Mexico's dismal trade balance prospects. Offered three options, half of the creditors opted for converting part of their debts into new guaranteed bonds with yields of 6.5 per cent, 40 per cent of them chose conversion to new saleable guaranteed bonds worth 65 per cent of their face value, and 10 per cent preferred to provide new money worth 25 per cent of their exposure on condition that they could get guarantees on their old debts.

The Economist observed (6 October 1990) that ''most Mexicans must be disappointed with the results so far with real wages having fallen for eight consecutive years to a point where they are barely half what they were in 1982, leaving some 30 per cent of Mexicans living in poverty, roughly the same proportion as in 1980. . . . (Meantime) Mexico has little immediate hope of financing the outflow (of $8 billion to service its remaining debt) with a trade surplus, so that, in one way or the other, it will have to borrow more to service its existing debt.''

Venezuela managed to bring in only $1.15 billion in new money under a deal similar to Mexico's. Bolivia and Costa Rica reduced their debts by buy-back at exceptional discounts, in Bolivia's case at 11 per cent and Costa Rica at 15 per cent, thereby reducing their annual debt-servicing obligations substantially. But *again there was little or no new money.* This has raised the question as to whether a country might not be better off to allocate its scarce foreign exchange for investment purposes unless it can do a buyback of all its debt at very exceptional discounts.[13]

Governmental involvement in the manner of the Brady Plan (as with the Baker Plan before it) can be regarded, therefore, as only a mixed blessing for the debtors. These countries might have been better off, after all, by continuing to let the arrears on interest payments—now amounting to over $22 billion—continue to mount, and meantime allocating the foreign exchange thus ''saved'' towards meeting their urgent domestic priorities.

These cases have been trial runs for the Brady Plan. After the failure of the Baker Plan initiative with its exhortations to private bankers that went unheeded, the United States has been anxious to demonstrate there is now a workable approach for the 39 countries that are eligible to reduce their debt burdens by taking advantage of the discounted value of these debts on the secondary market. In the course of negotiations, however, the discounts emerging from long negotiations have not matched the valuations on the secondary market at the outset. Even if the debtors had been able to secure the benefit of the large discounts indicated by the secondary market—reducing the debts to less than half of their face value—servicing the debt that would still remain outstanding to commercial banks alone would continue to absorb more than one third of the value added of their export earnings, or about one tenth of their GNP. The Mexican case, in particular, is a case in point.

The Mexican negotiations were exceptional but advertised as a showcase initiative. Few other countries could expect the level of intervention in the negotiations by Governments and the IFIs, which were unprecedented and unlikely to be repeated. Notwithstanding this favourable treatment, the net results were modest. Much of the reduction in total debt servicing of the commercial bank debt (about $4 billion per year) has been replaced by borrowing from Governments and the IFIs that offered new money ($3.9 billion) and guarantees. At the same time, Mexico had to allocate over $10 billion from its reserves for the purchase of United States zero-coupon bonds and other guaranteed instruments that call for Mexican deposits in escrow accounts, a less-advertised part of the price that Mexico had to pay to make the much heralded "breakthrough" of reducing its debt to commercial bankers. As the first test case of the Brady Plan, the bankers were pressured to accept large discounts in favour of Mexico, a practice unlikely to be repeated.

In any case, there are severe political constraints limiting an ambitious programme of *socializing* the risks of *private* bankers who lend to third world countries with such abandon, motivated by greed. This process of guaranteeing might well be interpreted by the public-at-large as a form of bailout of private bankers with public funds. The skepticism is supported by an analysis of the reasons for the 180 degree turn in United States policy when it shifted from opposition to acceptance of the idea that guarantees be given to private bank creditors either by themselves, the Japanese or by public entities such as the World Bank.

The most plausible and persuasive reason for the new United States stance appears to be the fear that Japan, and other countries with large trading surpluses and a commensurate capacity to lend and donate funds to the third world, are now capable of usurping the leadership role of the United States in relation to the third world by implementing such proposals even *without* United States endorsement and support.[14]

United States fear was evident at the outset, as Peter Kilborn reported in a news story about the Miyazawa initiative:

"Japan, which is not constrained by budget deficits, stands ready and willing to assume a disproportionate share of the burden of the guarantees, (with) American taxpayers. . . . sharing the liability for some (disproportionately smaller) portion of any bad debts."

In making this U-turn the United States policy followed the maxim, "if you can't beat them, join them—the better to temper their policies in victory and to share some of the glory, if any."

This shift is symptomatic of a sea-change in the global economy. Japan's voice has become more powerful by virtue of its trade surplus position and by the greater involvement in world affairs through its enhanced contribution to the third world. Its aid programmes are being channelled through bilateral aid programmes and multilateral institutions where they seek more voting strength in line with their increased contribution. In effect, as a Japanese commentator observed, "the United States 'stole' the Miyazawa Plan for third world debt relief and renamed it the Brady Plan. . . . (but) Miyazawa was not resentful; the Finance Ministry was only too happy to offer its support for the Brady Plan (to gain) recognition of their efforts to assume greater global economic responsibilities, especially in the area of international economic assistance."[15]

The Venezuelan debt-inspired riots in March 1989 seem to have also prompted an exceptional burst of re-thinking in Washington that led to this turnabout in United States policy. Within a week of the rioting in Venezuela, the United States Secretary of the Treasury, Nicholas Brady, announced the "new" initiative that put the accent on debt relief and on a return to growth in the debtor countries. Needless to say, Venezuela was one of the first beneficiaries of the Brady Plan. The United States urged the World Bank to provide a loan of $150 million and to release $285 million of "set-aside" funds from previously approved loans. This could enable creditor banks to exchange old debts for new instruments and enable Venezuela to achieve a 20 per cent reduction in the face value of its debt. But the banks, having the choice, opted for the conversion menu items that provided very little additional money.

The shift of United States policy was also evident in the decision by the United States Administration not to be a hold-out any longer in authorization of the long-sought General Capital Increase (GCI) for the World Bank and in pushing for the Bank Board's approval for that institution's first guarantees. These ice-breaking guarantees were first made on a token basis to Mexico and Chile for a total amount of $800 million. The World Bank and the other IFIs had been moving cautiously in providing such guarantees. The Senior Vice-President (Operations), Moeen Quereshi, has made clear the reason behind this cautious approach:

"The Bank is prepared to accept a larger share of the responsibility and burden of making the international debt strategy work, but *we will not take over the responsibilities of other creditors.*" (emphasis added)

As a public institution with a management obliged to respond to the wishes of their shareholders whose votes are weighted by their contributions, the Group of Seven nations have exceptional influence in shaping the Bank's policies. The issue of whether or not to play the role of guarantors for the debt conversion process had been under consideration for some time. In mid-1988, Ernest Stern, Senior Vice-President (Finance), of the World Bank, asserted that "if commercial banks are active in providing funds to debt-ridden countries, the Bank might consider supporting them in the future." He acknowledged that the Bank had already provided some guarantees. In early 1989, Jean Baneth, during his tenure as Director of the International Economic Department of the World Bank, is reported to have said that the Bank intended to study the mechanism of guaranteeing commercial bank lending to the developing countries.

Meantime, economists outside the World Bank, such as Bergsten and Williamson of the Institute for International Economics, were advising that the World Bank should assist the debt conversion process by offering its good offices as a guarantor, even if this meant allocating some of its loanable funds for this purpose rather than to their traditional lending programme. They maintained that the guarantee role would not be necessarily at the expense of the Bank's lending programme once the General Capital Increase had been approved and the Bank's "sustainable lending level" (SLL) raised accordingly because it would take a few years before the Bank's lending capacity could be raised to the limit of its newly-expanded SLL.

However, as the experience of the first few years of the Brady Plan era demonstrates, with or without guarantees there is no realistic prospect of the commercial banks ever again venturing into third world lending to any appreciable extent. The bankers themselves had made that abundantly clear through words and deeds. Furthermore, they would not begin to lend for medium-term and long-term development purposes without charging a risk premium that would raise the charges even further above what the borrowers could ever hope to service, let alone repay. The bankers' policy of restraint toward third world lending is, in any case, merely making a virtue of necessity. They are too weak from previous write-downs on third world loans and on misguided forays into financing real estate and other speculative ventures or are attracted to lend nearer home. German and other European banks are not likely to venture far when the Eastern European demand for capital is so compelling on geopolitical grounds alone.

Unless there is an unexpected surge in global savings that would change the situation on the supply side, prospects are less-than-rosy for lowering interest rates of commercial bank loans, whether through guarantees and other sweeteners, and still expect them to play a major role in the transfer of long-term capital to the third world. This bleak assessment has turned attention to the possible impact of the proposals that would change the *ownership* of the claims, namely, swapping debt-for-equity or for other forms of assets in the debtor country.

Lowering debt through debt-equity swaps and other forms of conversion;

This category of proposals takes the previous set of ideas a step further by reducing the debt through a process of converting the creditors' claims to repayment to claims on assets in the debtor country.[16] These assets can take the form of equity holdings in enterprises or in some form of local currency fund or into debtor government obligations to establish and maintain nature conservancies or some agreed-upon set of policies with related budgetary commitments. This type of conversion became possible on a significant scale with the development of the secondary market for third world loans that has enabled the debtors to take advantage of the prevailing discounts and provide a means of encouraging private investment inflows, particularly in the form of the return of flight-capital.

Turkey first initiated the straight-forward debt-equity swaps on a small scale in 1980. This was followed by Mexico and Brazil in 1982 and 1983 and by many countries since then. At one end of the spectrum are the small sub-Saharan African countries that have entered into the debt conversion programmes only recently. Five of these countries have passed enabling legislation and ventured to initiate such a programme, achieving in 1987 a modest reduction of about $10 million in the annual level of debt servicing obligations. Six months after the announcement of its interest in a swapping programme, Nigeria received applications for conversion of almost $2 billion that would, if consummated, lower its foreign debt by an appreciable percentage.

The swapping process has been most widely applied in Chile. Since 1985 when Chile first initiated a debt-equity swap, it has pursued the approach vigorously and has been able to attract investors willing to convert a significant percentage of Chile's external debt for an equity stake in the country. Chile, however, provides an exceptional case. Bankers or investors have normally been cautious, given the risks in venturing into largely unknown territory where it is difficult to assess the feasibility of investment opportunities. Chile promised stability under dictatorial rule. A great deal of flight capital thus was tempted back with the bait of promising returns. In any case, the banks were anxious to make deals with venturesome investors. The swaps held the promise of reducing the outstanding debts on their books, and doing so in a manner that would shift the debtor's economy towards greater reliance on a market-oriented approach. For the debtors the key attractive element in these swaps has been the possibility of capturing some or all of the discount on their loans as reflected in the secondary market for such loans.

The discount issue is the contentious factor in the equation, and therein lies one of the most serious deterrents: the difficulty of persuading major creditors to accept the secondary market valuation of its claims on the third world debtors, or if need be to share the discount between the new investors and the debtors. For reasons of its own, the Chilean Government was willing to be accommodating in striking a swapping deal. But for all the apparent success by 1986 of reducing their $20 billion debt by $6 billion, their debts to official creditors increased so by the end of 1988 the total external debt amounted to $19 billion. In addition, its options were more limited by the terms of the swaps that permitted profit reparation beginning in 1990 and by the increase in domestic debt.[17]

There is another and more serious dampener for most debtor countries. In Chile's case as a dictatorship, it played a lesser role. The dampener is the inflationary impact of such swaps when undertaken on a relatively large scale. In the swap arrangement, the investor is provided the full value of the swapped debts in domestic currency, so there is an expenditure that could add fuel to the inflationary fires already difficult to control.

None the less, under intense stress and anxious to reduce their foreign debt burden, many debtor countries have undertaken ambitious divestiture programmes. They have put on the auction block a range of non-strategic industries, such as hotels, breweries, ships and the like that are now open to ownership by foreign investors under debt-equity swapping programmes. For example, Argentina initially resisted privatizing its steel industry and opening its ownership to foreigners but has since removed that constraint. Brazil has declared its willingness to sell state-owned enterprises to foreign investors in the form of participation in joint ventures whereby ''foreign bank creditors could utilize part of the several billion dollars which have accumulated in the Central Bank as a result of the debt rollovers.'' The scope of the industries or other assets eligible for swapping against debt has been widening, but there remain serious constraints related to the degree of control that the political leaders are willing to allow foreigners to exercise.

To make the process more attractive to both the debtors and potential investors, Donald Lessard and John Williamson, Senior Fellows of the Institute for International Economics, have suggested an approach that would involve ''quasi-equities.'' They give the investor a share of the income of an enterprise but not a share of its ownership.[18] Norman Bailey, a former member of the United States National Security Council, has come forward with the suggestion that the creditors acquire a quasi-equity asset through a contractual arrangement whereby they agree to accept exchange-participation notes entitling them to some agreed-upon proportion of a country's export earnings during the life of the loan. The entitlement would be given in exchange for foregoing the payments of principal due on the loan and would in effect make the payments on the loans fluctuate with export earnings.[19]

Ingenuity in innovative arrangements might extend the acceptance of debt-equity swapping to a wider range of industries, but there would remain a hard core of resistance to alienating some assets that symbolically are an integral part of a country's "patrimony." And for the creditors, the idea has mild appeal given their lack of expertise and more importantly their view that because of the risks involved, not many projects are made available to foreigners that they would judge as suitable for investment even at the bargain prices that the swaps would make possible. They have been more inclined, therefore, to entertain other swapping ideas.

These other swapping variants involve converting debt into exports, an arrangement that is sometimes known as a debt-for-export swap and sometimes as a debt-commodity swap. The idea has been extended to other indebted developing countries: Brazil and Mexico have signed an agreement to boost their trade by $100 million with the use of debt vouchers for part of the payments, vouchers obtained by buying each others debts on the secondary market and exchanging them for the full face value of the debts.

The list of swapping arrangements is getting longer and longer:

- One proposal envisages Governments paying commercial bank creditors to reduce their debt claims in exchange for receiving the debtor's local currency. The local currency would be obtained by the Government as the debtor's payment for the receipt of surplus food from the donor country.[20]

- A "debt-for-good-works swap" has been arranged whereby Midland Bank "donates" its Sudanese loans with a face value of $800,000 to UNICEF which, in turn, enables them to obtain local currency for the financing of shallow wells and hand-pumps for about 5,000 villagers. When Sudanese debt trades at under 5 per cent of its face value—reflecting its export earnings at one tenth of its debt servicing obligations—this charitable gesture cost the bank very little, especially as the debt has been written off.

- Ecuador has arranged a debt-for-fellowship swap with Harvard University purchasing $5 million of Ecuadoran debt for $750,000 in the form of discounted loan certificates from United States banks. These are then donated to an Ecuadoran education fund.

It seems ingenuity knows few bounds. But the debt-equity conversion arrangements, having totaled less than $30 billion over the last few years cannot be said to have had a significant impact on the debt crisis, though they have proven helpful to a few debtors such as Chile. With inflationary pressures under control, Chile was in a position to use this means to substantially reduce its debt and debt servicing over a period of several years, particularly by attracting back the flight capital and offering attractive terms. By mid-1991 it became the first of the "problem debtors" to return to the international capital market. For most debtor countries, however, the down-side features of all such conversion schemes are great enough to confine it to a modest role.

Klaus Regling, a member of the IMF staff, writing in the March 1989 issue of *Finance and Development* in an article entitled "New financing approaches in the debt strategy," summed up the modest role of this financial procedure:

"(it) has become an important element in the evolving debt strategy (to) encourage the continued participation by banks, however, the benefits that can be derived from such financing techniques should not be exaggerated."

Notwithstanding such disclaimers, a *Financial Times* news item reported that this swapping idea had been described by both Margaret Thatcher and George Schultz as "the best solution to the debt crisis."[21] The endorsements and the invitations for swapping continue to be issued, but few seem anxious to come to the party. Not surprisingly, the concessions offered through swaps and other menu arrangements have not amounted to much: The cashflow savings for the 19 countries that have participated in these exercises have totalled $100 million a year in the last two years. This is less than one per cent of their export earnings and less than two per cent of their debt servicing obligations. The Brady Plan agreements have been favourable to a more significant degree only for Mexico and Venezuela. But even these savings have amounted to less than 10 per cent of their export earnings.

Greater hope vests in a swapping arrangement that seems to have a great deal of emotional appeal, namely, the concept of debt-for-nature swaps for establishing nature conservancies, and wildlife refuges, and for "protecting" the Amazon tropical rain forest from exploitation so that it will continue to absorb CO_2 and thus play a role in slowing climate change. The appeal lies in the expectation that such a swapping concept envisages benefits for the debtors and for the global environmental cause. This idea and other market-based proposals will be considered in the next chapter where the theme is the debt-environmental connection and proposals that follow from their close relationship.

CHAPTER 8

MARKET-BASED PROPOSALS— THE ENVIRONMENTAL CRISIS

THE SPECIAL CASE OF DEBT-FOR-NATURE SWAPS

The idea of debt-for-nature swaps has great appeal. It is included in President Bush's "Enterprise for the Americas" initiative. In October 1990 the United States Congress authorized the conversion of $125 million in P.L. 480 debt that third world countries owe for United States surplus food shipments, a gesture that would provide a cash flow from the budgets of these countries of about $1 million a year for nature conservancy projects. A further $5 billion of United States aid credits is slated to be released for such purposes when congressional approval is secured in 1991. Meantime, William Reilly, the Administrator of the United States Environment Protection Agency, has suggested that $12 billion of United States aid be used to mobilize about $100 million a year for "conservation projects" in debtor developing countries.[1]

Many of the smaller debtor countries, such as Bolivia, Costa Rica, Ecuador, Jamaica and the Philippines, were fast off the mark in response to this opportunity, quickly reaching agreement in principle to convert part of their debt to conservation endowments for stipulated acreage that would be set aside for conservation purposes. Sobering second thoughts, however, are dulling the appeal-on-first-sight of these debt-for-nature swaps. Though the first agreements have succeeded in establishing the principle and the modalities of such swaps, there are several reasons to expect them to be limited in significance either in terms of the amounts of money or the land areas involved:

- Few commercial bank creditors can be counted upon to make a community gesture, let alone one that is so far from home and so indirect in its benefits to them;

- The terms would generally involve the creditor accepting a heavy discount with no assurance that the terms of the agreement will be enforceable and be respected for a long period;

- From the debtor's perspective, the use of aid funds for this purpose would be seriously considered only if the aid is *additional* to what they would otherwise expect to receive, but few aid agencies have been prepared to offer this assurance;

- Again from the debtor's perspective, given the need for annual budget allocations in local currency that would support programmes for their operation and maintenance, the inflationary impact of the process makes it an arrangement of limited scope when the need is to dampen inflationary pressure already difficult to handle.

One or more of these considerations could torpedo the tentative agreements and abort future ones, or if the agreements are consummated, could downsize them. The much publicized Costa Rica swap provides a case in point. Costa Rica's Minister of Natural Resources, Mario Boza, endorsed the proposal of United States conservation groups of a $100 million debt-for-nature swap to be implemented over five years. Under pressure to cut deficits and reduce inflation, however, the Governor of the Central Bank vetoed the proposal. This kind of reaction provides strong grounds for doubting that the debt-for-nature swaps will become a widespread procedure: once there is skepticism about the debtor country's willingness to maintain such natural conservancy areas in their pristine condition, the swapping arrangement loses its appeal. The merits of such a budgetary allocation have to be seen by all the key officials of the country concerned as exceptionally great or the finances for maintaining the conservancy will not be provided year in and year out. Bribing them to do what the creditor countries consider "desirable" is hardly a prescription for the ailment, especially since there is no way to assure compliance with the terms of the agreement.

The critical obstacle is simply that there is no way that debt can be reinstated on grounds of non-compliance. Non-compliance may not be due to a lack of goodwill or of ignorance on the part of the officials, farmers and other parties involved in the recipient country. They may be well informed about the dangers of environmental damage ensuing from inappropriate pricing policies, land tenure systems and land use practices but be unable to take the appropriate actions if strong political, economic and/or social pressures militate against the desired corrective action. In such a case any contentious or difficult-to-implement commitments contained in a signed document will likely be ignored. Pressure for non-compliance is increased when the debt servicing obligations continue to leave little room for meeting immediate needs.

Despite these reservations, proposals of this nature continue to come forward. For example, one by Professor David Bigman is advertised to "end the debt crisis and save the environment too."[2] The essential elements are familiar: (1) partial re-payment of the outstanding debt in local currency, part to be allocated to an "Environment Fund" (EF) for financing projects for population control, for environmental enhancement and for general development purposes, and (2) the funding of the EF would be supplemented by a globally uniform carbon tax equivalent to five cents a gallon. This is judged sufficient to provide financing for environment-enhancing research and for environmental protection measures undertaken by third world countries for themselves and for the global community, presumably including the global-scale programme that would "save" the Amazonian tropical rain forest. A similar idea of an environment fund has been suggested by Professors Bulow and Rogoff. They label their proposal the International Citizenship Fund (ICF). Their proposal differs, however, in an important respect: it would eschew both the feature of intermediation of a guarantee-granting debt discounting facility and debt-for-nature swapping arrangements.

For all the appeal in the idea of such double-barrelled debt-environment proposals, the prospects for their realization are likely to be rather disappointing. This is especially evident in the case of swapping debt for measures to reduce global carbon emissions by maintaining the tropical rain forests that act as an absorber of a significant part of such emissions. This case merits special attention because of its scale and what such a swap implies with respect to a transaction that yields high global benefits and low ones for the countries concerned while their national costs are high given the constraint in exploiting large tracts of standing tropical rain forests while their benefits are low in terms of environmental enhancement.

THE SPECIAL CASE OF THE SPECIAL CASE: THE DEBT/ AMAZON TROPICAL RAIN FOREST SWAP

Concerted pressure is coming from the international community to apply this conversion idea to Brazil but on a far larger scale. In Brazil's case the swap would include a large part of the regions of the tropical Amazon rain forest, the world's largest remaining block of that type of ecological area that is deemed exceptionally valuable *in its present* state for global environmental reasons. The rationale for and the scope of this gigantic debt-for-nature swap has been well expressed in the proposal put forward in an editorial in *The New York Times* of 3 February, 1989 entitled, "Brazil's debt can save the Amazon:"

". . . . as much in the West's interests as it is in Brazil's, donors in the West would raise $4 billion with which they would buy discounted Brazilian debt with a face value of, say, $8 billion which would be exchanged in Brazil for bonds worth $8 billion in local currency (which would, in turn) be donated to endow a Brazilian environmental institute charged with protecting the rain forest. . . . Because aid can be so highly leveraged through debt exchange, the forests are cheap to save."

The Brazilians, however, were initially divided on this matter. As one Canadian journalist noted in a story from Brazil datelined early 1989:

"foreign activists have been insensitive to Brazil's historical preoccupation with maintaining its hold on the Amazon region, fearing encroachments by other South American countries. . . . (and) suspicious that foreigners are planning to grab the Amazon's riches from under a sleeping nation's nose. No matter how you dress up the debt-for-nature swaps, the scheme (to the Brazilians) still looks like foreigners buying a piece of Brazil . . . (and this applies as well to) recent proposals for the supervision of Amazon preservation measures by an international body."[3]

Brazilian officials were riled at what they perceived to be a double standard applied by the Governments of the industrialized world which had opened their own frontiers in an expansion that showed little or no regard for the environmental factor. And they are hardly doing enough now about correcting the environmental damage to which they have been the principal contributors. In protesting "outside interference," the Brazilians were joined in early March 1989 by seven other members of the Amazon Pact.[4] Like the Brazilians, they outlined ambitious plans for the exploitation of the region's hydro, mineral, timber and other resources. Included were 136 potential dam sites identified for development—70 in the Amazon region—to meet more than one third of Brazil's projected electricity needs by the year 2010. Meantime, the largest migration of this century has been underway, with the region's population doubling in the last two decades to reach over 15 million. Thus, despite the strong intellectual appeal of the debt-nature swap idea, Brazil by its very size and dynamic has posed an intractable problem. Yet that scale makes the swap proposals significant in global ecological terms.

If the swaps are to be significant in reducing Brazil's debt and the servicing payments, the amounts of money involved raise another set of problems, even if the acreage were to be bought at heavily discounted prices on the secondary market. Furthermore, it is one thing to consummate an agreement of such size and scope, but it is quite another to ensure that such an agreement would be maintained for long. Although the Brazilian Government is agreeable about taking measures under international pressure and on the basis of its own convictions, it would be next to impossible to enforce such an agreement should the Brazilians, at a later date, not have the funds and the resolve for the maintenance phase—or the political power to do so. Frontiers are exceptionally tempting. It is a rare politician that can resist or be strong-armed enough in the face of pressure from the energy-hungry industrial-urban interests, the hungry landless, the covetous powerful landlords allied with the mining and timber barons.[5]

But even if the Brazilians are genuinely sympathetic to the international concerns—as they appear to be—the arrangement would involve a reversal of the "polluters pay" principle because payments would be made to the potential polluter so as to induce actions aborting the polluting activities. The issues then would be: how much of the debt to forgive for not undertaking the environmentally-damaging activities? Paid by whom? Under what institutional arrangements?

These issues are being addressed. A thoughtful proposal is contained in a 1989 working paper draft prepared for the World Resources Institute and the UNDP. The authors suggest the establishment of an International Environmental Facility (IEF) under World Bank auspices that would be "an intermediating, regulating and implementing institution for raising the necessary funding, initiating and maintaining the nature conservancy or forestry projects" that are the objects of the debt-for-nature swap transactions.[6] The proposal would have the IEF act as a "conservation project assistance programmer with its main purpose being "to help identify, design, and finance 'sound' conservation projects in the third world." Funding would be derived from user fee charges on the preparation, operation and monitoring of the projects with which they are associated. The recently established Global Environment Facility funded by the World Bank and other organizations is the realization of this proposal, incorporating as it does most of its essential features.[7]

The operation and supervision of the debt-for-nature swaps are not a one-off type of transaction that can be signed and left as a fait accompli. Though these swaps may not be large enough financially to be anything more than a modest boost to ease the debt problem, their double-bonus attribute makes them attractive and likely to find sponsorship beyond the funds involved in the swaps themselves.

THE POTENTIAL AND LIMITS OF ENVIRONMENTAL MARKET-BASED PROPOSALS

A plethora of market-based proposals have been put forward bearing on environment policies and programmes at the national and international levels of governance. Leaving aside the ideological appeal of a system that can be guided by an "invisible hand" ostensibly to promote the common good, there is a practical side that makes reliance on so-called market forces attractive to many: the inertia principle of opting for the minimum amount of change that might be necessary to realize any given objective—or its converse, *opting for a downgrading of the objective to conform to a minimal degree of change*. For those with this outlook, the environmental threat does not appear to provide a sufficiently compelling reason to get off the inertial pathway of reliance on the prevailing market-based system, albeit slightly modified.

Many of those who are strong environmental activists have recognized the scope of the changes required. They have noted correctly that the prevailing economic system engenders a cultural condition that one of them has characterized as a "consciousness of unsustainability;" they have written and spoken of the need for a "new growth" approach, for "fundamental changes" and for "revamping of institutions."[8] Market forces, when they are free or reasonably competitive, can be powerful allies when constrained to achieve desired social as well as economic goals. There is a danger in placing too much confidence in them, however, as institutional arrangements in the world with its vested interests and other limitations. When structural change is necessary, the much advertised beneficence of these market forces may well be a travesty, the product of ideology-mythology or wishful thinking. This appears to be the case in connection with the environmental crisis.

The concept of "market forces" in relation to the environment: how applicable?

The principal environmental measures proposed include the following:

- Reforming tax, subsidy and pricing policies to encourage environmentally-enhancing activities and discourage environmentally-damaging activities, particularly those related to the use of fossil fuels;
- Restructuring the administration of all levels of governance involved in environmental policy-making so that environmental factors are treated as an integral part of policy-making, a change that implies the incorporation of environment policy-making functions into a central ministry, say finance or planning so that fiscal policy, budgetary and major project and programme investment decisions can be made on a longer-term basis and thus incorporate the relevant environmental factors; and
- Allocating more research funds toward the development of alternatives to fossil fuels and other environmentally-damaging gases and pollutants and wastes.

The market-based category of proposals are encompassed in the first item. Most of the proposals of this type fall into two main groups, both of which have been articulated by William Ruckelhaus rather succinctly:[9]

- Those that would oblige consumers to pay the "full cost" of a resource use, that is, "internalizing the externalities" and thereby "bending the market system towards long-term sustainability."
- Introduce the notion of "environmental resources" as "capital" on the grounds that "(the refusal) to treat environmental resources as capital (induces us to) spend them as income."

The policy implications of the first are rarely clarified by a definition of the ambiguous notion of what compromises "full cost," nor by operational guidelines as to how to measure and allocate such costs. Though it seems a logical and attractive idea, it is operationally an empty box. Many who endorse the market system approach do so without a conception of the market process as it actually operates. A typical example of this naivete can be found in a World Bank publication:[10]

"The environmental challenge calls for the application of sound principles of cost internalization, provision of public goods, and correction for market failures, (all of which) can improve economic efficiency and increase economic welfare."

Correcting for "market failures?" Providing for "public goods?" The necessary measures would then call for profound institutional changes with policies that have far-reaching political, social and economic implications. The policies to achieve these corrective measures within the framework of a "market economy" likely would be treated by the principal decision makers like bad-tasting medicine and thus not be taken willingly—with profound institutional implications that the so-called "market system" would find very difficult to accommodate.

The recommendation of treating environmental resources as "capital" also appears to be logical. In application, however, it is a naive suggestion. It does not recognize the *critical* distinction that must be made between what we call "natural resources" that yield an income flow (and by virtue of that flow are deemed to be "resources," or, in certain uses or *non-use*, prevent a loss in income), and those natural resources that are valued for their "environmental" contribution in the sense that they are indispensable and/or irreplaceable and have no measurable market value or even a notional price. The first concept of "natural resources" is itself elusive enough in terms of valuation. But how does one measure the value of a "resource," for example, that takes the form of a beautiful landscape, or of forests that provide watershed cover (thus regulating run-off and preventing floods) or act as carbon dioxide absorbers that have a value in terms of slowing the long-run direction of climate changes? No objective guidelines exist for measuring the concept of "ecological capital" and how such a measure could, in any case, be of any possible use in policy-making.

Nor is there much help in referring to attractive sounding but *operationally* empty boxes such as the concepts of "sustainable development" and "conservation" that abound in the literature and slogans. The over-simplification of the issues does rally the troops and raise consciousness and zeal. One should be wary, however, of trying to understand a movement by the banners under which it marches. This is especially so when dealing with "public goods" or "common property" that are key attributes of environmental services and as such severely limit the role of the market as the main institutional instrument of environment policy. If the objective is the achievement of outcomes that are socially, economically and environmentally desirable, the factor of "external diseconomies" must be taken into account. In the case of environmental diseconomies or damages beyond the cost incurred by the perpetrator, the outcome could be collective disaster. A dramatic example centuries old involves the relationship of goat-herding and the desertification of much of the Middle East that was once lush in forests and vegetative cover. Herding goats was sensible from the perspective of the owners, but given the environmental external diseconomies from the foraging of these animals on "the commons," the outcome was an ecological disaster. What was sensible for the individuals turned out to be catastrophic for the society of their descendants.[11]

Such deplorable outcomes do not necessarily arise from a lack of intellectual appreciation of "external diseconomies" by the users of the environmental commons. They might well be aware of the possibility or even the probability of such an adverse environmental and socio-economic impact, but their reasons for neglecting the adverse impacts on the global collectivity is found in their difficulty in integrating such environmental considerations with economic and financial factors that play so large a role in the private decision-making process as it operates in the real-world market system. Even when there is an intellectual appreciation of the importance of environmental externalities, the private decisions cannot take adequate account of either non-market "cost" phenomena such as ecological deterioration or damage, depletion of irreplaceable resources and other deleterious effects, or the benefits related to recreation, aesthetic, health and other conditions that are not counted in the operations of the market process. In the final analysis, it is clear that no amount of ingenuity can render the market capable of adequately treating *environment quality* as a factor because here we are dealing with a "public good."

Operational fuzziness of relying on "market" forces in relation to the environment

Every movement needs strategists and tacticians who have their feet on the ground, so to speak. The environmental movement has benefitted from the analysis and proposals of a great number of professionals. Most have affiliations with universities or institutions that are either policy think-tanks or action-oriented to carry out technical and capital assistance programmes for third world countries or to raise consciousness and money by educational and other means. Many of them provide policy advice at several levels of governance.

In concrete policy-programme terms, there are many common elements in the approach of these analysts/activists. We might limit our focus to one example, a critical aspect of the global environmental *problematique*: the carbon emission rate believed by many to pose a serious threat to human life on this planet by virtue of its likely implications for global climate change. The large majority of proposals contained in programmes of action that attempt to address this problem place great reliance on market forces. Two are particularly popular: a carbon tax, and an auction or marketing of "tradable pollution permits." Both measures are meant to reduce dependence on fossil fuels by raising the costs to the users of these energy sources. This expectation is based on the assumptions about the high price elasticity of demand for these energy forms.

Initially a society is locked into the technologies tied to specific energy sources, and the elasticity or responsiveness to price change is problematic. The drop in demand in response to the rise in price was not expected to be as great as it proved to be when the 1973 oil price shock hit the global economy. The experience from 1973 to 1983 demonstrated that far from being inelastic, there was a surprising responsiveness; the amount of fossil fuels used per unit of GNP decreased significantly. This inspired hope that at least in one aspect of life the underlying "culture of unsustainability" had changed for the better and had done so *largely* in response to market forces. Consumers did indeed respond to the higher energy prices by buying smaller cars, improving the insulation of their homes and factories and adopting other energy-saving measures. The result was that the energy/output relationship changed perceptively. Studies indicate that in the United States, to take one example, there was a 20 per cent reduction in the use of fossil fuel energy after 1973, with two-thirds of the conservation response being attributed to higher prices and the remaining third to a variety of measures such as automobile fuel economy standards.[12]

But subsequent developments have cast doubt on this assessment. In the United States, which consumes about 40 per cent of the world's production of oil, the energy/GNP relationship has regressed since 1984 almost all the way back to the state of affairs pre-1973. Despite the rise in environmental consciousness, consumer patterns have not changed significantly. A great deal of skepticism then is warranted in referring to past experience that might be only a temporary response to a shock. Like swings on a pendulum, the exaggerated fears of a severe shortage of oil and natural resources in the early 1970s had been replaced by an exaggerated confidence in the effectiveness of the market process wherein the price rise was perceived to have reduced significantly the dependency on oil, and thereby yielded both an economic and an environmental dividend.

But these were modest achievements, hardly large enough to make a significant impact on the overall demand for fossil fuels. The limited progress and subsequent regression can be attributed to the powers of inertia and of vested interest; both have operated to maintain the status quo in terms of the sources and uses of energy. Some success was achieved in reducing the fossil fuel/GNP relationship, however, and this was done with minor institutional change. Many have leapt to the conclusion, therefore, that the changes necessary and sufficient to resolve global environmental crisis need be only very limited and therefore consistent with the prevailing economic and social systems in all its essential features.

Looking back from the advantage of the 1990s, we find the vaunted reduction in fossil fuel use has been modest and far from sufficient to address the environmental crisis in a serious way. Therefore, the sanguine assessment as to what is *necessary* and *sufficient* should give way to a recognition that the underlying institutional arrangements are in need of radical change. This applies with particular relevance to the reliance on "market forces" as they operate in the real world.

The energy-environmental connection provides a clear example of the nature of those market forces and why it is mislabelling to refer to the market as "free" or "competitive." An appreciation of this reality is pertinent for environmental policy-makers. The electricity facet of the energy situation is revealing. In almost all countries the utilities generating electricity do not operate at arms length from their political masters; furthermore, there are institutional rigidities severely constraining the price setting process from operating "freely" and from operating in a way that takes account of environmental costs.

The facts of life are such that it would be naive to dismiss as exceptional the host of market failure symptoms that this state of affairs gives rise to; they are the norm, as can be appreciated when account is taken of the following:

- Electricity and natural gas pricing for households and for gasoline for cars and public transport are usually set below cost on the grounds that these commodities are basic goods and thus raising their prices would be regarded as "regressive," that is, as imposing an additional strain on the poorer segments of society,
- The source of power generation is generally determined on the basis of its employment-creation in the region, rather than on the basis of comparable costs for alternative fuels or *costs that take account of the environmental diseconomies*,

- Prices are rarely allowed to rise commensurate with rising costs due
  to poor management that could be attributed in turn to factors such as
  nepotism, corruption and the like.[13]

The pervasiveness of such conditions should give pause to policies that place
great weight on the price mechanism and the so-called ''market forces.''

This factor of public-consumer responsiveness to price changes is a critical
element in one of the main proposals in the environmentalist kit-bag, namely,
the imposition of a carbon tax to discourage the use of fossil fuel and other
energy sources that are the largest sources of carbon emissions, principally
CO_2 . To the uncertainty regarding the elasticity of demand for fossil fuels
and the effect on demand of a tax that raises their price, one can add the
additional complication of the political or distributional implications of such
a tax. Notwithstanding, the carbon tax has many advocates and is being applied
in a modest way initially.

The United States Congressional Budget Office has proposed a $28 per
ton carbon tax on carbon-containing or carbon-emitting types of fuels. This
tax is estimated to generate revenues of over $300 billion or more for federal
and state governments and reduce CO_2 emissions by 20 per cent by the end
of the century. Problems arise less with the arithmetic than with the *operational* difficulties in setting the level of the tax so that it can have the desired
effect in reducing carbon emissions, and weighing this factor against its
regressivity and its political acceptability. In the Worldwatch Institute's report,
State of the World, 1990, Christopher Flavin observes that

> ''Picking the correct tax is a complicated exercise...(but) a conservative
> estimate is that large-scale efforts (that is, on a scale that can be expected
> to be effective) will cost on average at least $50 per ton of carbon.''[14]

There are others who claim that a tax high enough to drive down carbon
emissions would have to be at least $100 per ton of carbon. All are bold
guesstimates.

Whether taxes of this order of magnitude—from $28 to $100 per ton
levels—would be politically feasible is an issue that revolves around the
questions of its adverse impact on growth and employment and of its regressivity. The idea of incorporating this tax in the price of carbon-emitting
fuels is of course rationalized, as Christopher Flavin phrases it, ''as the cost
of avoiding climate change.'' That benefit is, however, notional and highly
uncertain as well.

In any case, pricing changes clearly have to be reinforced by regulatory constraints. That is the key feature of the tradable-pollution-permit type of proposal calling for the establishment of an auction market for tradable transferable pollution permits whereby polluters can sell the "unused" part of their pollution allowance and thereby profit from measures they take to reduce their pollution levels. According to one enthusiastic advocate,

> "The power of the market (is thus) being harnessed to economic incentive policies for the achievement of environmental goals, (in effect, turning) the market into a powerful environmental ally."[15]

The process is one that, in effect, legitimizes activities that are environmentally damaging. This is rationalized as a bow to reality: all economic systems have their environmental downside that cannot be reduced beyond a certain point except at unacceptable costs, one of the unacceptable costs being a slowing down of growth or "no-growth." This approach might well be considered analogous to "burning down the house to cook the pig trapped inside."[16]

Leaving aside the issue of principle, there is the troubling matter of *operationalizing* this idea, that is, determining the limits at which the regulatory environmental constraints should be set and the related problems of enforcement. The regulatory limits should be guided on the basis of estimated social costs and benefits associated with the environmental externalities. This approach can go part way to addressing some types of environmental problems, but the critical question is whether it goes far enough in terms of its environmental targets. And is it, at the same time, fair enough? In setting these regulations there is the issue of "the public interest." This issue *should* guide the legislators in setting the limits in cases where the constituency is international and where it is national and regional, depending on the level of governance. The lack of scientific information and the weakness of the analytic underpinning does not provide a firm base for achieving the overwhelming consensus that the acceptance of severe regulatory limits might require, especially when the public interest is pitted against the power of vested interests.

To be made operational, therefore, the proposers have to specify *the minimal institutional changes necessary* to achieve the cultural/political framework for "market forces" to work in the hoped-for manner to attain the hoped-for objectives. Clearly this calls for factoring environmental effects into the decision-making process at the level of the private firm and household and of Governments. But when the characteristics of the market for such tradable pollution permits is closely examined for its possible mode of operation and its distributional and efficiency outcomes, the initial appeal fades. In the light of the inherent difficulties with such market-based schemes in *operational* terms, the proposal is feasible and desirable only under special circumstances. These special market conditions are so limited as to make the proposal rather trivial in the scheme of things environmental.

To illustrate, many questions must be answered before this approach can be said to be practical on a scale significant enough to be taken seriously as a policy option:

- How are the permissible pollution levels to be set?
- How are the licensees to be regulated as to levels of compliance?
- How is the market to operate to set a price for units of the permitted quota when there are too few parties on either the supply or the demand sides within a market-trading region?

In most circumstances, the schemes are open to great corruption possibilities, especially as the permit limits can be virtually licences to print money if set higher than they *need be*—but who can say where they "need to be." This is an issue with scientific, political, social, economic and financial dimensions.

Thus both proposals have to contend with the issue of gauging and handling the pressures of vested interests or of political-economic power counterbalanced against the interests of both efficiency and equity. These aspects are especially difficult to resolve in cases where the environmental problem is global, and to be both effective and fair the measures call for the participation of many Governments. For the developing countries aspiring to higher living standards and in a phase of development with high requirements for energy that may be environmentally damaging to the global community, the issue of a global accord imposing taxes and regulatory constraints and selling right-to-pollute permits is contentious. *In light of the debt overhang pressures*, the issue is compounded, further diminishing the faith that should be placed on the so-called "market forces" or "market system" as an institutional arrangement to achieve the daunting environment-development objectives.

These limitations of the market process have stimulated the ingenuity of economists to invent ways of applying a market approach to environmental policy. In the final analysis, while helpful, reliance on the market forces will not suffice either at the national level of governance or at the international level. There are initiatives, however, that can be taken and are being put forward as part of the global agenda for action, such as a World Atmosphere Fund, a Planet Protection Fund, an International Environmental Facility and others. These will be discussed in Chapter 11 where that agenda is the main theme and, to a lesser extent, in Chapter 12 where the focus is on the role of the international agencies in carrying through on this agenda to ease and to resolve both the debt and the environmental crises.

CHAPTER 9

"ACROSS-THE-BOARD" PROPOSALS: DEBT RELIEF AND DEBT FORGIVENESS

The case-by-case approach for easing or resolving the debt crisis has provided some modest measure of debt relief through downward adjustments of interest rates and stretching the repayment schedule with longer grace periods and maturity dates. But this favourable outcome of the "muddling-through process" has been limited, as is evident from the continued rise in the third world's total debt and the annual debt servicing transfers of scarce capital from these debtors to the creditors. Thus proposals have been put forward to take the same elements of interest rate reduction, longer maturities and such but apply them in an across-the-board fashion so as to have a positive shock impact by virtue of the *larger scale* and *faster speed* of implementation that such an approach makes possible.

The implementation of this across-the-board approach need not imply more ambitious or radical institutional changes. However, by virtue of its wide scope, this group of proposals would call for a degree of coercion in the case of those commercial bank creditors that refuse to cooperate. This type of proposal is confined, therefore, to government-held debt or to commercial bank debt when Governments are prepared to buy the debts from these banks at a negotiated or unilaterally imposed price. The across-the-board approach is, consequently, a form of shock treatment. Its rationale lies in the maxim: "desperate conditions call for desperate measures" — or at least bold and imaginative ones.

This category of proposals is comprised of three basic variants:

1. Capping interest rates on variable-rate loans or issuing variable maturity loans that become operative when the interest rate exceeds a

predetermined limit set in relation to measurable indicators such as debt service-exports ratios or the interest component of the debt service-exports ratio;

2. Capping the percentage of export earnings to be devoted to servicing foreign debt;

3. Cancelling all or part of the debt and/or declaring a moratorium for a stipulated adjustment period in an across-the-board fashion to all debtors or groups of debtors.

All of these actions may be taken unilaterally by a debtor and not as part of a generalized approach. It is of course more likely to succeed in its objectives and with less pain if the action is taken on a more generalized basis. All these measures offer immediate debt relief and could do so on a significant scale if undertaken by many of the major debtors on an agreed-upon basis, with or without creditor approval.

The first two measures focus on setting a limit on debt servicing payments that would enable the debtor countries to attain a minimally necessary rate of growth. They are thus flexible in response to variables such as their principal commodity exports, the level of interest rates, the terms of trade and the like. The third, defaulting on debt obligations, is the classical last resort of debtors, a phenomenon with many historical precedents.

CAPPING INTEREST RATES

The proposals calling for "capping" are a means of providing instant and assured debt relief. They have evoked some positive responses among editorial writers and columnists, even from those who are members of the creditor community or who write for journals or newspapers owned by those who belong to or are sympathetic with the creditor community. The capping idea has great appeal for politicians in the debtor countries; they can thereby declare that they regard the objective of meeting the basic needs of their own people as a matter of first priority. Ranking the obligations to service debts on a lower rung in their scale of priorities is additionally appealing when the debts were incurred by a previous regime and when the proceeds of the borrowings had been used for capital flight or for other non-productive or nefarious purposes.

Setting a ceiling on payments could take the form of issuing variable maturity loans where the capping becomes operative when the interest rate exceeds some predetermined limit, the unpaid portion of interest due then being added to the life of the loan, or less preferably from the debtor's viewpoint, to the total debt. The determination of the appropriate level to cap the rate puts the focus on what is deemed to be the tolerable limit of their debt burden. Several variants of such limits can be chosen from: the debt service-export ratio, the interest-export ratio, the debt-GDP ratio and so on. These conventional yardsticks could be used as early indicators of trouble, but the most directly relevant in the short term is the interest-export ratio and, over the longer term, the debt-GDP or the debt-wealth ratio (wealth being defined as an indicator of the *present value* of the future stream of national income).

These proposals to cap interest rates have almost as many advocates as variants: Anthony Solomon, a former president of the Federal Reserve Bank of New York; Preston Martin, a former Vice-Chairman of the Federal Reserve Board; and Henry Kissinger, who could be counted among the ranks of the payment-cappers on the basis of his proposal for a Western Hemisphere Development Plan (WHDP), which he characterizes as "the modern philosophical equivalent of the Marshall Plan." The key feature of the WHDP is an agreement by the commercial banks to a ceiling on interest charges with the cap on interest rates set at "the historical real interest rate (of) around 3 per cent," the debtors paying the difference between that figure and current interest rates in local currency to help fund the WHDP or having the difference added to their outstanding debt.[1]

Dragoslav Avramovic has been in the forefront of those advocating "concerted international measures to introduce ceilings on interest rates and restore the regulation of capital markets," a move that he sees as a necessary condition to reducing interest rates. As steps to achieve the desired reduction, Avramovic advocates that "the key Governments, in particular those of developed countries, agree on a proportionate reduction of the interest rates they offer for their borrowing and that of their agencies (which should cause) market rates to fall under the pressure of this collective monopsony of the buyers of funds."[2]

The interest-capping proposals have not been endorsed as yet by any creditor Government or bank. Though advocated by some debtors, its application in an across-the board manner has been aborted by a lack of agreement and cooperation from the creditor side.

Capping payments at a fixed percentage of export earnings

This idea has received wide support from the outset of the crisis. As early as September 1984, the Latin American Economic System (SELA) presented a study to its ministerial conference in Mar del Plata. It suggested that a proposal be put before the forthcoming meeting of Commonwealth Finance Ministers that would limit Latin American countries to paying no more than a quarter of export revenues as debt service. In mid-1986 Brazilian officials proposed restricting the debt servicing payments to a fixed percentage of the debtors' GDP, 2.5 per cent to be the upper limit in 1987 and 2 per cent in 1988. Others have tied the debt servicing payments to some ratio related to export earnings or the domestic requirements for foreign exchange reserves and import payments to maintain a certain minimum rate of growth.

The most celebrated case was the 1985 decision of Peru's former President, Alan Garcia Perez, to limit the percentage of export earnings devoted to debt servicing, stipulating 10 per cent as the cap in the initial stage. The speech was newsworthy in being put forward in an assertive manner by a head of state and declared to be an operative decision. Not surprisingly, in the ranks of the debtors this decision was welcomed as a long-overdue idea that was waiting for some brave leader to initiate. The decision thus took on the attributes of an act of open defiance.

Even in the North American press the declaration received a favourable press. Columnist Tom Wicker, commenting on "the message from Garcia" in a op-ed piece in *The New York Times*, described it as

"the most imaginative idea yet offered by the leader of a debt-ridden Latin American nation, a possible way out of the region's dangerous debt crisis that avoids both extremes—default or years of extreme austerity threatening political upheaval."

On the same date in the normally staid and politically conservative *Globe and Mail* of Toronto, the editorial declared:

"the decision of the new President of Peru to flout the IMF is not the act of an angry young man. *How does an impoverished nation with a crumbling economy justify interest payments to foreign bankers while its own people decline into misery and social chaos?...Though it seems provoc-*

ative, (the Peruvian decision) contains an obvious element of common sense. The question is whether the international financial community can accommodate such candor (especially as), in this circumstance, the moral, practical and political logic of the present international debt management system seems clearly inadequate, deserving of challenge, requiring innovation.'' (Emphasis added.)

It is not difficult to understand the amalgam of compassionate concern, frustration and fear that had made President Garcia's gesture strike so responsive a chord. The idea has been looking in vain, however, for wider endorsement and adoption as debtors have backed down in face of the strong opposition of the creditor community.

The creditors have taken exception to this approach on three grounds: (1) It is too rigid a formula or too cumbersome or unworkable given the difficulties of determining the ''acceptable'' ratio of exports earnings to debt servicing, (2) It is too unfair in its application in so far as it shifts onto their shoulders the risks of fluctuating commodity prices and the other factors affecting the foreign exchange earnings of the debtor countries, and (3) It is bound to prove counterproductive in as much as the opposition of the creditors will further reduce the flow of capital to the debtors in general and the defiant ones in particular. The creditors did indeed respond by further reducing the availability of capital and/or hardening the terms for whatever capital could be borrowed, even those borrowings that take the form of suppliers' credits. Peru felt the sting of this retaliatory action.

The Peruvian experience has been painful, and this pain has been exacerbated by the fact that it has been incurred in vain as their economic plight worsened after a brief period of euphoria. The Peruvian example has brought home the message to other debtors that one or a few vulnerable debtors cannot embark alone on this path. It is hardly surprising, therefore, that few other countries have dared follow through with this type of unilateral action in an explicit declaration that becomes tantamount to throwing down the gauntlet to the creditor community.[3] With the Peruvian experience as a precedent of what the creditor community could do in retaliation, few countries have dared to follow the same route, though Nigeria and Zambia have declared similar intentions and then backed off. As an explicit tactic, the debtor countries have had to take recourse to other ways of lowering their debt burdens, among them the more radical ones of debt moratoria and debt default or cancellation.

DEBT CANCELLATION AND/OR DEBT FORGIVENESS

As late as three years after the debt crisis erupted in August 1982, the issue of debt relief in the form of debt forgiveness was an unmentionable idea in creditor circles. In 1985 John Williamson was able to state:

> "Debt has been renegotiated, reconstructed, rolled over and stretched out, but it has not been forgiven. . . . My own view is that a policy of categorically denying the possibility of debt relief is inadmissible on humanitarian grounds, unjust inasmuch as the banks have on occasion contributed to the problem of excessive indebtedness, and unrealistic since in extremis countries will be unable to service their debts however hard they try. . . . Moreover, it seems paradoxical in the extreme to deny to sovereign debtors a possibility that creditors with stronger enforcement mechanisms often find it in their own interest to extend to corporate debtors."[4]

It was not until 1987 that the proposals to provide debt relief in an overt fashion in the form of debt forgiveness for a *group of countries* began to be taken seriously by the creditor countries—or at least acted upon, even if only in a modest way. The catalyst was not an awareness of and a compassionate reaction to the festering conditions of misery and tensions in many of the debtor countries that had become too blatant to be denied. Rather, the catalyst was the awareness that the debts of many of the most debt-distressed countries would not be serviced *under any foreseeable conditions*, and the wisest course then would be to make a virtue of necessity.

The idea of debt default or of debt forgiveness has been floated as a trial balloon from the debtor side by some officials of Latin American countries, including Cuban President Fidel Castro and by Celso Furtado, a former Brazilian Minister of Planning. The Soviet Union's President, Mikhail Gorbachev, has proposed a 100-year moratorium on interest payments, effectively reducing the *present value* of the debts to zero. But such unthinkable thoughts as default have been met with warnings about the frightening counter-productive consequences of such unilateral actions, namely, a complete cut-off of credit *forevermore*.

This dire outcome of debt defaults or moratoria is not, however, supported by the historical record. That record could in fact support the opposite case, namely, that past defaults did not *necessarily invite calamity either for the*

defaulter, the creditor banks or the global financial system. In this century
alone, the list of defaulters is a long one: Mexico (1914), Brazil, Chile and
Colombia (1931), Cuba (1933), and in the 1930s, Britain, France and Germany. By 1937 about half of the United States loans made between 1925 and
1929 were in default and were largely written off, while the debt incurred by
Germany as reparations (set by the Treaty of Versailles at about $250 billion
in current dollars) was cancelled outright. In more recent times, the United
States reduced the German debt acquired under the Marshall Plan by two
thirds and stretched repayment over 35 years at the concessional rate of 3 per
cent. In these events there are illuminating correlations between defaults and
recovery for both the debtors and the creditors, especially the industrial export
sectors of the creditor countries.[5]

If historic precedent is a guide, it appears that the costs of default have
been exaggerated. In any case, there may well come a point where there is
little creditworthiness to jeopardize, and·the benefits of default outweigh the
costs of default. For many debtor countries this point already may have
arrived, and they and others may be said to be playing the game of what one
commentator, W. Cline, has labelled, "benign arrears."[6] The analysis, therefore, points to an alternative that is not unthinkable and may become probable
if conditions for the debtors deteriorate to a point where the availability of
credit is, in any case, virtually nil—and the outflow of capital to service the
debts exceeds any prospect of a commensurate inflow.

Until the present, the interests and circumstances of the debtor countries
have been too varied for them to take a united stand on what is regarded as
an extreme position that —they are warned—would brand them as parriahs
in the eyes of creditors, both present *and future*. The perception of that risk
has been a sufficient deterrent—so far. However, conditions for some of the
debtors, particularly the desperately poor sub-Saharan African countries, have
become so extreme that debts are not being serviced, and the creditors have
been forced to turn a blind eye to the accumulating arrears. There is a growing
acceptance, therefore, on the part of all Governments as creditors of the need
to offer a substantial degree of debt forgiveness across-the-board for these
debt-distressed countries as a *group*.

The task of deciding which debtors are to be favoured by the gesture of
debt forgiveness is now quite simple: harsh reality has forced the creditors
to bypass the thorny operational questions as to how "poverty" and "ability
to pay" are to be defined, how to determine the proportion of the outstanding
debt that is to be forgiven, and the scope, manner and timing of such an
action. Professor Jeffrey Sachs has advocated across-the-board interest forgiveness on a limited scale—5 years for 35 countries which would have the
effect of reducing the *present value* of their debts:

"The key to achieving adequate debt reduction is to avoid the voluntarism of the Brady approach, to insist on an across-the-board participation of the banks with no free riders. . . . and to instruct the IMF to give official forbearance to arrears which play a strategic role in bringing about debt reduction, an action that would send a strong signal to the banks that they will not gain by holding out."[7]

For the commercial bank creditors the most important issue has been the impact of such defaults or forgiveness on their own solvency and bottom line, and for their Governments, the risks for the global financial system. The commercial bankers are willing to forgive when the debtors are clearly desperately poor, the debts involved are relatively small, and *are not being serviced nor are likely to be in the foreseeable future*. Some smaller countries have lightened the burden of debt servicing by an unadvertised suspension of payments, while the creditors have treated the accumulation of arrears with a policy of tolerance, knowing full well that the alternative for desperately poor debtor countries is a declaration of moratorium or default on all or part of the loans outstanding.

As early as 1983 Danish banks collectively announced that they would forgive their share of Togo's debt. Few bankers followed this pathbreaking initiative until 1987 when two American banks, the Bank of Boston and the American Express Bank, declared they would forgive some outstanding debts. The amounts were not significant either for the banks involved or for the countries affected; most of them were in Latin America. Other banks have simply increased their reserves to better meet the eventuality of having to write-off bad debts. They have, at the same time, declared their intention to try to collect on them as best they can. The banking community regards this tactic as one that strengthens their bargaining position to maintain or even increase the pressure that can be placed on the debtors in the debt rescheduling process.

Except for the Danish banking community's initiative, the governments as creditors have been faster off the mark in the debt forgiveness tortoise race. In 1973 Sweden and the Federal Republic of Germany declared their support for debt forgiveness at a Special Session of UNCTAD, but only under circumstances where the debt servicing burden was deemed by them to be out of line with capacity to pay. This ambiguous declaration was soon followed by the Government of the Federal Republic of Germany declaring that it would write off its modest African debts. In 1986, the Netherlands took debt relief measures amounting to about $100 million. Canada followed suit in

1987, forgiving several hundred millions of debt owed by the poorest sub-Saharan African countries.

The most dramatic official gestures have come in the last few years. In 1987, six years after the debt crisis erupted, at the summit meeting in Toronto, French President Francois Mitterand proposed an across-the-board forgiveness of one third of governmental and government-guaranteed debts of the poorest sub-Saharan African States. The gesture amounted to about $12 billion (one third of $35 billion), or less than 1 per cent of the $1,300 billion third world's debt. The reduction in debt servicing would have been about $100 million a year if the debts were to be serviced. These proposals, including the later ones for Poland and Egypt, have marginal global impact though the favoured countries stand to benefit significantly. The significance lies in the fact that these proposals can be characterized as being "across-the-board."

The United Kingdom Prime Minister, John Major, in his previous position as Chancellor of the Exchequer proposed an even more radical gesture in late 1990 in Trinidad at a meeting of Finance Ministers of the Group of Seven: an across-the-board write-off of a significant percentage of the debts of these poor country debtors, most of whom are in sub-Saharan Africa. These 26 countries owe about $116 billion. A substantial cut of say two thirds would amount to $78 billion or approximately 5 per cent of third world debt. Since about 70 per cent of their debt is owed to Governments or official creditors, this would hardly offset commercial creditor claims except possibly to increase their secondary market value. But even this is uncertain because these countries were unable to service their debts after the first write-off in 1989. They serviced about 40 per cent of the $8.5 billion owed on interest for the reduced debt.

The significance of such proposals is that they are less and less unthinkable as initiatives that are "across-the-board" in scope and manner of application.

The issue of debt forgiveness is still contentious and will remain so as long as the debt overhang casts its pall over the global economy. The divergent views on this issue are dramatically illustrated by the squabble that ensued at the meeting of the Group of Seven Finance Ministers in late April 1991. On that occasion the United States announced that 70 per cent of Poland's foreign debt and all of Egypt's military debt owed to the United States would be forgiven on an exceptional basis and requested other creditors to forgive as much or at least 50 per cent of Poland's foreign debts owed to these Governments. The Japanese were adamantly opposed.[8] The French proposed that such forgiveness initiatives be extended to other debtors such as the least developed countries that are not able, in any case, to service their debts. The United Kingdom suggested that up to two thirds of such debts (amounting to $26 billion) be forgiven.

What is significant is that across-the-board initiatives are becoming more thinkable to creditors, but so far the designated group does not include the middle-income debtor countries. In global terms they are the so-called "problem debtors" because of the size of their outstanding debts owed to commercial banks that have been rendered fragile by the unserviced or poorly serviced debts on their books.

Congressional voices have taken a different view, however, among them Senator Bill Bradley and Representative Charles Schumer, a member of the United States House of Representative's Banking Committee. One part of the proposed approach advocated by Senator Bradley in 1986 envisaged granting creditors a 3 per cent interest rate reduction and forgiving 3 per cent of the principal annually for three years to those debtor countries agreeing to economic reform at a specially convened trade/debt summit. Congressman Schumer, in an op-ed article in *The Washington Post*, went so far as to urge that debtors "be helped as a group, rather than case-by-case:"

"What is needed," he wrote, "is a creative solution such as. . . . writing off outstanding loans as nonperforming by 30 per cent or a percentage that is in line with the average discount at which the banks are currently reselling some of their third world debt."[9]

In all the years that have passed, there have been faint echoes from the United States Administration. The hesitation stems most probably from a reluctance to break the taboo against approaches deviating from the case-by-case muddling-through process. The United States Administration changed its tune in 1991 when for geo-political reasons it advocated an across-the-board write-off of 70 per cent of Poland's debt. This time the Japanese dug in their heels, fearing to set an example. A 50 per cent compromise was reached with clear declarations about the special case.

This stance has the appearance of a King Canute gesture. The case for significant write-offs across-the-board is becoming more compelling as the situation continues to fester with high interest rates, little movement on trade barriers and shrinking markets as recession takes its toll. Debt forgiveness on a massive scale was once, and might once again be, one of the essential preconditions for global recovery.

Much depends on whether action is taken on a scale commensurate with the danger. But it would have to be undertaken as part of a broader programme of action that could lead to global recovery.

The authors of the *World Development Report* 1988 put the issue succinctly:

''There is no simple, single solution to the debt problem; *a comprehensive framework is needed. . . .*''

We shall consider this ''comprehensive framework'' in the next chapters where the focus is on the concept of a ''new Bretton Woods'' (Chapter 10), on a global programme of action for addressing the debt and environmental crises separately and together as one mega global crisis (Chapter 11) and on the past and potential role of the international institutions to facilitate and implement the suggested policies and programmes (Chapter 12).

PART FIVE

THE GLOBAL-SCALE DIMENSIONS OF PROPOSALS TO ADDRESS THE GLOBAL CRISES

"The biggest politico-economic challenge to statesmen is to integrate national policies into a global perspective, to resolve the discordance between the international economy and the political system based on the nation state. . . . In (today's) circumstances the international economic system operates — if at all — as crisis management. The risk is, of course, that some day crisis management may be inadequate. The world will then face a disaster its lack of foresight has made inevitable. . . . *My major point is that the world needs new arrangements.*

The spirit that produced Bretton Woods reflected the realization that in the long run the national welfare can only be safeguarded within the framework of the general welfare." (Emphasis added)

—Henry A. Kissinger [1]

"Ultimately an effective greenhouse treaty will need the voluntary co-operation of sovereign powers. . . . including developing countries without whose co-operation the growth in the output of carbon dioxide would swamp any cuts by industrial countries. . . . In the case of global pollution, no world government exists to make polluters pay. . . . The prospect of a convention to start work on a treaty on global climate change. . . . has drawn economists into unfamiliar fields of international politics."

—The Economist [2]

CHAPTER 10

GLOBAL SYSTEMIC CHANGES

One category of proposal goes well beyond those dealing with the debt crisis on a case-by-case basis and even those that provide debt relief across-the-board. The premise of this broader approach is the belief that the prevailing global economic-financial *system* has fostered the emergence of the present troubling situation with all its fragility, instability, unsustainability and in-equity. This approach puts the emphasis on the need for change in the pre-vailing global rules of the game for trade and capital movements *as a system*.

The objective of this approach is not limited to ''a return to debtor's creditworthiness'' but is rather designed to avoid catastrophic breakdown of the economic-financial system and to improve that system. The improvements would be multidimensional: faster global growth in real incomes or well-being, a more equitable sharing of this growth, and a growth pattern com-patible with standards of environmental quality, locally and globally, to sustain such growth over the long-term. For some of the necessary conditions to attain this state of affairs with respect to trade and capital flows is the estab-lishment of rules or a system analogous to the one established at a conference held in Bretton Woods, New Hampshire in 1944.

THE OPERATIONS AND BREAKDOWN OF THE ORIGINAL BRETTON WOODS SYSTEM

The agreement that emerged from that conference addressed a limited but key set of issues facing the post-war world, namely, the rules for international movement of goods and services and of investment. It was a system in the sense that the parties involved in across-border trade and capital movements were coerced or willing cooperants agreeing to conduct their affairs according to these rules. Professor Richard Cooper has referred to it, therefore, as "the Bretton Woods bargain," or "an understanding" whereby the United States was to take on the obligation to act as a stabilizer by exercising an overwhelming degree of control over key features of the international financial system such as money supply and exchange rates.[3]

To carry through on this agreement, there was a need for new institutions. Two were established: the International Monetary Fund (IMF) and the World Bank, the official name of which is the International Bank for Reconstruction and Development (IBRD). The "reconstruction" function reflects one of its early responsibilities with regard to lending for post-war reconstruction with France as its first "customer." A third institution, the International Trade Organization (ITO) was proposed and aborted by the United States in favour of a truncated entity that was labelled, the General Agreement on Tariffs and Trade (GATT). As Professor Heilleiner aptly describes it, GATT was "a small secretariat authorized to do little more than 'service' the 89 contracting nations (out of the IMF's 146)," and to do so with respect only to some of the trade-related issues because there were "major gaps in the coverage of GATT that were left out by (force of) political events such as the final defeat of the ITO."[4]

The IMF was conceived as the pivotal institution with a facilitating and surveillance role for the operations of a dollar-reserve system somewhat analogous to the pre-war gold standard or gold-exchange standard that had the British pound as its dominant reserve currency. It was "an adjustable-peg system" intended to be less rigid than the gold standard in providing for periodic adjustments. The Bretton Woods system's rules were designed to provide stability by fixing the foreign exchange parities among the major industrialized countries and allowing only periodic adjustments when the consent of the IMF could be obtained. This system vested the IMF with the authority, as one commentator so aptly put it, "as champion of virtuous finance." But the IMF, despite its international board of directors and shareholders, had limited power. It was the United States that was vested with the responsibility of "virtuousness" in keeping the United States dollar, as the saying goes, "as good as gold." The IMF had the power to comment, to propose but not dispose; but this "power" of commentary was exercised by IMF management with constraints, and even when there was an independent view, its influence was severely limited.

The United States dollar as the reserve currency was to be backed by gold reserves in only a loose sense because the relationship of the United States money supply was not itself fixed in relation to gold except figuratively. Congress could and did change the legal "obligatory" connection between its gold reserves and money supply. But none the less, United States policy makers were expected to exercise the necessary discipline incumbent on a reserve currency country. To ensure this confidence, anyone could obtain gold bricks from the Fort Knox vaults in exchange for the paper dollars at a market price set on the free market of the London bullion exchange.

The United States was also expected to keep the international system sufficiently liquid by running a trade deficit. The early post-war years were characterized by perennial bouts of dollar shortage stress as the United States ran trade surpluses that absorbed a large percentage of the available dollars. Despite this there was no severe generalized dollar shortage beyond the immediate post-war years. Beginning in the 1960s there was a surge of United States investment abroad, as dollars moved off-shore to escape governmental regulatory constraints on banking operations. This off-shore process gave rise to a new institutional arrangement, known as the Eurodollar phenomenon, that made it unnecessary for the United States to continue to run a chronic trade deficit in order to ensure the necessary liquidity that the rapidly expanding trade flows required.

The Bretton Woods constraints obliged the United States to maintain global *confidence* in the dollar, so there was a sense of limits to the permissible bounds of money supply expansion. In the late 1960s, at the time of the Viet Nam War, United States policy makers tested the limits of monetary expansion "allowed" under the Bretton Woods "rules" when they pursued domestic policies that brought on inflation at a rate greatly exceeding that of the other major industrialized nations. Downward pressure was exerted on the dollar. By the end of the 1960s a gold rush was set in motion reflecting rapidly waning confidence in the dollar. This confidence factor was dramatically reflected in events that can be dated almost precisely. On 1 March 1968, the upward spiral of gold prices commenced, ending only after several years when the price per Troy ounce that had fluctuated in the $300-400 range reached its peak at a level in excess of $800.

Under the circumstances, United States policy makers had to choose between adhering to the obligations the country had assumed under the Bretton Woods agreement by reining in the inflationary forces through the imposition of tough fiscal and monetary policy measures, or breaking the agreement. The United States chose the latter course by "closing the gold window" and thus, after a quarter century, ended the Brettons Woods era.

Freed of the constraints, when the opportunities arose in the early 1970s to recycle petrodollars, the commercial bankers acted as the principal intermediaries between the oil-exporters unable to absorb much of their sudden foreign exchange windfall due to the oil price rise and the oil-importing developing countries that became anxious borrowers to pay their increased oil bills. From 1973 to 1980, syndicated Eurocurrency lending to the developing countries increased from less than $4 billion to almost $50 billion, an increase of 1,200 per cent. The process has been aptly described by a London banker, Minos Zombanakis, as "a lending orgy." (He did not characterize the "morning-after" syndrome.)

In the syndication process the major commercial banks took the lead—and the fees that go with that role—while the smaller banks jumped enthusiastically but blindly onto the syndication bandwagon. By 1980 these banks, that had never before ventured into international lending, accounted for about one third of the total volume of such syndicated loans. This was made possible by the technical and organizational strengthening of the network of interbank deposits. This network had expanded so rapidly by 1983 that it accounted for more than 40 per cent of the volume of Euromarket deposits and 50 per cent of the Asian dollar market. As the main depositories of petrodollars, the major banks were eager to lend both directly to countries and indirectly to the interbank system. By virtue of this indirect process, very few of the hundreds of smaller banks that participated could obtain, or cared to obtain, any knowledge, let alone a measure of control, over how the funds were to be used by the borrowers. The banks plunged into these international financial waters knowing there was danger in doing so, but the *systemic* imperatives overpowered caution and good judgement.

The bankers were aware that the international lending process depended heavily on the Eurocurrency market, and the reason for this reliance was simply that the arrangement by-passed the national controls for reserve requirements and other constraints. Particularly after 1974, the commercial bank syndicates thus had access to a form of financial marketing centres that enjoyed the advantage of "international monetary indiscipline," to use a felicitous phrase of Dr. Raul Prebisch.

Indeed, the banking community forcefully and openly opposed any international collaborative approach to examine the implications of this lending mania and the institutional arrangements that made it possible. Prominent bankers even went on record opposing those nervous "ninnies" who were calling for so-called "safety nets." The process has continued to this day, but with fewer illusions than those entertained in the heady days before 1982 when Walter Wriston, former Chairman and Chief Executive Officer of Citicorp, could assert that it was sound policy to lend, even to *push* lending to third world countries; as he put it in a classic phrase, "sovereign debtors don't go broke."

The demise of the Bretton Woods system in the late 1960s and early 1970s gave way to a floating rate of exchange system. The regime of capital and trade flows has been characterized since then by a troubling degree of exchange volatility and a *mega* global change in the trade deficit-trade surplus relationship. This has led to a major shift in the debtor-creditor relationships and all that that implies. The 1970 decade of this post-Bretton Woods period of a non-system was the gestation period for the debt crisis that broke out in the summer of 1982.

THE RATIONALE FOR A NEW BRETTON WOODS

After the collapse of the Bretton Woods agreement in 1970, no adequate *control* mechanism was in place to prevent the chain of events that led to the enormous pile-up of the mountain of debt. Under a properly functioning global economic and financial system, the countries that went on a borrowing and lending binge in the 1970s would have been brought up short by the Bretton Woods reins. Thus there is understandably a nostalgic view of the earlier (1945-1970) international regime with its greater stability and growth. This then is the basis for the advocacy of a "new Bretton Woods:" to secure an agreement that once again sets out "rules of the game" with respect to trade and capital flows and involves a comprehensive framework of institutional changes. The call is for rules such as those that held sway for a quarter century until 1970, but adapted of course to current circumstances.

When the stability of the Gold Standard's prime years, 1880-1910, is contrasted with that of the 1960 to 1990 decades, as shown in Figure 18 in terms of long-term interest rates, wholesale prices and trade balances, the implications are clear. But given the lessons of the breakdown of these systems, and of their limited achievement in the unequal sharing of the putative benefits of the large increase in global average per capita incomes, the new Bretton Woods would be broader than the old one in the scope of its objectives and its means of achieving them.

The rationale for the calls for global monetary reform is rooted, therefore, in the excesses that followed when no effective response mechanism was in place to dampen the changes in the speed and direction of speculative currency movements that destabilized exchange rates. The absence of any form of braking and steering mechanism to influence the mobility of capital movements has posed a danger as the speed and mass of the amounts of foreign exchange being transferred has risen to a point beyond any Government's ability to control.

Figure 15: *Volatility of Long term Interest rates, Wholesale prices and Current Account Balance amoung major industrialized countries 1880-1910, 1960-1990*

Than and Now

| ■ Britain | ■ Germany | ■ United States | ■ France | ■ Japan |

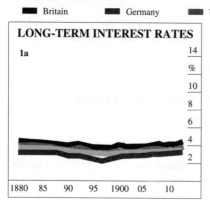

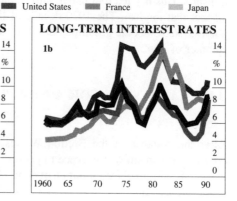

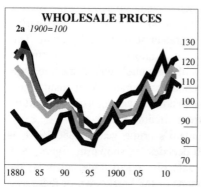

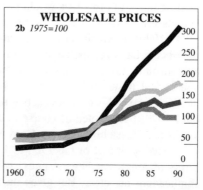

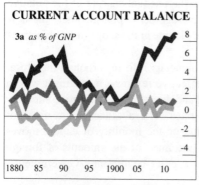

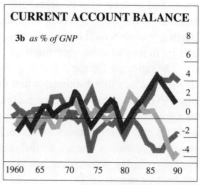

Source: Human Development Report 1990 UNDP   *Source: Human Development Report 1990 UNDP*

Some numbers tell the story: the global flow of trade in financial assets, that is, trading in the foreign exchange markets of London, New York and Tokyo has grown three-fold over the decade of the 1980s, more than doubling since 1986, to reach a volume valued at almost $100 trillion, or about $500 billion of every working day, and the world's banking systems now transfer more than $1 trillion a day in foreign exchange between themselves.[5] *This dwarfs by a factor of 10 the amount of reserves that the central banks of the major industrialized countries, the Group of Seven, could put into the market to influence the exchange rate in any desired direction,* unless the market players change their expectations by virtue of such token moves accompanied by Group of Seven declarations. Furthermore, the daily turnover in the global foreign exchange markets is about $500 billion or six times the reserves of Germany and Japan and over 10 times the United States holdings of D-mark and Yen. The dynamic of this phenomenon is even more troubling: the present transactional volume is double what it was only five years ago, and an exceptionally high proportion of this currency movement is speculative or "hot money" unrelated to the productive aspects of financing trade and private foreign investment.[6]

This capital movement also dwarfs the global flow of trade in goods and services by a factor of 25 even though global trade had increased 13-fold in real terms since 1950, and for the 1980s by about 20 per cent a year, to attain a volume valued at about $4 trillion by the end of 1990. *It is this relationship of $1 of trade in goods and services to $25 of trade in financial assets that has made it so essential for the global economy to have a financial system with control features akin to those of the Bretton Woods agreement* and before that, the Gold Standard and the British pound as the reserve currency. This is especially so in light of the relative proportions of capital and trade flows that indicate only a small part of the capital movement is devoted to financing legitimate trade and legitimate investment activities. Much of the flow had taken on the attributes of what has been labelled "hot money." Thus, there are dangerous implications both in the unprecedented magnitude, in both relative and absolute terms, and the speculative nature of the capital flows between countries.

The record of exchange rate volatility since the early 1970s is evidence of the importance short-term factors have played in the movement of capital, factors such as differential in interest rates and expectations of future movements in exchange rates. The long-term equilibrium of these exchange rates that theoretically should gravitate towards purchasing power parity is submerged, however, by the speculative capital movements. Accordingly, the focus of attention for reform of the international economic-financial system is understandably placed on the interplay of financial factors that have a highly speculative character.[7]

The damage these post-1970 emergent financial institutional developments have wrought on the global economy is, in the final analysis, reflected in the current debt crisis and the instability and fragility that goes with it. The days of Bretton Woods are being recalled with nostalgia when it is realized that during the period when its rules held sway there was a much more mutually supportive relationship between the global economic and financial system. During those two decades the increase in the global flows of trade and incomes exceeded 150 per cent, while the real value of international trade expanded by 250 per cent. Furthermore, the benefits of this growth were being shared as well by developing countries that on average year-in year-out were growing at a much faster rate than the industrialized ones.

True, this favourable distributive aspect expressed as an average does not reveal the great unevenness of the advance in income levels, not only between developing nations but even more so between the rich and the poor in these countries. But notwithstanding this important qualifier—which explains how 40 per cent of humankind experienced virtually no advancement in all those years and are still existing in conditions of absolute poverty—the Bretton Woods years were a great improvement over the years of the post Bretton Woods decades of the 1970s and 1980s when average incomes dropped dramatically and the gross inequities in income distribution became more pronounced.

With this experience as precedent, in face of current conditions it is understandable that many are posing the question: what should be the appropriate response at *this time?* There is a simple answer: more coordination and more constraint. But how? In terms of membership and procedures and such, what *form* should this coordination take under present circumstances?

At one level is the issue of the relationship of the major economies one to the other, characterized as it has been by a major shift of economic-financial hegemony. This has created a problem of leadership. Where at one time one country, the United States, could dictate terms by virtue of its overwhelming economic-financial dominance, there are now several (Japan and Germany or the European Community) with clout enough to force the hegemony to turn from acting as a Sergeant-Major to a pleader for cooperation. Stephen Marglin phrased the current challenge clearly and succinctly in these terms:

> "the central issue is whether there (is). . . . a set of practises, a system of behaviour which one or more major powers can follow in order to induce cooperative behaviour on the part of the others?"[8]

At another level the issue is broader: how is this cooperative framework to include the global community of nations beyond the small club of the major economic powers that have been meeting and attempting some form of ad hoc cooperation through Group of Three and Group of Seven meetings and other fora? The issue of widening the Group of Seven membership is now on the international agenda. Legitimate protests have been expressed about the fact that the few have arrogated to themselves responsibility for the many, a presumption especially flagrant with respect to the third world debt crisis that the Group of Seven discuss, propose and attempt to dispose *without the participation of those most affected, the debtors*. The protestations have been growing louder. Worsening this situation, the process is not working to dissipate the debt overhang with its depressing impact both economically and morally. This negative effect has brought to the fore the issue of broadening the membership of the policy-making club to achieve a truly internationally representative approach to the current global *problematique*.

HESITANT STEPS ALONG THE COOPERATIVE ROAD TO PROVIDE THE "INTERNATIONAL PUBLIC GOOD"

It has long been recognized that if the concept of *coordination-constraint* is to be more than a pious hope, leadership must provide what has been called an "international public good," that is, the establishment and maintenance of a global milieu characterized by the rule of law, acceptable modes of behaviour in commerce and everyday activities and other attributes of a desirable world in terms of stability, fairness and openness. Providing this public good calls for a significant change in the behaviour of the leaders of the major industrialized nations who alone are economically powerful enough to provide such leadership.

Professor Charles Kindleberger described the current situation succinctly:

"After about 1981, the United States, like Britain from about 1890, had shrunk in economic might relative to the rest of the world as a whole, and more importantly, it lost the appetite for providing *international economic public goods*—open markets in times of glut, supplies in times of acute shortages, steady flows of capital to developing countries, international money, coordination of macroeconomic policy and last-resort lending."[9]

Formal coordinating meetings between countries to discuss economic and financial issues have been going on for a long time on a more or less regular basis within the framework of the IMF, the World Bank, and the United Nations and its agencies and on an ad hoc basis through global and regional conferences such as those on environment, new sources of energy, food and so on. In addition there are the OECD meetings on aid, trade and a range of economic and financial issues; and there are the most publicized of all such conclaves, the so-called summit meetings. But these have had—and undoubtedly will continue to have—negligible effect so long as the major players on the economic and financial stage pursue highly divergent policies and rely on the current process. The comment of Professor Kindelberger on summitry reflects a widely-shared assessment of the manner in which the Group of Seven "leadership" is being conducted:

"What I worry about mostly is exchange policy and macroeconomic coordination (especially as) the commitment to consultative macroeconomic policies in annual summit meetings of seven heads of state has become a shadow play, a dog-and-pony show, a series of photo opportunities — whatever you choose to call them — with ceremony substituted for substance."

The first signs of change in this regard were evident in September 1985 when United States Treasury Secretary Baker requested a meeting of the finance ministers of the five leading industrialized nations, the Group of Five, in New York at the Plaza Hotel, presumably choosing the site to suggest the appearance of informality. The present process thus might be said to have started with the Plaza Hotel meeting of the Group of Three in the mid-1980s, a time when the post-Bretton Woods non-system began to show severe strain in terms of exchange rate volatility, mounting defaults and arrears in the servicing of third world debts. The ad hoc process has been followed-up at the Louvre, Akasaki Palace and other such exotic venues. But as a mode of achieving cooperation, judged on the basis of results this process has fallen far short of what is needed despite some appearances that the Group of Seven coordination was effective. As Professor Paul Krugman has noted,

"in retrospect, *the apparent success of the Group of Seven at enforcing target zones* after the Louvre (meeting of February 1987) appears to have been something of a fluke: the Group of Seven's actions had a major effect only because the market expected them to, *not because they were powerful in their own right, (thus) meaningful monetary reform on a global scale remains to be achieved.*"[10]

As the volume and speed of transfer of funds in Eurodollar accounts have accelerated with the help of electronic-informational technological advances, it has become clearer that the ability of Governments to influence financial decisions has become more and more limited. There is first the capital movements involved in the process of multi-country manufacturing and services. Its growing importance is indicated by the investment trends of United States firms. In 1990 they increased their investment in domestic facilities by 6 per cent and in foreign ones by 17 per cent. With each passing day, Governments find themselves less and less capable of influencing the investment decisions that play such a large role in the transfer of capital.[11] When to this is added the increasing importance of the phenomenon of speculative movements fueled by hundreds of billions of laundered drug dollars, "capital flight" and other forms of "hot money," the controls of any one nation have virtually disappeared.

A great divergence of views exists with regard to *procedural* specifics. An exception is the general point that *the concept of Bretton Woods serves as a shorthand way of referring to the formalization of the process of coordination that would guide and constrain the conduct of economic and financial affairs among nations.* But the contentious issues with regard to the procedural aspect are secondary. A series of meetings might culminate in one big meeting along the lines of the 1944 event in Bretton Woods, New Hampshire, but there is no best path to reach the desired end. The Bretton Woods meeting was arranged under conditions that were historically unique, and the preliminaries, conducted during wartime, took four years.

Apart from the procedural aspect, there is the *organizational*: if the agenda is to be broadened, the participation of other nations outside the membership of the Group of Seven and the OECD must be included. Stephen Marris in a report of the World Institute for Development Economics Research of the United Nations University (WIDER), aptly observes,

"The most important collective decisions in international financial policy in recent years have all been of an ad hoc type—the Louvre and Plaza accords and the Baker Strategy on the debt problem—(involving). . . . only governments of the large developed economies (that have the requisite) financial kind of clout. . . . *Yet the limitations of ad hoc co-op-*

eration as a means of running the world economy are becoming increasingly clear. . . . The Group of Five, with its link to the Summit, has an inevitable bias towards damage limitation and the short term political interests of those currently in power.''(emphasis added)[12]

Beyond process and participation, the most important issue is *substantive*, that is, the nature of the desired institutional arrangements or system that would enable and encourage policy coordination among all parties in the global community of nations to achieve agreed-upon objectives. Thus the process, the organization and the objectives have the following three components:

- First, there is the aspect of *substance* and *scope*, that it be focussed on key issues and be wide enough to include consideration of a broad range of policies and changes in the existing institutional arrangements to achieve a greater measure of coordination and cooperation in the economic and financial spheres generally recognized to be essential for contending with the formidable problems of the global economy;

- Second, there is the aspect of *modalities*, that the way to reach meaningful agreements for such coordination and cooperation could take many paths and forms, from a series of meetings to the preparation for and the convening of a full-scale conference along the lines of the one that took place in Bretton Woods in 1944;

- Third, there is the aspect of organization-participation to include representation from the nations outside the Group of Seven in the deliberations.

The world has long lived with indecision, inefficiency and inequity. Few of the advocates of a new Bretton Woods would be moved to urge changes on that account, but they make common cause in feeling that—as a matter of pragmatism and morality—the present arrangements are unsustainable. The necessary policy and institutional changes will be made, therefore, by volitional decisions in a controlled and orderly way to take advantage of the greater integration of the global economies. Or they will be changed by *force majeure*, that is, in an uncontrolled and precipitous manner. Should the changes come about in the second manner, the solution or outcome is likely to be a retreat from the 40-year-old trend toward interdependence to autarkic policies as each of the industrialized countries endeavours to minimize the damage to itself by adopting ''beggar-thy-neighbour'' policies. The possibility of the last outcome gives the problem and finding a solution an element of urgency.

Voices in support

The list of advocates for consideration of a Bretton Woods approach includes eminent persons from both developed and developing countries and from the two solitudes, the business-financial and the academic world. However different the vantage from which they speak, the voices calling for a new Bretton Woods—whether they use the term or not—share a common concept: the need for some form of cooperative arrangement beyond what now exists.

The list even includes former President Reagan, who proposed in the February 1985 State of the Union message to Congress that his Secretary of the Treasury undertake a study on the international monetary system to consider whether an international conference on the issue should be convened. His position was applauded at the time by the Democratic majority of the United States Congress' Joint Economic Committee in its annual report issued in mid-March 1986. The Committee's report went on to urge "speedy action on a new conference patterned after the Bretton Woods meeting of 1944."[13]

Similar signals about the need to consider a new Bretton Woods also emanated from Japan. In its November 1985 issue the Japanese daily *Mainichi* revealed the following news item:

> "One of the proposals to emerge from a ministerial consultative committee set up by Prime Minister Nakasone was a call for a 'new Bretton Woods' to reform the international monetary system and to aim for the creation of a world fund to harmonize the interventions of central banks on exchange markets."

From Europe, on a state visit to Brazil in mid-October 1985, the President of France, Francois Mitterand, sent forth the same basic message:

> "There is no durable solution to the foreign debt problem without. . . . reforms in the international monetary system."[14]

This statement reaffirmed his comment on the subject two years before when he called for "a carefully organized international monetary conference at the highest level (to establish) common rules of the game and clear perspectives without which we will not emerge from the (present debt crisis) situation. The work of overcoming the crisis is not that of a single conference or of a single year, but an immense task on the scale of a generation."[15]

Thus there has been a strong measure of support in governmental circles in the Group of Five nations for *considering* the reform of the international monetary system. The group of 24 third world ministers have also added their voice:

"The convening of an international monetary conference (is). . . . an important and essential step. . . . in moving towards a thorough-going reform of the international monetary system which would secure the objective of exchange and monetary stability on the one hand, and address itself to the special concerns of the developing countries on the other."[16]

Members of the financial community such as Felix Rohatyn joined the chorus in declaring that "a successor conference to the Bretton Woods agreement should study a more orderly international monetary system."[17]

In 1984, Sir Robert Muldoon, formerly New Zealand's Prime Minister and Minister of Finance, sponsored a resolution to have the Commonwealth secretariat prepare a study focusing on the desirability and feasibility of a new Bretton Woods. It was his view that:

"(we must commit ourselves to) start a systematic process which looks to significant changes in the structure of trade, payments, development efforts and exchange rates. . . . Basic preparatory work would be undertaken first by a small group of 20 to 25 experts — who have the political backing of their Governments — with the IMF, GATT and maybe UNCTAD sitting in. . . . *A second Bretton Woods conference (would) come out at the end of this process rather than at the beginning.*" (Emphasis added.)[18]

This view was reiterated by Professor Gerald Helleiner, the Chairman of the Commonwealth secretariat's Study Group that prepared the 1983 report, *Towards a New Bretton Woods: Challenges for the World Financial and Trading System.* In a follow-up article, he suggested "a carefully planned World Economic Conference—what some are calling a new Bretton Woods. (This) may provide a framework and the 'beacon' needed to give focus and a sense of overall direction to international economic reform. This is one case in which the process may be more important than the ultimate destination. . . . Such a process as it proceeds could generate changes in the practises of existing institutions, alter government policies, and strengthen existing regimes. . . . The new Bretton Woods, now widely discussed, should therefore be seen not so much as a conference but as the initiation of a negotiating process involving a re-examination of the world's financial and trading machinery in light of current and prospective needs..in the same spirit of optimism and creativity as characterized the preparations for the original conference at Bretton Woods."[19]

Several years later, with no evident progress on the follow-up to the new Bretton Woods conferencing idea, the World Institute on Development Economic Research (WIDER) prepared a report on economic summitry, and suggested that new institutional arrangements are overdue. Among the suggestions put forward is the establishment of a Group of the Non-Five that would represent those countries left out of the Group of Five inner circle, including, of course, third world countries. The purpose of this innovative idea would be to broaden the base for decision-making and exert pressure to hold a high-level world summit that "should not be a meeting that is simply another ad hoc bout of global summitry" but have concrete objectives for the Group of Non-Five to pursue. Examples are, (1) to resist further erosion of the multilateral institutions, (2) to lobby for the creation of an Interim World Economic Council, (3) to develop joint positions on all the main issues pertaining to the management of the world economy, and (4) to develop proposals for a major reform of the existing international institutional framework.[20]

In a phrase, the intent is to halt the retreat from multilateralism so clearly evident with the onset of the debt crisis as the United States turned to Japan and the Federal Republic of Germany to support coordinated policies of short term damage-control. "Trilateralism" has become the mode for decision-making for the short and medium-term. Advocates of greater international cooperative arrangements such as Fred Bergsten, Director of the Washington-based Institute for International Economics and former Assistant Secretary for the Treasury for International Affairs, has pointed out that the de facto basis for effective global management rests on Group of Three cooperation, though the participation might be wider. To achieve the "effective, cooperative global system that we're aiming for," he has suggested the launching of

"a new global negotiation for monetary reform in parallel with the European discussion of the European Monetary Union (EMU). . . . The Europeans have agreed to start their EMU negotiations in December of this year (1991), and have talked about moving to stage two of the process by the start of 1993 or 1994. Somewhere during that period there should be launched a parallel negotiation towards what I would call GMU—global monetary union—that would parallel European monetary union."[21]

There seems to be broad agreement that in a world of great interdependence international cooperation must be put on a *regularized* basis for consultations and for coordination of policies. This implies "new" institutional arrangements to achieve the required global management on trade, capital and environmental issues. The "newness" relates to the strengthening-expanding of the operations of the existing international agencies or the establishment of additional institutions on their own or as adjuncts to those already in operation. But decisions as to what ought to be done in this regard call for a framework concept within which a package of separate but related proposals can be put forward, all designed to improve the management of the global economic/financial system.

The *system concept* implies discipline to constrain national actions inimical to their planetary neighbours and promote mutually supportive actions. This has special relevance to the United States, not because it is the most delinquent in this regard, but simply because the country with the largest economy and the reserve currency "privilege" has an exceptional obligation with regard to the welfare of the international community—and thereby to itself. The history of the past two post Bretton Woods decades, starting with the "oil shocks" of 1973 and 1979 and the surge in interest rates in 1980 to the onset of the present global debt crisis in 1982—attests to the high price paid by the global community for the United States abdication of the responsibility incumbent on it as the leading nation.

Commentators as far apart in their vantage on the world scene as Drs. Raul Prebisch and Henry Kissinger speak with one voice on this issue:

Dr. Prebisch:

"The use of the dollar as an international as well as a national currency has given the United States the privilege of creating international money and obtaining free of charge part of the product of the rest of the world in exchange for this money. At the same time, it has imparted to the United States the responsibility of following principles inspired by the needs of the world economy. Full use has been made of the privilege, but *the way in which the responsibility has been carried out can hardly be the subject of admiration.*"(emphasis added)[22]

Dr. Kissinger:

"We live with the paradox of a global economy which lacks a system for setting agreed long-range goals. . . . (a system characterized by) incongruity between the internationalization of the world economy and the dogged strengthening of national autonomy in economic decision-making . . . A case in point (is) the unilateral decision by the United States in 1971 to suspend the convertibility of the dollar and to impose a 10 per cent surcharge, the effect (of which) was to overthrow the Bretton Woods arrangement affecting all countries—without prior consultation or notice to anyone."[12]

In today's highly integrated economic world there is obviously a compelling need for a more cooperative form of leadership. The establishment of an international economic and financial *modus operandi* based on collectively acceptable and enforceable behavioural rules would temper the pursuit of short term, narrow, self-serving national policies by factoring in broader global obligations. If shared leadership is called for to provide those international public goods that are so desperately needed, the questions that must then be asked are: how is it to be achieved? and what is to be done substantively?

KEY ELEMENTS OF THE REQUIRED GLOBAL SYSTEMIC CHANGES: ADVANCE ON THREE FRONTS

On the aspect of "how," it might suffice to say that the choices now open to the global leadership are limited. A global crisis has occurred that portends major changes. The cynics may be complacent. Unfortunately, it might take a shock to bring the point home that such changes will be undertaken consciously or they will be forced. Since illusions based on wishful thinking die hard, *force majeure* may dictate the time and intensity of the adjustment process.

Actions must be taken on several fronts to engineer a "softer" adjustment:

- *The global financial regime*—reversing the direction of capital flow transfers back towards the developing world rather than away from it; changing the terms for its acquisition, or the *real* interest rates for non-concessional capital granted or borrowed and the *real* rates of return for foreign investors capital; establishing rules that control the movement of capital so as to dampen exchange rate volatility and achieve currency alignments that are sustainable and fair;

- *The global trading regime*—lowering protectionist tariff and non-tariff barriers to third world exports, and improving the terms of trade for the benefit of the developing countries; and

- *The income-sharing regime*—reversing the trend from increasing polarization of incomes between industrialized and third world countries and eradicating the scourge of "absolute poverty," and accelerating the transfer of scientific, technological and managerial knowledge and the up-grading of human resources through training and technical assistance and capital transfers to build the self-reliant capability to achieve a lessening of dependence and income disparities as global income grows.

- *And all this with sensitivity to the environmental implications of the speed and pattern of growth.*

These are the broad headings of objectives on the global agenda. The challenge is to devise feasible programmes of action. The global dimensions make it imperative that changes be made in the international institutional framework to enable mutually supportive policies and programmes to be designed and implemented. These policies and programmes would, in the short term, address the debt crisis as a manifestation of a global economy out of balance and out of control, and especially in terms of income distribution, moving in the wrong direction. Taking a longer view but not ignoring the short term as a transitional period, the policies and programmes would need to address the environmental crisis. The key attribute of the necessary changes would be policy *cooperation* and *coordination*, a mode of operation best achieved on a regularized or institutionalized basis under a system of rules rather than on an ad hoc basis, as now, without such rules to impose mutually beneficial obligations or constraints.

We turn, therefore, to a global agenda in Chapter 11 and in Chapter 12, to the role of the international institutions in terms of the past performance and their potential to devise and implement the policies and programmes required to attain the objective of resolving the debt and the environmental crises. "Resolving" implies a process of easing the pain first, but then taking steps to avert a catastrophic *denouement*. The ultimate objective is the improvement of the global economy. That implies taking those institutional and policy measures necessary for growth with greater equity and greater sensitivity to environmental constraints.

CHAPTER 11

THE
"NEW BRETTON WOODS"
—DEBT

The debt and environmental crises rank separately and together as over-whelming top priority issues. The likely implications of not addressing them soon and fully are too tragic to contemplate. The environmental crisis may well threaten humankind's very survival. The debt crisis is already adversely affecting humanity's future as it widens still further the gap between the haves and the have-nots; furthermore, it has been reducing hope for more than two billion of the people who constitute "the bottom 40 per cent" of humanity that have not been able, as yet, to share in the world community's growth over the past several decades. In a phrase, these two crises reflect a massive global disfunction.

The suggested agenda items to address this situation include the full range of issues directly affecting, and affected by, these two crises. Their intent is to establish both the *necessary* and the *sufficient* global conditions for easing and resolving both these crises in a manner that not only avoids breakdown but in a more positive way achieves a growing, more crises-free and equitable world that is also environmentally stable. The core ideas with respect to the global debt crisis aspect are limited to a few:

- How to achieve the policy discipline at the national level and the policy coordination at the global level so as to bring interest rates down to their historic levels, dampen fluctuations in exchange rates, lower the trade barriers facing third world exports and improve the terms of trade in their favour;

- How to get *net* aid up to the 0.7 per cent of GNP target, and beyond that to a level equivalent to the 1.3 per cent of the Marshall Plan aid by the United States to Europe after the Second World War, and how to substantially increase other capital flows.

The approach to the global agenda for a programme of action might start with the financial aspect, especially with lowering real interest rates and increasing the flow of capital on low interest and concessional terms, then focus on the trade regime and, lastly, on the distributional implications of all this to suggest what might be done to close the income gap and eventually eliminate the scourge of absolute poverty that now afflicts millions of persons on this planet.

THE FINANCIAL ASPECT: COORDINATION OF POLICIES TO LOWER REAL INTEREST RATES, STABILIZE EXCHANGE RATES, ETC.

To lower global real interest rates to a *sustainable* level, stabilize exchange rates and achieve all the other desired conditions, the main focus must be on what needs to be done with the international institutions, policies and operations that affect the volume, the pattern and terms of capital and trade flows. Two features of the global economic condition are salient: the strong demand for capital contrasted with a relative weakness on the supply side, in a phrase, a severe global shortage of capital as reflected in its high price, and the close interdependence of the national economies juxtaposed with parochial short-sighted leadership of United States policy makers and those of the Governments of the other major economies, acting alone and *together*.

Given the high degree of interdependence in the world, the days are gone when one nation, the United Kingdom or the United States, could act alone as the world's financial sergeant-major and expect others to fall in line. The "leader" must now ask for the cooperation that it needs when the intended effect of policy decisions can be offset or nullified by the actions of other countries. The greatest difficulty arises when coordination requires policy changes on the part of each nation that run counter to deep-seated political and cultural patterns affecting consumption, savings and investment.

The main onus of responsibility to make this coordination possible, effective and globally beneficent must be placed on the policy makers of the world's largest economy, the United States. Lowering the level of global real interest rates calls for substantial and sustained reductions in the United States budget and trade deficits which continue to be exceptionally large by historical standards. In the fiscal year ending 30 September 1990, they totalled over $220 billion, a 43.7 per cent jump from the 1989 level and likely to rise in the next year by as much as $40 to $75 billion to reach the highest level ever. And the savings rates of annual household incomes in the United States continue to be exceptionally low—under 5 per cent as contrasted with that for Japan of about 17 per cent.[1] This is reflected in a trade deficit that, to take one example, has meant that in the past decades Americans have bought from the Americans. Thus the United States economy's growth continues to be dependent on importation of a high percentage of the global pool of available *foreign* capital just to cover a trade deficit that still annually exceeds $100 billion.

This condition of dependency is likely to continue given the great disparity among the major economies between their rates of domestic savings, consumption and investment and the productivity of that investment. On all aspects, American policy makers face hard choices: measures to increase savings by raising taxes or by cutting back government, household and business spending would pose the downside risk of precipitating or deepening a global recession; measures to raise productivity hardly provide an answer in the short term. What is needed is an ambitious programme of rebuilding infrastructure, strengthening and refocussing research, improving education and health and the like, all of which can be achieved to the required degree over the longer term. The obviously preferable corrective none the less is to start on the road to improve the rate of productivity by bold new policies and programmes. There is little sign on the part of the United States Administration or Congress of the political will and courage to take the requisite corrective measures. There is a concern about the high rates of interest and plans made for the policy makers of other major economies who respond to parochial interests. Even as they talk of cooperation each is pursuing a policy of high rates that reflects the reality of capital shortage as the need for capital mounts.

In the face of this policy paralysis, the urgent need to take the corrective actions to lower the global level of real interest rates has revived consideration of a *forcing* mechanism: what global system of rules would most likely *put irresistible pressure on* the United States—and on the other major players—to take the steps necessary to correct these troubling trends? There is, thus, an alternative: If the appropriate policies to achieve the sustainable balance in trade and capital movements cannot be enacted and implemented voluntarily, the answer is to *oblige* the United States and the others to comply with rules for global conduct with regard to such flows. The rules would compel the necessary adjustments.

This set of rules or "system" is familiar, having been in operation since the 19th century in the form of the gold exchange standard and, post-1945, in the Bretton Woods Agreement and today in the European Economic and Monetary Union (EMU).

When United States policy makers decided in 1970 not to continue to play their key role as the reserve currency country under the Bretton Woods "system" a heavy price was paid. What is being suggested is a return to a "new Bretton Woods," a move that would entail a sublimation of sovereignty or, as Flora Lewis has phrased it, "pooling some sovereignty for mutual benefit." This trade-off, she has observed in commenting on the European example, involves "ceding some power and independence to gain influence, prosperity and security."[2]

There are skeptics who would argue that at this time United States policy makers are unwilling or incapable of making that choice. True, they would argue, the United States played a key role in the establishment and operation of the Bretton Woods agreement following the Second World War, but the United States enjoyed the privileges of being the major hegemonic power in this arrangement; and that prior to the prewar period, the United States played by the Gold Standard rules, but it was a time when it was weaker economically and the dollar had no choice but to defer to the British pound as the major reserve currency.

The answer to the skeptics is simply that the United States now faces a Hobson's choice: either the path of economic contraction or bold imaginative policies that would require systemic or structural institutional changes to strengthen its economy, enabling its living standards to rise and be sustained on a solid foundation. If the second course is not pursued out of fear, inertia, risk aversion or bowing to vested interests that favour the *status quo*, the other contractionary route will follow as a way of reducing living standards to conform to the shrunken means. This forced contraction will lead in all likelihood to a condition analogous to the Great Depression of 1929-39.

There is an old adage that says quite logically that the horse can be brought to the water but cannot be forced to drink; the appropriate response might be: "Watch what happens if the horse is left standing in the blazing sun for a day or two." The history of the last several years, starting with the 1985 meeting of the Group of Seven Finance Ministers at the Plaza Hotel in New York and the so-called "Plaza accord," indicates that the need for coordination is recognized. But it also indicates with the wisdom of hindsight that the present method of ad hoc meetings of Finance Ministers is incapable of assuring the desired adjustments in exchange rates and dampening their volatility, not to mention the more ambitious challenges of correcting the persistent imblance in trade and capital flows and of lowering real interest rates.

This difficulty of achieving policy coordination—especially the ability of any one of the major economies to dictate a "common" policy—was clearly illustrated on the occasion of the Group of Seven Finance Minister's meeting in late April 1991. The United States Treasury Secretary asked the German and Japanese Finance Ministers to take measures to reduce their interest rates. Unless they did so, the United States decision to lower interest rates would widen the difference in rates and reduce the inflow of capital. This likely adverse consequence constrains the United States from stepping too far out of line no matter what domestic considerations would call for. The response to this United States request was hardly cooperative.

The German view was direct and to the point. They were criticized for putting their own national interests ahead of the global interest:

Germany should not be blamed for draining global savings (that have kept rates high). The only answer can be: increase savings, since what we are experiencing is a shortage of capital. It is not Germany that is contributing to that shortage since Germany's savings rate is high enough to finance its own needs including the investments being made and planned for Eastern Europe. We are not against lower interest rates, *but they must be earned.*" (emphasis added)

The commentary of the United Kingdom *Financial Times* of 30 April, 1991 displayed the same indignation but in less moderate terms in an editorial entitled, "Group of Seven under pressure:"

"It is outrageous for the United States to ask that other Group of Seven countries adjust...and to complain about high global real rates of interest when it has done everything it can to persuade Germany and Japan to eliminate their savings surpluses of the 1980s. It makes little sense to complain about a global "credit crunch" when it is most evident in the mismanagement of its own financial system. . . . The solutions (the Americans) seek are virtually all to be found at home."

The critics have been quick to point out that during the last nine years the United States has imported about $670 billion (in 1990 dollars) and has run up current account deficits of over $1,000 billion, that is, they have imported that much more than could be paid for through exports.[3]

In any case, the example provided by the European precedent will undoubtedly speed up United States acceptance of an agreement involving the "pooling of sovereignty." The Europeans have been assaulting the bastions of sovereign rights by lowering the barriers throughout their continent to allow a freer movement of goods and services. This was formalized in the mid-1980s in the Single European Act. Movement on the financial side has also occurred with an early prospect of establishing a central bank known as Eurofed that will operate by binding procedures under a European Council of Finance Ministers. This will constrain national fiscal and monetary policy-making within agreed-upon limits and strengthen monetary cooperation among Europe's central banks by recommending policies, but without the power to force them except through the exercise of Eurofed's powers to impose conditions on countries in financial trouble that come looking for a Eurofed loan. The process of establishing the European Economic and Monetary Union or EMU is evolving towards adoption of a single currency and, eventually, a European political union or EPU.[4]

This institutionalization or formalization of the policy coordination process among the European nations is being driven by the pressures of economic competitive realities. While the European process is testing the limits of what is possible, the global community is standing by, possibly emboldened by the precedent. Few now doubt that a similar course towards greater cooperation and coordination at the global level is on the agenda. As two commentators observed in a review of the current state of the world economy, in 1990-91:

"The EMU is likely to transform the international economic coordination process that the industrialized countries have fitfully pursued over the last decade and a half. . . . At the technical level, creation of a European central bank, with one currency and one bureaucracy, will presumably make the coordination easier, but in reality co-ordination could become more difficult. . . . (as) the new European currency increasingly challenges the dollar's role as the world's key currency...(and) the EMU fundamentally changes the power relationships among Europe, Japan and the United States on monetary issues."[5]

Designing the most congenial set of institutional arrangements to realize the desired improvements in the global financial regime must go beyond the coordination of policies by the Group of Seven nations. Almost any arrangements are preferable to the present non-system with its absence of a framework of agreed-upon rules for international trade and capital flows. The lack of control in capital movements, given the amounts involved, has revealed all too clearly that the global financial situation is much too fragile. This has made many policy-makers in all the major industrialized countries more receptive to the idea of going beyond the ad hoc process of meetings of Finance Ministers. They have already put in place procedures for follow-up that involve collecting data, monitoring and publicizing the key indicators of global economic and financial conditions and relying on "enforcement" through shaming those who are publicly revealed to be delinquent in not adhering to summit agreements.

There is, however, no provision for action for failure to deliver on promises made. So far the frequent promises of closer economic policy coordination have remained just that: promises. Even on the conservative side of the political spectrum, there are now voices urging institutional changes to achieve the coordination through implicit enforcement:

> "Common objective indicators of economic well-being already developed by the Group of Seven nations. . . . (should) be used to *guide and enforce* economic co-ordination so that interest rates, exchange rates and other key economic indicators do not dramatically diverge. . . . By institutionalizing coordination, the United States can derive some of the domestic benefits of *externally imposed economic discipline* while ensuring that the economic policies of other countries are tempered by the needs of the American economy."[6]

A global regime of institutionalized economic policy coordination affects smaller industrialized countries and the developing countries, all of whom have been left out of the inner circle. The design of such a system must be sensitive to their needs and concerns. The issue of broadening the coordinating group's membership beyond the small club of the Group of Seven nations is now on the agenda. The universality of membership in a global coordinating arrangement raises questions as to *whether* the United Nations itself and its agencies might play a role in pursuit of the common interest on the part of all the players and, if so, *how*.

Tripolar leadership is now effectively provided by Germany, Japan and the United States by virtue of their size and/or their relative strength. As the three major economies, they cannot be expected to agree to rules that are inimical to what they perceive to be their own short-term interests. But even between themselves, there are troubling differences so that a fragmented leadership is provided when coherence is essential in face of the crisis conditions. There is a growing realization, therefore, that a global framework needs to be put in place to overcome the volatility and the fragility of the present arrangements.

It is in the design of this framework agreement that international participation is called for. The scope and the way it operates must be seen to serve the global community at-large and especially the developing countries that are under intense stress. The framework agreement must provide a more congenial milieu for trade and capital movements in which the rules and related institutional arrangements promote greater equity and environmental standards mutually agreed upon.

The negotiations would be favoured as an assessment of the experience of the Bretton Woods era from 1945 to 1970, a period that has been referred to as "the glorious years of growth in trade and GNP." An additional positive feature makes its operation of special relevance: the average incomes of the developing countries as a group grew faster than those in the industrialized ones, thus reducing the income gap between the North and South. However slow this convergence might have been—and it was much too slow—the record on this score was infinitely better than the post-1970 years when global incomes slowed, the average incomes in the developing countries fell further and further behind those of the industrialized countries, and the number of desperately poor increased from an estimated 700 million in 1970 to about double that number by 1990.

Providing more funds at low concessional interest rates

An essential precondition for easing and remedying the third world debt problem is capital inflow on a scale and on terms that can enable them to grow while servicing their debts. The litany of woe has already been sketched:

- At present the *flow* is from the developing to the developed countries at a pace that, since 1982, has amounted cumulatively to more than $300 billion;
- Net flows of commercial bank lending and private investment have been declining over the past several years in *real* terms;
- The IMF, which is mandated to provide balance-of-payment support for needy countries, has become a recipient of capital from these countries rather than a contributor as the repayments on past loans exceed the new disbursements;

- The other international financial institutions have not been doing much better with only modest prospects of increased levels of lending by the World Bank and the other multilateral development banks, an improvement occasioned by the recent authorization of a $74.6 billion general capital increase for the World Bank that has raised its sustainable level of lending to over $20 billion;[7]
- Official development assistance (ODA) has virtually stagnated in real terms at an annual level of about $50 billion and shows little prospect of rising significantly in the near future without some extraordinary initiatives beyond that of the Japanese Government that has increased its ODA to over $10 billion annually, making it the largest donor nation in absolute terms.[8]

The prevailing situation has been aptly characterized as "a crisis of commitment" or as an "aid supply crisis." The outlook is as bleak with forecasts of an annual increase in real terms of only about 2 per cent over the next few years, leaving a serious shortfall in meeting even minimal capital requirements to sustain let alone increase per capita incomes. This situation has given rise to emergency aid programmes such as the World Bank and the IMF's "special facilities." This approach is typified by the "special programme of assistance for IDA-only debt-distressed countries in Africa." This initiative was established towards the end of 1987 and channeled an additional $7 billion over three years for these countries. This is a response to a desperate situation for the most distressed segment of the debtor community of nations which, together with a measure of debt forgiveness, eases the pressure to prevent breakdown but hardly provides the basis for a cure. The situation has evoked bolder and more imaginative approaches.

1) Aid à la Marshall Plan

The United States Marshall Plan of the late 1940s has inspired many proposals because matching its volume in relation to the United States GNP would call for a seven-fold increase in the United States ODA programme that now amounts to about 0.2 per cent of GNP. It is, therefore, an impressive antecedent. The following proposals have been put forward with the example of the Marshall Plan serving as a point of reference as to the amount and the degree of concessionality and conditionality of the suggested aid flows:

- As early as 1977, in testimony before a congressional committee, Professor Ronald Muller of the American University submitted a proposal for a "third world Marshall Plan" but without particular reference at the time to the debt crisis;[9]
- In 1984, Henry Kissinger suggested assisting the heavily indebted Latin American countries by establishing a temporary international credit facility that would lend for long term at low interest rates, a proposal he referred to as akin to the Marshall Plan;[10]
- James Robinson III, President of American Express, has advocated a new version of the Marshall Plan with, however, the Japanese making the major contribution of donated, loaned or invested capital to the third world debtor countries;[11]
- Felix Rohatyn, a New York investment banker, advanced a plan that would have Japan allocate about $175 billion of new money over five years for Latin American debtor nations, a Japanese variant of the Marshall Plan concept;[12]
- Saburo Okita, Chairman of the Institute for Domestic and International Policy Studies and a former Foreign Minister of Japan, in 1986 proposed that the Japanese provide substantial funding as part of a programme allocating Japan's foreign exchange surplus to sustaining the United States bond market, aiding third world countries, and meeting some of Japan's own needs.[13]

These proposals have all fallen on deaf ears.

2) *Issuing special drawing rights for the developing countries*

The capriciousness of legislative bodies with their parochial and short-term perspectives on the issue of aid has prompted proposals for more "automatic" or "delinked" sources of funding. One frequently advanced proposal of this kind has focused on substantially increasing the allocation of special drawing rights (SDRs) and doing so in a way that would mainly benefit the developing countries rather than the industrialized countries that have higher quotas under current IMF rules. Spokesmen for the developing countries often have gone on record proposing the issuance of about $50 billion in SDRs over a period of several years and channeling the overwhelming percentage of this allocation to developing countries only. Dragoslav Avramovic has suggested that such an allocation be for two years and observed that

> "This is one of the quickest, most efficient and probably the only way in which the urgent financing needs can be met. . . . (and in which) a concerted long-term approach to the debt problem and a recovery programme for Africa can be organized."[14]

The SDR issue has long been on the global agenda within the forum of the United Nations and has also been given a thorough hearing before congressional subcommittees. The Managing Director of the IMF made a plea for an allocation of SDRs in light of the inadequate response of the financial markets to the needs of the debtor countries for greater liquidity. But the proposal did not make any headway in the face of opposition by the major industrialized nations. In any case, on the basis of present policy, the share the developing countries could be expected to receive would amount to no more than $3 billion over the next three years. As William Cline, a fellow of the Washington-based Institute for International Economics, has realistically observed, "SDR creation hardly seem likely to be equal to the task."[15]

3) Taxing users and polluters of "global commons" (oceans, upper atmosphere, and the like)

Other suggestions have been put forward that would tap non-conventional sources for funds. One of the recurrent proposals centres on the funds to be derived from the rights to levy taxes and royalties on commercial operations utilizing the "global commons" — the oceans, outer space, Antarctica, and areas not under any one nation's jurisdiction. The authors of the Brandt Commission reports of 1980 and 1983 put forward proposals of this kind, calling for the establishment of a World Development Fund to collect and administer the incomes generated by such royalties and taxes.[16]

The core idea has already been incorporated in the seabed mining provisions of the United Nations Convention on the Law of the Sea which could yield, according to one estimate, more than $6 billion per year. Tapping this potential must await the United States signature to the United Nations convention, an unlikely event, unless and until the United States Administration ceases to heed the self-serving lobby of transnational corporations that do not wish to be encumbered by regulations and royalties of any sort, let alone those imposed by an international body. To them it seems to count for very little that the proceeds are intended to benefit the international community at-large and the developing countries in particular.

The precedent of the Law of the Sea Convention is now being applied to the atmosphere. An international meeting of some 300 scientists and policy makers convened in mid-1988 to discuss "The Changing Atmosphere." They put forward a resolution to establish a World Atmosphere Fund to be administered by an international body that would support research, technology transfer, investment and aid for the attainment of "sustainable, low-emission development in the developing world," the funding of which would come from the auctioning of pollution-emission permits, and a fossil fuel tax with "a compensating transfer of resources to the developing nations:"

> "Inevitably there will be those who argue that this proposed scheme has not the ghost of a chance of acceptance, that any such notion of multi-nation consensus reflects the most outrageous academic naivete and woolly-mindedness. . . . The likeliest objection - that such a large re-source transfer from the industrial to the developing world is politically impossible and not worth pursuing - is not tenable. Current energy use trends are not sustainable and portend planetary catastrophe. . . . If the scheme proposed here won't work, we had better direct ourselves to thinking up something better, not abandoning the search as impractical. Perhaps there are now growing signs of the political will necessary to mount such a global initiative."[17]

Former Prime Minister of India, Rajiv Ghandi, suggested the idea of a planet protection fund. The benefits from these and other initiatives focused on protecting the planet's atmosphere could be only conceptually measured. There is no monetary value that can be placed on the prevention of environmental damage that is, by its nature, incalculable. The benefits are assumed to be greater than the funding for the organizations needed to set standards, monitor, carry out research and the like. The proposal envisages deriving the necessary funding from the sale of pollution-permits and pollution-curbing taxes as well as from the imposition of a system of royalties and taxes on the use of the global commons upper atmosphere for satellite communications and other purposes.

4) "Peace dividend" for development and the environment

While the immediate prospects for deriving significant funds for transfer to the developing world from this source are not bright—as is so vividly demonstrated by the resistance of the United States to a seabed mining agreement —there is the beginning of a new consciousness related to an awareness of the need to take action with respect to the environmental threats having to do with emission of CO_2, CFCs and gases. Thus the search goes on for other special sourcing of funds to turn around these deplorable trends.

This search has led to proposals to divert a stipulated percentage of disarmament "savings" to development purposes. To cite one source among many, the Manley Commission report, *Global Challenge—From Crisis to Co-operation: Breaking the North-South Stalemate*, has proposed that a commitment be made to divert the savings from disarmament towards special development funding by an amount that is equivalent to about 10 per cent of global arms expenditure, that is, an additional $100 billion a year for recovery and for development.[18] The report notes,

> "We are not suggesting a naive formula by which the world would decrease its arms spending each year by a tenth in favour of spending for development. But we do advocate that the target for a global budget should, over 10 years, be at least equivalent to current global arms spending."

The conceptual link is apparent when the contrast between the two levels of expenditure is examined: the current amounts spent on the military ($1000 billion) and that budgeted for aid ($50 billion). In *constant* dollars in per capita terms, while military expenditure almost doubled over the past quarter of a century, there has been no increase in the amount of aid.[19] Neither these trends nor their implications have, as yet, become universally apparent. But with the ending of the cold war, the anomaly of the current levels of military expenditures has begun to permeate the public consciousness sufficiently strongly to inspire hope that serious disarmament is about to commence and substantial savings are about to be realized. The diversion of the funds thereby "saved"—referred to as "the peace dividend"—is being placed on the international agenda with the impoverished billions in the third world as prime contenders for a significant share. They will now be competing for such funds with Eastern Europe, which has already secured a pledge of $38 billion from the European Community for its rehabilitation and transformation, with the poor within the industrialized nations themselves and with domestic environmental programmes.

The distant dream may not be as far as it seemed yesterday, but there are roadblocks and diversions on the way to its actualization—as the political developments in the Middle East demonstrate. When the peace dividend is available, and when it takes the form of allocations for debt forgiveness on a large scale and for large sustained capital transfers on low interest terms and other favourable and politically acceptable conditions, there will be a sea change in the global prospects on the debt and on the environmental fronts.

Improving the global trade regime

Global trade in goods and services may not match capital movements in value terms, but it is as critically important an element in the global economic-financial system. During the Bretton Woods period trade expanded by a robust 20 per cent annually to reach a total annual value of about $4 trillion. Trade in manufactured products grew along North-North lines most rapidly. South-South trade lagged far behind. It now constitutes only about one fifth of global trade though the South holds about four fifths of the world's population. With the increase trade flow has come an increasing degree of trade interdependence. This increasing dependence of each economy on trade applies even to the United States. In 1960 it relied upon exports for only a 4 per cent contribution to its GNP, but by 1990 *net* exports accounted for about 90 per cent of its growth in that year and about 40 per cent of all growth since 1986. Exports had become, as one commentator observed, "the country's prime economic engine of growth."

Trade being so vital, it is not difficult to understand the concern of all governments about the persistence of high non-tariff barriers. This concern has been most acute in the developing countries, especially those grappling with heavy debt burdens. These barriers to the markets of the industrialized countries have been intensified by discriminatory treatment that impedes the growth of the industrialized sectors of the developing countries and, consequently, slows their participation in the more lucrative side of international trade. They have thus been the most vocal advocates of non-discriminatory rules and enforcement mechanisms applied to international trade. The cost to the developing countries of the trade barriers imposed by the industrialized countries has been estimated to be about twice the annual volume of official development assistance (ODA) that they have received and about twice the annual interest owed on their foreign debts.

GATT had been relied upon as the institutional arrangement that held the promise of lowering protective trade barriers. However, its role has proven disappointing in as much as its coverage in terms of rules and codes, its surveillance and its enforcement powers were limited at the outset. In practice they proved to be even more limited as non-tariff barriers and other restrictive trade practices worsened even as nominal tariffs were lowered through successive negotiating rounds. The non-tariff barriers of the industrialized countries have remained higher against manufactured third world exports than against those of other industrialized countries and in many cases have been virtually insurmountable beyond a limited quota. The developing countries have thus come to question the underlying rationale of the GATT, and "trade liberalization" has come to be seen as an empty box with a misleading label.

GATT has been further weakened by the acrimonious trade disputes between the United States and Japan and the European Community in the current GATT Uruguay Round. The struggle is being waged over export subsidies for agriculture, dispute resolution measures, and trade in services, patents and such. With the collapse of the Uruguay Round there is now, quite understandably, a questioning of the merits of the prevailing institutional arrangements by the major trading nations as well as by the third world countries. Long before the collapse of the talks, Professor Lester Thurow of M.I.T. had dared to pronounce GATT dead.

Super-GATT and the resurrection of the International Trade Organization

Many others now share Professor Thurow's assessment that GATT has outlived its usefulness. Two economists, Clyde Prestowitz and Robert Jerome, recently echoed the same message in an op-ed piece in *The New York Times* entitled, "GATT's not where it's at." They urged that

"the world trading system. . . . be brought into the 1990s. . . . (recognizing that) trade liberalization is a questionable assumption, either as a matter of realism or of equity. . . . a 'super-GATT' (be established) composed of a small group of like-minded countries willing to take on the new obligations that would be reciprocal, unlike the prevailing system of 'national treatment' and 'most favoured nations treatment'."[20]

This line of thought has brought back to the light of day the long-buried idea of the International Trade Organization (ITO) that was mooted in 1944 at the same time that the World Bank and the IMF were conceived. Thanks to United States opposition, the ITO was truncated to become GATT, an "agreement" with a small secretariat to service the negotiations and articles of the agreement, rather than a full-fledged international institution. Because there is a growing awareness that the global trade agenda calls for bold institutional change undertaken in the same innovative spirit as that which characterized the Bretton Woods discussion of 1944, suggestions are emerging that are being advanced by politically conservative voices for the resurrection of the ITO. Though the label is somewhat different and its functions, given the changed circumstances, are also somewhat different, in the 1991 issue of *Foreign Affairs* that focuses on the theme, *America and the World 1990-91*, C. Michael Aho and Bruce Stokes proposed the creation of a World Trade Organization without making any reference to the abortion of the ITO.[21]

The formation of regional trading blocs is a reflection of policy makers resorting to second-best options. The reduction of trade and investment barriers within these regional institutional arrangements does little to help the outsiders. They can expect to face even higher barriers in exporting to this regional marketing group of nations. While Mexico can be invited to enter into a North American Free Trade Agreement and other Latin American countries can be given promises of a similar nature, the reality in terms of increased market access for third world products into the United States and Canadian markets will likely prove illusory. In any case, many developing countries will still be left on the outside looking in as the global economy is fragmented into protectionist blocs that provide entry for limited quotas under special agreements. This trend has made the trade issue a pressing and contentious one demanding some overarching approach that could reduce the protectionist barriers of the industrialized countries whether they take the form of tariffs, quotas or export subsidies.

There is another rationale for the resurrection of the ITO concept that pertains to the trade imbalance among the industrialized countries, an imbalance reflected in the massive foreign debt of the United States and its persistent growth. The issues are structural, as is recognized in the United States-Japan Structural Impediments Initiative. It is an example of discussions undertaken for questionable motives but appropriately normal range of barriers, including cultural ones though they are not labelled as such. The core of addressing causal factors of a systemic nature now needs to be extended to probe structural impediments in the larger context of global trade that includes North-South trade and the impact of the debt overhang on the policies and practices of the debtors under stress. The ITO framework could be made broad enough to include this structural-institutional aspect and the related environmental implications of export policies under conditions of severe debt stress.

Improving the sharing of the global growth of incomes: the equity factor

Beyond stability and growth, the issue of equity is central. It makes a mockery of the concept of "resolution" of the present global malaise with its crisis stresses if the corrective measures do not address the plight of the 40 per cent of humankind that are not yet able to share in the bountiful output of production of goods and services that the statistics of global GNP growth would seem to signify. The past few decades of the post-Bretton Woods era have not been glorious for these bottom 40 per cent, and the future continues to look bleak for them. Tables 18a and 18b indicate what their *real* GDP per capita is forecast to be by the year 2000.

Sub-Saharan Africans can look forward to a further drop in incomes while the citizens in the developing countries that are classified as "severely-indebted middle-income" will find their incomes stagnating. At the same time, as shown in Tables 19a and 19b, the gap between the rich and poor will continue to widen, except for those in the few Asian countries classified as "newly industrializing" or NICs who, on the average, have had a relatively rapid rise in incomes by virtue of special circumstances.

A global economy operating for a quarter century under the Bretton Woods rules saw a slight closing of the gap in per capita incomes between the industrialized and developing countries. Though a modest improvement, the trend stands in sharp contrast to the experience of the two decades of the post-Bretton Woods period when the gap widened dramatically and shows little sign of change for the better without some dramatic shift in policies and institutional arrangements, eliminating barriers to trade and investment flows and establishing a uniform set of rules to facilitate this movement. The most dramatic testimony to the income equalizing effect is evident in the American experience. Despite the highly divergent resource endowment of the different regions of the continental United States, over a period of about 60 years, from 1930 to 1990, the United States virtually eliminated significant discrepancies in personal incomes between these regions—as shown in Figure 20.

This achievement prompts the question: Is it too fanciful to believe that

Table 18A: Real GDP per capita in year 2000 for groups of least developed countries

Country group	Relative to regional average in 1980 (index 1980 = 100) Baseline	Low case
Low- and middle-income countries	168	157
Excluding China	129	120
Asian newly industrializing economies	285	267
Severely indebted middle-income countries	116	106
Sub-Saharan Africa	86	81
High-income OECD countries	160	151

Source: The World Bank, *Bulletin, Vol. 1, No. 4, Aug-Oct. 1990*

the technologies of production, information and communication have now entered a phase that would allow the same sort of convergence to happen worldwide, say by the year 2100? Noting this trend, *The Economist* has ventured a response:

"The obvious analogy, on a global basis, is a world government. This is implausible. . . . The basic unit (of governance) is going to remain the nation-state. . . . but organizations like the European Community, the GATT, and the United Nations will continue to promote internationalism, and start becoming the scenes of *a slow pooling of societies and sovereignties*.(Emphasis added)[22]

Table 18B: Real GDP per capita growth rates *(average annual percentage change)*

Country group	Per capita income (in US$) 1987	Trend 1965-88	Recent experience 1980s	Scenarios for 1990s Baseline	Low case
Low- and middle-income countries	725	2.9	2.3	3.2	2.5
Excluding China	1,143	2.3	0.4	2.2	1.6
Asian newly industrializing economies	2,685	6.0	5.9	5.0	4.4
Severely indebted middle-income countries	1,691	1.9	−0.5	2.0	1.2
Sub-Saharan Africa	333	0.5	−2.2	0.5	−0.1
High-income OECD countries	16,530	2.4	2.2	2.6	2.1

Source: The World Bank, *Bulletin Vol. 1, No. 4, Aug-Oct. 1990.*

Figure 16: *Convergence of Personal Income per head in the United States as a percentage of United States average.*

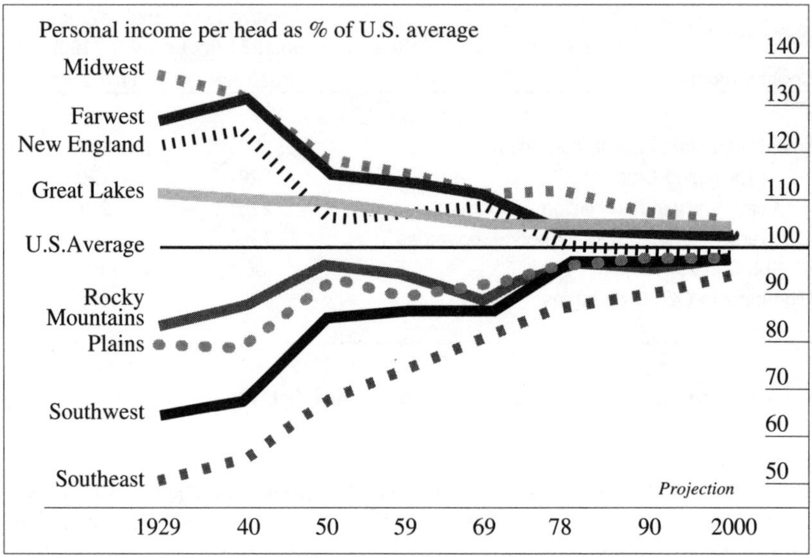

Personal income per head as % of U.S. average

Source: U.S. Department of Commerce

The example is suggestive. But in the United States case, the free movement of *people* is one of the outstanding attributes of the system that contributed to the equalizing process. Globally the pooling process has been exceptionally slow with respect to the movement of people despite exceptional cases such as the migration of Mexicans to the southwestern United States, of the Turks to central Europe, and of the Vietnamese boat-people to Hong Kong. While this movement of people has helped contribute to the income equalization process, the scale is relatively miniscule. This migration factor needs to be addressed, but for the shorter term the onus for income change must be placed on those making policy with regard to the other factors in the equation, namely, the movement of goods, services and capital, and with capital, the relevant technology.

Clearly, boldness and imagination is called for when the need is for *systemic* measures to facilitate the movement of these factors on a scale and in a manner that will have the intended equity effect. The changes necessary to achieve this outcome should be designed not only to stabilize exchange rates and harmonize interest rates. The *loosening* of the constraints on the movement of the many factors at play needs to be accompanied by a *tightening* of constraints in accordance with rules established for the promotion of the common welfare world wide. Enforcement of the rules is tantamount to governance arrangements that assure the provision of the "international public good." That would be the primary obligation of those in positions of power, in the economic-financial sphere, at one level, the Group of Three or Group of Seven, and at another, the world community of nations acting through a *reorganized* United Nations system.

Three elements of this programme to achieve greater equity merit special attention:

1. The arrangements whereby capital can once again flow to the third world either on concessional terms through official development assistance (ODA) programmes, or lent at a *real* rate of interest in the 1 to 2 per cent range, effectively ruling out commercial banks as providers of long-term capital, or invested on terms that enable the recipient countries to share equitably in the returns;

2. The arrangements whereby commodity prices that constitute the main sources of foreign exchange earnings can command a higher real price, that is, relative to the price of manufactured goods that are imported;

3. The arrangements whereby innovative programmes can be undertaken on a vastly expanded scale for accelerating research and implementing programmes for the promotion of such key developmental factors as education (e.g., utilizing cost-effective modern informational and telecommunicational technologies as part of technical assistance programmes) and for energy *in situ* for the areas outside the grid networks (e.g., utilizing stand-alone forms of energy that are abundantly available, environmentally preferable and could, with appropriate research, be produced and marketed at much lower prices).

These arrangements will be difficult to achieve unless and until the United States joins the ranks of Japan, Germany and other countries in contributing to the supply side of the capital flow equation, and the world community devises institutional modalities to establish a more effective means of transferring scientific, technological and managerial knowledge along with the technology and the capital. These non-financial aspects should be included, therefore, as integral elements of any negotiations establishing a new Bretton Woods agreement.

The drafters of the guidelines for such an agreement will have two advantages: the perspective that comes with experience and the existence of seasoned institutions, the World Bank and the International Monetary Fund and a panoply of related regional development banks and agencies within the United Nations system. The formidable challenges on debt and the environment place a special responsibility on the major economic-financial powers, but other countries on their own behalf and through the system of international institutions must also play key roles in charting new paths and implementing new programmes. This implies profound changes in these institutions, changes best justified on the basis of what must be done at the global level of governance to conceive and implement a broad-based agenda for action that promotes growth with equity and environmental quality.

CHAPTER 12

THE
"NEW BRETTON WOODS"
—ENVIRONMENT

Just as there are a few core ideas with respect to the global aspects of the debt crisis, there are a few that can be identified as central issues with respect to the global aspects of the environmental crisis:

- How to achieve the policy discipline at the national level and the policy coordination at the global level so as to reduce emissions of environmentally harmful gases and wastes without impeding growth (though changing it);
- How to shift to the forms of energy use that are environmentally benign (with commensurate lifestyle changes and other institutional changes) at both the national and international levels.

Environmental issues global in scope call as well for an international approach whether through ad hoc agreements between nations on a regional or global basis and/or permanent institutional arrangements to ensure their implementation and enforcement. In as much as the environmental crisis conditions have an intimate connection with the debt crisis, the scope of a "new Bretton Woods" that would address that institutional issue must be extended beyond the establishment of rules for trade and capital flows to include consideration of their impact on the global environment. The rules regime could take the form of setting agreed-upon emission targets and/or regulatory constraints with regard to the emissions of CO_2 and chlorofluorocarbons (CFCs) directly correlated to the rate and manner of development, particularly with reference to the use of energy in specified forms (differentiated, say, as to carbon emissions characteristics) and for specified purposes (differentiated, say, with regard to households, transport modes and power-generating utilities).

199

These activities would require financing either to subsidize the appropriate technologies for the production and use of energy and emission and waste control tie-in with the trade and capital aspects, or to compensate for benefits that some countries would have to forego to comply with the international rules. The prime example of this latter case is well-advertised, namely, the request to Brazil and other countries with extensive tropical forest regions either to cut back on the exploitation of these regions or to develop them in a manner that would be more costly because of the environmental constraints and would yield benefits for the international community well beyond those accruing to the countries called upon to take the requisite measures. This funding aspect, especially in light of the asymmetry of the costs and benefits, has yet to be addressed.

There would need to be commensurate institutional changes for the financing and the implementation and monitoring functions that are necessary. The Brundtland Commission, officially labelled the World Commission on Environment and Development, has suggested that a foundation for managing the global commons already exists in the coordination underway between several of the United Nations agencies, the Organisation for Economic Co-operation and Development (OECD), the European Economic Community, and other organizations. The World Commission on Environment and Development suggested the establishment of programmes such as a Global Environmental Monitoring System and a Global Resource Information Database within the framework of these existing institutions.[1]

Such suggestions are part of a long list of proposals that have been advanced, are under consideration and/or are already being implemented:

- *Organizing and funding international-scale programmes for research into the scientific, technological, economic, financial and socio/cultural aspects of environmental change that would be of most immediate environmental benefit for the developing countries;*
- *Providing substantially greater financial assistance through debt relief measures including debt-for-nature swaps;*
- *Undertaking international research programmes to accelerate the introduction of technologies and related production processes in agriculture and industry that are environmentally consistent with more rapid growth,* such as low impact alternative energy systems and institutional innovations as a CGIE^{2}R (the E standing for energy and environment that are closely related in the rural sector) modelled after

the internationally funded Consultative Group on International Agricultural Research that has proven exceptionally successful;[2]

- *Offering technical assistance to help the developing countries to formulate development plans and related policies, regulations, model contracts and guidelines with regard to the exploitation of their resources so that appropriate consideration can be given to environmental aspects;*[3]

- Establishing minimal acceptable international environmental standards to tackle global aspects of the environmental challenge such as regulatory constraints and taxing with regard to CO_2 emissions and other activities contributing to global warming, ozone depletion, waste disposal and effluent discharge into the oceans, etc. *through international agreements* such as the recent Montreal accord related to ozone depletion,[4] the United Nations Code of Conduct on Transnational Corporations, the United Nations Law of the Sea, and the like.

In the industrialized world it is unlikely that the quantum leap in the public's concern about the environment will find a corresponding echo in the minds of those in power, be they in industry or legislatures, especially when budgetary constraints impose difficult political choices. Radical institutional adaptation is not their thing. Nor can much be expected from the debt-burdened developing countries where policy makers are under extreme pressure to service their country's debts and accordingly put environmental concerns on the back burner. Environmental objectives cannot be realized, however, without a congenial policy framework. This calls for an approach broader in scope than one focussing narrowly on the economic-financial aspects of global cooperative arrangements. Thus there is another proposal that needs to be added to the action programme list:

- *Launch negotiations for a "global structural adjustment programme"*
  This would be a proposal to consider an environmental analogue to the Bretton Woods agreement of 1944 that could set out procedures under a system of rewards and penalties designed to secure adherence to the agreed-upon environmental norms of good behaviour.

To this list of items on the global environmental programme there should also be a proposal included to address the debt overhang effect that works against debtor countries taking the requisite steps with regard to the environment:

- *Undertake a generalized debt reduction scheme on a scale that will effectively and significantly relieve the debt burden pressures* that militate against the adoption and implementation of environment protection policies and programmes and that encourage or tolerate environmentally harmful practices, but are considered necessary to meet debt servicing obligations. This scheme should be tied in with debt-for-nature swaps with due regard to the limitations associated with any such large-scale project(s) within a country.

All of these proposals have high costs that must be factored into any action programme. Christopher Flavin notes in the Worldwatch Institute report, *State of the World 1990*, that "there are no reliable estimates of how much climate change will cost the international economy, and scientists doubt whether accurate projections will ever be possible" but he refers none the less to "hundreds of billions of dollars." The Brundtland Commission has ventured an estimate of an annual outlay of $154 billion from 1994 onward for this one programme alone. Professor Nordhaus cites studies showing a price tag of over $300 billion annually to attain a 60 per cent reduction in greenhouse-gas emissions and $100 billion for a 40 per cent reduction. Financing a programme to stabilize and reduce CO_2 emissions by 20 per cent by the year 2005 is now a declared target for an internationally-announced agreement, but the target has a soft quality with the omission of that key cost item and the lack of enforcement teeth. Good intentions too often are mocked by reality, especially the financial reality that will enable the programme to be implemented, monitored and enforced. This puts the spotlight on the source of whatever funds might be needed to carry through on the agreement.

The suggested sources of funds include establishment of a special funding programme, sometimes referred to as a "Global Marshall Plan for the Environment" akin to that suggested for easing the debt crisis.[5] The same idea has also be put forward under various labels such as the "Environment Capital Facility," "Conservation Financing Facility," and the "Bank for Sustainable Development." These would be separate or tied to the World Bank or some such established institution that would help in raising the necessary funding through the issuance of environmental mutual funds, tax-free environmental bonds, environmental flow-through shares, environmental capital venture funds and an emergency environmental fund. In addition, proposals for additional funding have suggested such sources as taxing the users of the global commons (principally the upper atmosphere, oceans and Antarctica) and diverting part of the peace dividend, or even a percentage of the capital flow under aid and multilateral lending programmes. Meanwhile, the Global Environment Facility established by a collaborative arrangement between the UNDP, UNEP and the World Bank incorporates some of these proposals.

The aid programmes have been gradually shifting more of their funds towards technical assistance programmes designed to help the developing countries to buy, build and use energy-efficient technologies that they could not otherwise afford. These programmes help them technically in formulating and implementing environmentally-sound policies, programmes and projects, in particular those that are obligations under international conventions affecting climate warming, ozone depletion, waste disposal and the like.[6] There are severe financial, technical and organizational limitations on the side of the donor and the recipient country to undertaking these technical assistance programmes on a wide scale and to ensure that they are effective. The third world countries are required to make a far-reaching shift of their priorities towards greater environmental consciousness with all that this implies, but the formidable financial and other constraints they face at the best of times are now compounded by the severe pressure of servicing their heavy foreign debts. Financial assistance on a massive scale would undoubtedly help.

Thus, the sources of funds suggestions include the following:

- A global carbon tax on the users of fossil fuels which at $50 per ton of carbon emission would yield annually in the United States alone about $28 billion if 10 per cent of the revenues were allocated to environmental programmes;
- Taxes levied on the use of the global commons of upper atmosphere, oceans and Antarctica and, as military expenditures wind down;
- Allocation of some of the savings from the so-called peace dividend to environmental purposes;[7]
- Debt-for-nature swaps which can, in some cases, provide a substantial measure of financial relief directed to environmental programmes.

Some developing countries hold different views as to what constitutes an environmental problem, or as to their seriousness and the urgency of the need for remedial action. But the significant difference pertains to their respective capacities to take corrective action to tackle their part of these global environmental problems. This raises a thorny problem related to the non-reciprocal benefits and costs from some global environmental measures such as those called for with respect to deforestation of the Amazon Basin.

In the international realm, cooperative solutions require binding agreements, so there might well be a need for a *quid pro quo* that will entice the polluter to desist. This form of payment to developing countries could be troublesome because, as some commentators have noted, this practise "can easily turn the morality of the polluter-pays principle upside down (to become) the victim-pays principle."[8] If this type of arrangement or bargain is judged to be the only basis for reaching international agreements to obtain the necessary cooperation to tackle the issue of global warming and other global-scale environmental problems, it cannot be dismissed as unthinkable, distasteful as it may appear to be. The stakes are high, but the game must be played. Professor Dasgupta has posed the issue succinctly:

> "The private cost to Brazil in pursuing a carbon dioxide depletion policy will be far less than the global cost. . . . thus the idea of international compensation to the depleter for reducing the rate of depletion should no longer be regarded as far-fetched. Partial debt-relief for a lower rate of plunder of the Amazonian forest is something that will probably be on the agenda in the near future. This is a Pigovian subsidy. It is hard to imagine that there are many other options open to us."[9]

Many proposals are advanced without spelling out the necessary conditions for their implementation, particularly with respect to the institutions that would have responsibilities from fact-finding and research to policy-making and monitoring. Few of the proposals are amplified to take account of relevant cultural, political and financial constraints on the developing country side, and, on the industrialized country side, to take account of the resistance of the parties that have to bear the risks in making heavy expenditures for uncertain results. This is the familiar "risk-aversion" barrier compounded by the equally familiar and even more formidable barrier of "vested interests."

A clear and relevant example of how these barriers to change operate is provided by the experience of the large and ambitious United Nations Conference on New and Renewable Sources of Energy held in Nairobi in 1981. The conference theme and its analytic work and proposals had a direct bearing on the global environment: the two years of work in preparing background papers, conducting over 30 workshops and organizing a full-scale conference with a cast of thousands had as one of its principal objectives the promotion of environmentally-benign energy sources as alternatives to fuelwood, oil and coal. The oil-producing countries, including the United States and the USSR, with a vested interest in conventional energy sources, effectively scuttled any follow-through action by ensuring that the programme of action was confined to non-operational rhetoric.

Calls for "a decade of action against world poverty and environmental deterioration" are likely to be appealing. It is difficult to take issue with fine-sounding programmes such as the following rather typical example culled from a recent report:

"Encourage the shifting of technologies from resource-intensive, pollution-prone technologies,

Advise on tax and subsidy policies that take account of resource depletion and reflect a far more profound understanding of global sustainability,

Share more equitably the environmental and economic benefits, and

Institute a transition to a new arrangement among Governments and peoples that can achieve environmental security".

Unless the programme gets beyond the platitudinous terminology to specify the steps to achieve them, the real story is more likely to be a sad tale of lost opportunities, of wringing hands in a paralysis of despair in the face of a big threat or adopting the tactics that have been aptly called "panicky eco-action." The programme must take the measure of the opposition, of the scope of what has to be done including the altering or establishment of institutions, especially at the global level of governance where, given the global scope of the crises, cooperative action is essential.

Global economic conditions are *pushing* the community of nations to test the limits of the possible in searching for the desirable. The testing involves stretching the international agencies already in place to take on more responsibilities and perhaps to work in different ways, implying structural-administrative changes and/or policy changes. We turn to examine what institutional legacy today's world has inherited from the past, the better to assess what it might do in the future to carry through the proposed global agenda.

CHAPTER 13

THE ROLE
OF THE MULTILATERAL
DEVELOPMENT BANKS
(MDBs)

The exceptionally stressful condition of the global economic system has focused attention on the roles of the international the mandate to help the debt-distressed developing countries. Given the additional complexities introduced by concerns for issues of poverty, women and the environment, these international agencies have been going through the throes of introspective analysis about their past and present performance as a guide to charting their future course. Underlying the discussions is an awareness that the old patterns of behaviour will not suffice to meet the new challenges.

It was in 1985, well into the third year of the debt crisis, when Mahbub ul Haq, then Pakistan's Minister of Finance, Planning and Economic Affairs and formerly Director of the World Bank's Policy Department, expressed a widely-shared view:

> "This is certainly not the finest hour for multilateralism. But the fault is not that of the Bretton Woods institutions. They would have liked to do more, much more. They have often acted with rare courage. . . . The fault is really ours—the member governments and we, the Governors— for we have failed these institutions and betrayed our own heritage."

Time and circumstance have modified the objectives of the World Bank, the other multilateral development banks (MDBs), the United Nations Development Programme (UNDP) and some of the United Nations Specialized Agencies concerned with different aspects of "development," including health, education and culture. An overt shift has occurred from an overwhelming focus on the GNP growth aspect of "development" towards the inclusion of other objectives such as income distribution, the role and welfare of women and children and environmental quality. But at the same time, this broadening of perspective has been tempered by pressure to meet another objective, avoiding a major breakdown of the debt rescheduling process and of the threat that this poses for the global economic-financial system. (See Annex D (Glossary) for the list of relevant United Nations agencies, multilateral development banks and international financial institutions.)

The increased attention to the equity and environmental aspects is reflected in a proliferation of studies, publications and public relations activities devoted to them, but the main emphasis of the operational programmes of these international agencies continues to be on development and on mitigating the impact of the debt crisis. The rationale is that without stabilizing and easing the current crisis, the other concerns are not amenable to improvement, let alone resolution.

Given the broader impact of the debt crisis, since the summer of 1982 the debtor developing countries have turned increasingly to the International Monetary Fund (IMF), the World Bank and the other MDBs that might help them in grappling with the capital needed to meet the financial pressures of the debt crisis. To a lesser extent they have turned to UNDP and some of the more economy-oriented United Nations Specialized Agencies. For technical assistance they sought the help of the MDBs, UNDP and the full range of United Nations Specialized Agencies.

Understanding how adequately these institutions have responded to the needs of the third world and the reasons for their performance is a basic step in assessing the proposals put forward to deal with the debt and environmental crises. In many cases, these proposals have significant implications for the structure, policies and operations of the existing international institutions, often involving innovative features.

Dealing with the Debt Crisis

The World Bank and the International Monetary Fund (IMF), known as "the Bretton Woods twins," were established in 1945 to play major roles on the international financial stage. Therefore, there was an a priori reason to expect a response in the mid-1970s to the warning signals about the growing debt of third world countries. Yet when the debt crisis erupted in the summer of 1982, the response had to be improvised in the form of ad hoc rescue packages. Both these institutions reacted in a manner that evoked a comment by one of the leading members of the United States banking community, Rimmer de Vries, Senior Vice President of Morgan Guaranty Trust Company:

> "... it has to be accepted that LDC debt problems would not have reached such troubling dimensions had the major industrial powers and official institutions played a more assertive role in the initial period following the second oil shock. .... Of course, the IMF and the World Bank are limited by the wishes of their member Governments, but *passivity was an unfortunate response.*"

Before the shock of the initial oil price increases in 1973 and 1974 there were no institutional arrangements in place to handle a crisis situation in an appropriate manner. The 1969 Pearson report, *Partners in Development*, commissioned by the President of the World Bank, provided ample warning of impending problems, but the report seems not to have been read, and certainly was not heeded. At the time, before the oil shock of 1973, the traditional forms and methods of capital transfer to the developing world were showing signs of being inadequate in the required speed, volume and terms of lending. The financial intermediation process included bond financing and direct foreign investment, commercial bank lending mainly for short term trade purposes, concessional bilateral and multilateral aid as part of official development assistance (ODA) programmes, as well as the IMF's newly-minted special drawing rights (SDRs). (See Glossary) The post-1973 petro-dollar phenomenon had a dangerous potential for destabilizing the global economic-financial system; the situation called for a deliberately bold response. *The responsibility for the necessary financial intermediation could have been placed on the shoulders of the Bretton Woods twins, the World Bank and the IMF and other institutions of the United Nations system.* Instead, *the United States and the other industrialized countries, as a matter of policy, constrained these international institutions from playing a more active role.*

In making this decision to place reliance for the petrodollar recycling on the private banking sector and the so-called "forces of the market place," the governments were in effect opting for capital to be transferred through an unregulated commercial bank syndication process that would be difficult to control, would be biased towards speculative rather than productive use of the capital, and would incubate the debt crisis that erupted in the early 1980s. Accordingly, now we hear calls for greater reliance on the international institutional framework with commensurate strengthening and additions to handle the international initiatives on the global agenda of action. The assessment of what should be done by the panoply of international agencies operating in the fields of development and the environment requires an understanding of their present role to reveal both the limitations and the potential of the international financial institutions, the MDBs and the rest of the United Nations system.

The IMF's response

The IMF has had the mandate to deal with the *short-term* balance-of-payments problems and thus had an array of "safety straps" with which to handle situations of an emergency nature. They include the following: the Compensatory Financing Facility, the Standby Credit, the Extended Fund Facility, the Quota Entitlement, the General Agreement to Borrow (GAB), Special Drawing Rights (SDRs), the Oil Facility, and the Gold Trust Fund. (See Annex G: Glossary.) The organizational framework was already in place when the debt crisis erupted in 1982. But the IMF was initially constrained by the major shareholders, however, particularly the United States, from playing a major role either as a source of liquidity or as a regulatory and pro-active force in the international financial system.

During the years prior to 1982, frequent requests had been made by the Governors and Executive Directors of the developing countries, as well as IMF management, for enlarged access to Quota Entitlements, increases in the General Agreement to Borrow (GAB) and the creation of more Special Drawing Rights (SDRs). The opposition to these requests was always led by the United States, though often joined by Japan, the United Kingdom and the Federal Republic of Germany. The history of the establishment and use of the SDRs illustrates this opposition.

After four years of negotiations in the late 1960s, the United States was prevailed upon to agree to the creation of SDRs as an addition to but not as a replacement for the dollar and gold that were the bases for the system then in place. Even after agreeing, the United States sought to severely limit the increases on the grounds that the new SDRs would augment global liquidity and thereby rekindle inflation. Almost $10 billion of SDRS were distributed over the first three years and $12 billion after 1979. These were distributed on the basis of each country's quota, hence the developing countries, despite their greater need, received only about one third of the total distributed.

Over the decade of the 1970s, the private banking community forged new modes of operation, principally syndication on an unprecedented scale. This was reflected in a 10-fold expansion from $60 to $600 billion of the non-regulated Eurocurrency market's volume of operations. During this same period, the IMF was authorized to contribute about $30 billion (25 billion SDRs), enabling it to contribute less than 1 per cent to the expansion of global liquidity. This constrained role was not exceptional. From 1974 to 1981 the IMF was able to finance only about 3 per cent of the $427 billion total cumulative current account deficits of oil-importing countries and thus provided only about 4 per cent of the total gross capital flows in those years. By 1982 the IMF quota allocations as a percentage of world trade fell to less than 4 per cent, a dramatic decline when contrasted with the 1945 level of about 16 per cent. In effect, *the IMF was consigned to the side-lines with more of a role as a spectator and commentator than a player*.

When in the summer of 1982, the problem took on the dimensions of a crisis and pressure was placed on the IMF to provide capital to the debtor countries so as to prevent threatening defaults, the response was quick but modest. The IMF's resources were simply not adequate to meet a challenge on the scale of the debt crisis. At the spring meeting in 1983 of the Interim Committee of the IMF, a 50 per cent quota increase was approved amounting to about $30 billion over three years and an expansion of GAB from $6.5 to $19 billion. Thus when the debtor countries of Latin America came to the rescheduling table, the IMF was able to contribute over $16 billion. By the end of 1984 the IMF had disbursed more than $22 billion to over 60 countries and made commitments for another $8 billion. This amount went only a small way, however, towards meeting the emergency foreign exchange requirements of the oil-importing developing countries.

This policy of constraining the IMF was again evident in late 1985. At the Interim Committee meeting, the United States urged a reduction in the limits of the Quota Entitlement and a reduction in the limits for assistance under the Compensatory Finance Facility. That policy stance won the day through the concurrence of the other Governors from the industrialized countries whose weight in the voting arrangements of the IMF gave them a majority. It won the day even though at the time many of the major debtors were paying more to the IMF than they were receiving. Taking the 15 countries labelled "problem debtors" as a group, two thirds of the meager IMF funds received were being returned as repayments, leaving only one third to ease their balance-of-payments plight.

On each subsequent occasion when the United States agreed to increase the flow of payments, they were limited so as not to weaken the IMF in its debt *policing* function: limiting the access to *automatic* entitlements to IMF funds strengthens the leverage of the IMF in the provision of its limited funds. Thus, while the IMF's financial contribution was modest in relation to the need, *it was thereby enabled to play an important role as disciplinarian.* In combination with an organizational role, it assumed convening and servicing consortia for debt negotiations under the aegis of the Paris Club and other venues. This made the IMF a key agent for the exercise of the hegemony of the United States and its compliant partners in the cozy club known as the Group of Seven. The group is comprised of six other industrialized nations, Germany, Japan, Italy, the United Kingdom, France and Canada.

The more desperate their straits, the more amenable debtor countries are to accepting severe conditionality. Under the crisis conditions of the early 1980s, the IMF could play what one commentator, Sidney Dell, a former senior United Nations economist, characterized as a "grandmotherly" role. Through the conditions attached to providing loans, it could exercise supervisory powers over the recipient country's economic policies, including sensitive political and social aspects that went well beyond their balance-of-payments difficulties. The competence of the IMF to wield this kind of influence has been questioned on a priori grounds having to do with the qualms about the application of blatant hegemonic economic-financial power, and on the basis of the dismal results even when judged in terms of achieving the narrow objectives of renewal of balance in its balance-of-payments situation and of the growth rate in per capita income. As Sidney Dell has noted,

"the IMF's evaluations of its own programmes indicate a failure rate sufficiently high to warrant considerable caution regarding the capacity of an international organization to prescribe workable and acceptable domestic policies for countries; the Fund should, therefore, address itself much more to balance-of-payments than to domestic policies. . . ."[1]

The indictment is of course compounded when the factors of equity and environment are brought into the picture.

The distributional and environmental aspects have been considered as being more properly within the mandate of the World Bank, the other regional development banks and the agencies of the United Nations System. But the trend towards capital aid and technical assistance for dealing with macroeconomic aspects of development, including structural change and related institutional aspects, has brought both these development-oriented agencies and the IMF onto the same policy turf, sometimes in conflict in their advice and related conditionality provisions. But as the pressures have brought them more into a cooperative mode of work, the original demarcation of the roles of the Bretton Woods twins has become fuzzy, raising questions about their future roles as separate organizations.

The World Bank's response

The World Bank's response to the events of the summer of 1982 was so sluggish as to move Pedro-Pablo Kuczynski, a former World Bank official and now President of First Boston International, to voice a widely held critical view: "The World Bank has the image of having slept soundly through the first phase of the debt crisis." Former Federal Reserve Board Chairman, Paul Volcker, during a meeting with World Bank officials in which he described the efforts of his agency and the IMF to contain the debt crisis, took the occasion to ask a World Bank official, "Where have you been during all this?"

The recriminations were the opening barrage of a more broad-based attack on the World Bank led by the United States Administration. Taking a slightly different tack, a high ranking United States Treasury official voiced the "official" verdict on the World Bank's performance with reference to the festering debt crisis: "It's been our view for a long time that the World Bank has not been using its resources effectively." Of course, the criteria for "effectiveness" was not articulated.

In any case, by the summer of 1986, at the time of the announcement of Barber B. Conable as the United States nominee for the position of President of the World Bank, the United States posture had become pro-active: President Reagan declared that he looked to Mr. Conable to "*remake* the Bank into the lead agency coping with the third world's debt crisis." This United States policy thrust was designed to have the World Bank play its role in a manner most helpful to the creditor banks. This has raised a serious question as to whether the World Bank should meet short-term exigencies in the donor community even if this were to constrain the institution in pursuit of its *longer term* development mandate.

Two initiatives indicate the flexible response that has been adopted:

- The World Bank has assumed the role of guarantor and insurer so as to facilitate the conversion of third world debt into other financial instruments more acceptable to the creditors because of the guarantee feature, and

- The World Bank has shifted a fifth of its lending programme from projects to programmes, or what are called "structural adjustment loans" (SALs) to accelerate disbursements to the most stressed major debtors so as to enable them, or induce them, to continue to participate in the debt workout process rather than defaulting or declaring a moratoria.

The World Bank's involvement as guarantor raises troublesome implications on both the ethical and political grounds of putting *public* money at risk to underwrite *private* capital loans and investments. This ethical-political factor was once the argument used by the United States Administration to oppose this guarantor role for the Bank. But under the pressures to ease the debt burden, there has been a policy reversal: encouraging *additional voluntary* lending to the debtor countries by the commercial banks is a main pillar of the Brady Plan, and the assumption underlying this support for guarantees is that the commercial banks more likely would be forthcoming.

These original troubling objections were thus brushed aside by the United States and received support from Japan, as expected because Japan had previously put forward the same idea under the Miyazawa Plan. Debtor countries have been divided on this issue. Many realize that by taking on the contingent liabilities implied in its role as guarantor, the World Bank's lending capacity *for other purposes* was being reduced; at any one time, there is a well-defined limit to the Bank's sustainable lending level (SLL).(See Glossary)

In any case, this policy change with respect to the World Bank's role has had little impact on the volume and terms of capital flows. Given their own stressful conditions, few of the commercial banks have been accommodating. For them the guarantee factor is only one of many variables in their lending decisions. With so little additional capital from this source, despite the guarantees, the World Bank has been under pressure not only to stand by as guarantor but also to be pro-active by increasing the percentage of its overall lending to the major debtor countries. It has done so by using the strategem of shifting a greater proportion of its lending operations into quicker-disbursing modes under the labels of "programme loans," "sectoral loans" and "structural adjustment loans" (SALs).(See Glossary.)

The IFIs as "structural adjustors"

In mid-1982 the World Bank was severely constrained from actively participating in the emergency debt rescue by virtue of its mode of operation that was almost wholly focussed on project lending and long-term development.

By placing greater reliance on SALs, the World Bank managed to rapidly increase its lending and shorten the appraisal and disbursement time to transfer funds to debt-strapped developing countries.[2] The United States and other industrialized countries were strongly supportive of this type of programme lending, not only as a means of speeding up the lending process but also as a means of gaining greater clout in their lending operations with distressed debtor countries.

Only after interest rates shot up in 1980 did it become clear how troubling this new situation would be for borrowers with variable rate loans—and that included most of them. The oil shocks of 1973 and 1979 had already created a cash crunch for some oil-importing third world countries, prompting the IMF to set up an "Oil Facility" and the World Bank to set up a category of lending under the label, "special assistance programme."[3] By 1980 structural adjustment lending was initiated to enable quicker disbursement than was possible under the procedures of traditional project lending. The latter had an average gestation period of over two years while SALs could be disbursed in a matter of a few weeks. During the panic phase of the debt crisis from 1983 onward, SAL-type lending increased rapidly both in absolute terms and as a percentage of overall World Bank lending, reaching its current level of about one quarter of the World Bank's lending programme.

But the funds under this programme made only a modest contribution to easing the debt overhang pressures for most of the debtor countries. The reason for this can be found in part in the skewed geographic distribution of SALs towards countries that had large debts outstanding to private United States banks. In the first five years after their introduction, the cumulative total SAL lending amounted to less than $5 billion for 30 projects in fewer than 20 countries. However, of the 20 countries, five highly indebted countries absorbed more than 40 per cent of the total SAL lending. Thus, for example, by 1985 Brazil doubled the amount of its borrowing from the $2.3 billion level of 1980-82. It seemed to matter little to the World Bank's Governors from the industrialized countries that this increase violated one of the Bank's operational guidelines of limiting its exposure to any one borrower to 10 per cent of total lending. Nor did it seem to matter to them that in the same year lending to the other Latin American debtor countries *went down* by over 10 per cent, from $6.4 billion to $5.7 billion.

The example of World Bank lending to Mexico demonstrates the same point: the "privileged" recipients of SALs were countries that were under most pressure to repay loans to United States banks. In the spring of 1986, again under "special circumstances," Mexico was able to borrow about $1 billion from the World Bank at one time, (a $500 million SAL and a $465 million loan for reconstruction required as a result of the September 1985 earthquake). This special treatment was repeated again in later years when Mexico was being wooed to be a test case for the Baker and Brady Plans.

But the "favours" bestowed come with a price: more pervasive and "harder" conditionality. Categorized as a "trade liberalization" loan, the latest large Mexican SAL called for an unprecedented thorough-going interventionism to "encourage" Mexico to implement a programme calling for the reduction of import barriers and export subsidies and other measures which indicate "a commitment to market-oriented economic reforms." Though such motivations are usually implicit, the explicit rationale is often voiced. For example, a United States Treasury spokesman, in commenting on the latest large Mexican SAL, put the issue rather brazenly: "Only countries that commit to market-oriented economic reforms will get the (World Bank's) help."

In any case, this programme type of lending will likely plateau at its present level (as a percentage of total lending) for a short period and then decrease. The reasons for expecting this to happen are the following:

- Political limits to a skewing of the lending programme in this manner as countries outside the "problem debtor" category protest more and more loudly that they are not able to get their fair share or the share of World Bank lending that has been traditionally available to them;
- Greater risks in this type of lending, and danger signals have become evident that, if carried further, portend an adverse impact on the World Bank's credit standing in capital markets; and
- The results have been disappointing, particularly when any positive impact on growth rates has been at the expense of increasing the maldistribution of income in the recipient countries (despite efforts to include compensating programmes) and at the expense of the environmental, health and educational investments fundamental for the longer-term development of the recipient countries.

The down-side distributional aspects have been recognized, and as already noted elsewhere, efforts are being made by the World Bank to address them. But when the core purpose of SALs to promote a return to "creditworthiness" is assessed as disappointing, the matter takes on a new dimension. The core of the policy reform measures favoured by the donors, and its ex post justification, is indicated by the following tables, Tables 19 and 20, roughly depicting the correlation of "economic performance" and a list of policy reform measures for Latin American debtor countries from 1982 to 1989.

Table 19: Economic reform in Latin America 1982–89

	GDP growth per capita (percentage)			Consumer prices (annual percentage increase)			Accrued D debt interest/export ratio (percentage of exports)		
	1982	1986	1989(a)	1982	1986	1989(a)	1982	1986	1989(a)
Favourable Performance									
Bolivia	− 6.9	− 5.6	− 0.4	296.5	66.0	16.6	43.4	42.1	28.6
Chile	− 14.5	3.4	7.6	20.7	15.4	21.4	49.5	37.9	19.0
Colombia	− 1.1	4.8	1.4	24.1	20.1	26.1	25.9	20.2	21.1
Mexico	− 3.0	− 6.0	0.7	28.8	105.7	19.7	47.3	38.4	28.5
Uruguay	− 10.6	7.2	0.7	20.5	76.4	89.2	22.4	24.7	27.7
Unfavourable Performance									
Argentina	− 7.2	4.6	− 6.1	209.7	81.9	4923.8	53.6	51.0	47.4
Brazil	− 1.6	5.2	1.5	97.9	58.4	1779.1	57.1	42.4	29.2
Peru	− 2.3	6.0	− 13.1	72.9	62.9	2775.8	25.1	31.7	29.5
Venezuela (in transition)	− 4.0	3.7	− 10.4	7.3	12.3	81.0	21.0	31.1	27.1
Latin America (b)	− 3.5	1.4	− 0.7	84.6	64.5	1157.6	41.0	36.3	28.3

(a) Perliminary figures.
(b) Includes 19 countries. Debt figures reflect interest accrued, not paid
   for Latin America and the Caribbean (ECLAC/CEPAL).

Source: Economic Commission for Latin America and the Caribbean (ECLAC/CEPAL).

Table 20: The progress of policy reform in Latin America and the Caribbean (as of 1990)

Country	Fiscal discipline	Public spending priorities	Tax reform	Financial liberal- ization	Compe- titive exchange rates	Trade liberal- ization	Foreign direct investment	Privati- zation	Deregu- lation
Bolivia	+ +	+ +	+ +	+ +	+	+ +	+	0	+ +
Chile	+	0	+	+ +	+ +	+ +	+	+ + (a)	+
Peru	−	−	0	−	−	−	−	−	0
Argentina	+	0	0(a)	0	+	0(a)	+	+ (a)	+ (a)
Brazil	0	−	−	0	+	0	−	+	−
Mexico	+ +	0	+ +	0	+	+ +	+ +	+ +	+
Colombia	+ +	0	+	+	+ +	+	0(a)	+	0
Venezuela	0	0	0(a)	+	+	+ +	+	+ (a)	+
Jamaica	+	0	+ +	+	+	+ +	+	+	+
Costa Rica	+ +	0	+ +	0	+ +	+	+	+	+

+ + Substantial reform   + Some reform   0 No significant change (or mixed changes)
  − Retrogression   (a) More action expected shortly

Source: John Williamson, *The Progress of Policy Reform in Latin America.* Table 10.

The cause-and-effect inference is questionable when so many variables are at play. But the overall results are troubling in as much as there appears to be only slight "progress" — to use the World Bank's terminology—with regard to such critical aspects as debt servicing and the ratio of export earnings to interest payment flows.

This outcome can be attributed in part to a misplaced faith in market forces and a wide range of weaknesses in the recipient countries, but the more likely reason for the low success rate of SAL lending can found in looking beyond the individual countries to the global context: Individual countries cannot be expected to succeed with a structural adjustment in a hostile or uncongenial international context that itself needs to undergo structural adjustment.

The World Bank and the IMF have been playing a role in promoting an international economic order that, to put the best face on it, is hardly congenial for the third world countries they are striving to help. They and the other IFIs and MDBs have operated overwhelmingly with a "country focus" dealing with each recipient country on a case-by-case basis. But severe limits to country-by-country advice occur when the advice assumes global conditions that could nullify the hoped-for effects: If all or many of these countries were to heed the same advice, the "fallacy of composition" becomes operative.[4]

What may be good advice for one or a few countries—say, to adopt export-oriented policies—may not be possible to implement or prove desirable for a large number of countries. There are, after all no assurances that on the other side of the trade equation the industrialized developed countries are prepared to import the goods that the developing countries can export, and to do so at reasonable prices. Thus until there can be an appreciable World Bank and IMF influence *on the policies of the industrialized countries*—on issues such as raising commodity price levels, lowering non-tariff barriers, dampening exchange rate volatility, and reducing real interest rates and other factors affecting the development of poorer countries—the feasibility and desirability of this kind of policy advice is questionable. There is another questionable feature: most of the "success stories" are deemed to be successful in the key criterion of an improvement in their balance of payments. But in almost all such cases, the current account surpluses have been due less to export expansion than to severe import compression achieved at the expense of current consumption and of investment in health, education, research and infrastructure that are indispensable for growth. The one-dimensional emphasis on short term gains in foreign exchange earnings ignores the deleterious environmental impacts as the long-term aspect of sustainability in the interests of future generations has taken a backseat to the exigencies of the short term.

These shortcomings take on added significance when the World Bank is expected to play the starring role on the debt crisis stage *with closer collaboration or cooperation with the IMF*. Both institutions are already working in the same macro-economic territory. Indeed, SAL-type lending is closely akin to the IMF's "standby agreement." An informal off-and-on process of informational exchanges between the staff of the two institutions has long existed. But this is being carried further with the establishment of the first jointly financed programme, namely, the "Structural Adjustment Facility," a new lending pool of $3.1 billion derived from the reflow of funds to the IMF Trust Account and from some untapped money in the "soft window" World Bank affiliate, the International Development Association (IDA).

Logical as it may appear, on balance, this process of fusion of the "Bretton Woods twins" likely would prove to be a retrograde step. This may not be evident in easing the pressure in the short term, but when the perspective for making a judgement is long-term and is developmental in the broadest sense, it will become apparent that there is an inherent conflict between a cash-dispensing agency that works as a fire-fighting brigade handling short-term emergencies and one that works with a long-term responsibility and a broader developmental mandate. In accordance with Gresham's Law, the winner in this conflict of cultures can be foretold: just as bad money drives out good, the short-termers will tend to dominate the long-termers, and this will happen sooner when crisis and panic are in the air. The end result will be to exert even greater pressure on the debtor countries within a cul-de-sac global framework, and as importantly, neglect or downgrade initiatives on a global scale that are as imaginative and bold as called for by the magnitude and deep roots of the debt-equity-environmental *problematique*.

If the World Bank can escape being press-ganged into the short-term emergency phase of the debt crisis, it will, along with regional development banks and related United Nations agencies, sooner and more effectively become one of the main conduits for the long-term transfer of capital and technical know-how. Before that happens there will be a rough patch as the flow of funds of the Bretton Woods institutions increase from a level that was equivalent to about $1 per person during the 1975-1980 period to a little over $2 over the next five years.

But the responsibilities go further. As the leading international *developmental* institution, the World Bank must take initiatives on global and regional issues such as the level of real interest rates, trade policies and other factors that are exceptionally critical in resolving the debt crisis and meeting the need for long-term sustainable capital flows on acceptable terms. Not to do so would amount to accepting the status quo with all its fragility and inequities and leaving the way open for a diminution of the World Bank's role. In that case, the World Bank clearly would not be fulfilling the aspirations of the developmental mandate set out at its founding at Bretton Woods.

THE ROLE OF MDBS IN THE ENVIRONMENTAL CRISIS

The World Bank and the other multilateral development banks were slow in responding to the environmental implications of their lending programmes and have still not assumed a significant role in establishing and/or funding global scale environmental programmes or conferences. The World Bank was slow to appreciate the importance of the environmental aspects in its project work. It established a small division in the mid-1970s that had a retrospective role in the "project cycle," that is, after the identification, preparation phases were completed and the appraisal phase virtually completed. This monitoring role was expanded in the mid 1980s as pressure mounted through criticisms of the role of the Bank and its dominant philosophy that put the overwhelming emphasis on growth.

Since then the World Bank has expanded its environmental staff to 60 professionals, 10 times its original complement. The programme has widened in scope to range from the traditional review of projects in gestation to limit the environmental damage that might be the consequence of the project being financed, to the establishment and enforcement of environmental policies to guide World Bank lending, to preparation of theoretical and applied environmental issues studies on various aspects of the environment in its global, regional and national dimensions, to financing projects with major environmental components. These include projects focused on reforestation, afforestation, soil and water conservation, management of rangelands, wildlands, and watersheds, preservation of genetic diversity, sites and services for urban housing, slum upgrading, water supply and sewerage improvements, solid waste management, development of renewable energy and prevention of desertification. More than a third of the Bank's projects in 1989 contained significant environmental components.[5]

From 1987 to 1989, the Bank increased environmentally-related forest lending by 150 per cent, intending to triple it over the 1990s. The latest development is assuming responsibility to administer a Global Environment Facility to which 25 countries are pledged to contribute between $1 and $1.5 billion over three years from April 1991.

A seminal experience was a turning point in the Bank's approach to the environment in its project financing role. By the Bank's own admission, the Polonoreste project in Brazil was a case of misjudgement of

> "the human, institutional and physical realities of the Amazon rain forest as the area came under increasing pressure from migrants seeking their future on this Brazilian frontier. (While) protective measures to shelter fragile land and tribal peoples were taken, they were not carefully timed nor adequately monitored and enforced."[6]

The criticism of the World Bank still persists. The pressure is needed to influence an institution dedicated in the main to lending for development with built-in management criteria difficult to change. One aspect of the Bank operations in particular is rightly subjected to a critical eye by "environmentalists," namely the structural adjustment loans (SALs) which are quick-disbursing to relieve debt servicing pressures, and on that account, are likely to be too narrowly focused on the short term with a corresponding neglect or downgrading of the more subtle longer-term environmental impacts.

Beyond the expansion of their role as lender, the international financial institutions and the multilateral development banks need to be pressured to become involved in the organization and implementation of policies and programs that have global dimensions. Few such institutions, after all, are capable of playing a broader role in the global governance that this crisis calls for. Their current performance falls far short of the potential, especially in the case of the World Bank. As the major institution in both its mandate and its size, it has a responsibility to lead. But to realize this potential, there must not be a loosening of the ideological constraints imposed by its major shareholders.

THE ROLE OF UNDP
AND OTHER
UNITED NATIONS
AGENCIES

The United Nations system has had an explicit developmental mandate from its earliest years, in the United Nations itself through divisions such as the United Nations Development Programme (UNDP) and several divisions within the Economic and Social Council secretariat such as the Resources Development Group. The mandate was also explicit in the specialized agencies that focused on various sectors: on education, science and culture (UNESCO), food and agriculture (FAO), health (WHO), industrial development (UNIDO), trade (UNCTAD) and since the early 1970s, environment (UNEP). All the specialized agencies receive partial funding for their operations from UNDP when they are designated as "executing agencies" for various projects and programmes.

The funds of the World Bank and the IMF are substantially greater, so these institutions have concentrated on large capital transfers with a measure of technical assistance; the United Nations system has tended to put its emphasis on technical assistance with a measure of capital transfer, as for example, through the United Nations Capital Development Fund, which as part of the UNDP, undertakes small-scale projects in a manner similar to the World Bank in terms of procedures and analysis of feasibility.

The UNDP ON SHIFTING SANDS IN THE
DEVELOPMENT FIELD

Over the years since 1982, as the debtor developing countries have continued to be encumbered by an increasingly onerous burden of debt and concomitant high social costs, their dependency on both capital aid and technical assistance has become greater. It has long been apparent that the unfavourable and unfamiliar global environment of the 1980s necessitated changes in the type of assistance that the developing debtor countries require, and that they are asking for. Thus over the last few years there has been a significant shift in lending and related technical assistance towards a macro and sectoral policy approach and away from the technical and project-oriented approach that had been overwhelmingly dominant until recently.

This has shifted the need for capital to meet balance-of-payments debt servicing obligations and for technical assistance to meet the needs in fields related to crisis management. The shift has been clear particularly with respect to problems centred on debt scheduling and negotiations, policy analysis and planning, budgeting and its supporting information systems, personnel development and training, administrative structures and procedures and the like. In the case of Africa this growing dependency is reflected in the trend towards an increase in requests for technical assistance resulting in a rise in this type of aid to where it accounts for about one third of the total aid they receive.

Third world countries have long recognized that they can turn to UNDP and the specialized agencies of the United Nations system for a wide range of technical assistance. But since the capital resources of these institutions are comparatively small, even with regard to technical assistance, their first call is on the IFIs. The latter can link technical assistance with substantially larger lending programmes, whether the funds are delivered within the framework of loans for "structural adjustment," for special assistance to meet critically important needs or for conventional project and sectoral lending. Thus these institutions have been the main beneficiaries of a shift in the pattern of technical assistance that is requested and delivered. This is reflected by the fact that in recent years the World Bank has annually disbursed as part of its loans or credits about twice as much for technical assistance as UNDP's technical assistance expenditures in the form of grants.

A perusal of some salient statistics reveals the magnitude of that shift: during the two decades since 1968, UNDP's share of total expenditures allocated by all aid agencies for technical assistance fell from 65 per cent to 25 per cent.[1] For the two decades since 1970 when the technical assistance component of ODA amounted to $90 million, donor Governments have substantially increased their technical assistance contributions to both the IFIs and to UNDP and United Nations specialized agencies. They have kept their contributions to UNDP relatively stagnant in *real* terms. This shift has occurred despite (1) the comparative advantage enjoyed by UNDP by virtue of its extensive global network of field offices and the broad scope of its activities covering all aspects of development, (2) the fact that the demand for such assistance has been growing faster than the availability of concessional aid and, (3) the fact that generally there is a charge for the IFI's role in providing technical assistance.

The factors underlying this 20-year trend show no sign of abating. They should be understood if they are to be changed to enable the United Nations agencies and UNDP to play a more effective and significant role in contending with the global debt and environmental crises. The urgency is that the position of UNDP and other United Nations agencies in the constellation of aid agencies may be further undermined by the additional pressures being placed on the debtor countries. This is accentuated by innovative approaches to debt management and debt rescheduling involving new financial instruments and techniques—the "market-based menu approach." Surging concern about the impact of debt servicing pressures on global environmental conditions will be one of the central themes of the United Nations World Conference on Environment and Development scheduled for 1992.

The shortage of professional staff in third world countries to carry out the requisite programmes and projects has become more and more acute, especially with respect to both debt management and environmental specialists. This has placed additional pressure on UNDP in light of its mandate to be the lead agency in coordinating technical assistance. Without major changes in UNDP policy and structure and the additional budgetary and professional staff resources to achieve the changes, its marginalization will not be halted, let alone reversed.

Assessment and response

UNDP's management has been responding to this challenge with initiatives that address the *emergency* nature of the current global situation. Through a variety of special programmes UNDP has been able to act both as a catalytic agent to raise funds for specific purposes and as a coordinator for emergency aid.[2] None of the programmes have been designed to have a direct bearing on the debt or environmental problems of these countries, though they are of course responsive to a situation created by those problems and are proving indirectly helpful within their limited mandates. However, several initiatives have been launched by UNDP that bear more directly on the medium-term and the longer-term problems faced by these countries.

The two most relevant are the National Technical Cooperation Assessments and Programmes (NatCAP) and the Round Table programmes. The concept of NatCAP is said to have been born out of frustration with the disappointing results of technical assistance as reflected in continuing dependency on outside advisory help. NatCAP involvement with the third world countries includes surveying and assessing the recipient general economic situation, followed by a more detailed examination sector-by-sector where the linkages between technical assistance and financial assistance can be made. The rationale for NatCAP is that, on the basis of its intervention, the technical assistance needs could be more precisely identified, particularly in the area of debt management.

As part of its self-examination undertaken after the first pilot phase of the NatCAP Programme, an evaluation was commissioned. Known as the Kapur Report after its lead consultant, Shiv Kapur, who had been director of the World Bank's Evaluation Department, it had a broad mandate to examine UNDP's past and potential role, with particular reference to the developmental issue in light of the debt overhang. The report endorsed the NatCAP approach but offered critical commentary and suggestions to improve its implementation:

"The central issue (as) one of empowerment of the recipient governments in determining the direction of aid flows and of the UNDP (both) in assisting Governments and in providing leadership within the aid community. The empowerment of the UNDP will call for a new role for the organization that, in turn, raises questions of capability and organization."[3]

The findings of the Kapur Report are stark:

- The aspiration of UNDP to play the "lead agency" role has so far not been demonstrated;
- The experience of the NatCAP exercises has revealed that other key bilateral and multilateral development agencies are not prepared to play follow the leader and to pursue an agenda consistent with that set out in the NatCAP report. The result is that the technical assistance programmes of UNDP, the World Bank or major donors will likely proceed in an uncoordinated manner if there should be a divergence in the assessments and in the recommended policies and programmes of action of these other players in the development field; and
- In the event of such divergent views, UNDP is likely to come out second best.

The Kapur report recommends that the concept of NatCAP be reviewed in its overall concept, its methodology and its management. The fall-out of this assessment has not yet shaken either UNDP management or its political masters to action commensurate with the problem. The UNDP Administrator has proposed the establishment of a Management Facility for Technical Co-operation. The declared purpose would be to assist developing countries to improve their capacity for economic management, including debt servicing and negotiating issues and the relationship of development policies to environment programmes from data collection to monitoring. As a tentative budgetary suggestion, the facility would have $500 million over a three to five year period and be yet another mechanism for the coordination of the myriad technical assistance programmes being provided by different donors within the rubric of "economic management."

This initiative is also seen as tying in well with the NatCAP exercises seeking to identify the technical assistance requirements. Clearly the rationale is based on recognition of a need for change in the way NatCAP is presently operating. But the capacity to achieve this is still in doubt without other initiatives to strengthen UNDP in the key areas identified by the Kapur Report. If UNDP is to have any hope of playing a leadership role—and to be seen to be doing so—far-reaching changes must be made in redefining its mandate in relation to a realistic estimate of available resources, and in its organizational structure and operational procedures.

This issue of institutional reform is not new. Many reports and unofficial studies on this theme date back several decades. One of the most ambitious reports was commissioned in the mid-1970s when the United Nations established a group on restructuring composed of "experts on the structure of the United Nations system." Their report contained a host of recommendations for reform, most rather modest in scope. Notwithstanding, no significant movement occurred except for the formation of new specialized agencies. There is, therefore, continuing concern.

In a recent study by the WIDER organization, the current United Nations policy making process is considered sufficiently flawed to prompt a proposal for "the downgrading or elimination of some organizations and the strengthening possibly merging of others."

Meantime, the task has been complicated by an agreement, the Technical Cooperation Framework Paper (TCFP), signed by the President of the World Bank, Mr. Conable and the Administrator of UNDP, Mr. Draper. This agreement delegates to UNDP the responsibility of preparing the technical assistance programme for the Consultative Group meetings as well as those for the Round Tables. The issue of reorganization and of building an in-house professional cadre would appear to be even more pressing in light of this agreement, and at the same time more difficult because of limited financial resources.

In the view of some observers, UNDP has been assuming obligations that it cannot discharge adequately in its present state, a practice that has damaged its reputation. The recent UNDP-World Bank agreement provides a case in point. That agreement seeks to correct the inadequacies of the prevailing process by UNDP taking responsibility for decisions regarding the timing of both the Round Table and Consultative Group meetings and the technical assistance aspects of the agenda.[4] This arrangement likely will leave UNDP in a supporting rather than a lead role because the World Bank would be responsible for the preparation of the basic documents and the analysis on policy options and related debt negotiations. Rather than enhance the UNDP role, this administrative-procedural function will reinforce its minor status, subservient to those with the responsibility for substantive matters.

Finding a greater role in the debt crisis for the UNDP

UNDP understandably intends to assume a more substantive role in global efforts to resolve or ease the debt crisis. It has continued to act, however, as the financial conduit for projects or programmes that other agencies are to implement. In this case, UNDP has assumed again a supporting role to the World Bank, an institution that is hardly in need of the UNDP finances. A prime example is provided by the agreement with the World Bank to enter into a programme entitled, "World Bank/UNDP Cooperation on Structural Adjustment." Under an arrangement with the Regional Programme for Africa, the World Bank serves as the executing agency for a project aimed at surveying and monitoring over a five-year period the social impact of the structural adjustment programmes operative in sub-Saharan African countries. For UNDP the question became one of balancing off the mandate to cooperate but to do so without playing a subordinate role merely as a conduit of funds with no substantive contribution to the training and related support programmes designed to strengthen the debt management capabilities of the developing debtor countries. The most appropriate role for UNDP with respect to the debt crisis has been the focus of discussion within UNDP for the past several years. The issues debated include whether UNDP should address broad policy aspects or limit itself to providing financial aid that supports institutional strengthening of information systems, policy analysis through training and related programmes.[5]

UNDP's relationship to the debtor developing countries will unquestionably remain different from that of the World Bank and the IMF with regard
to issues relating to their debt and environment problems. *Whether welcomed
or not, advice with money and conditionality attached carries a great deal
more weight than advice of any other sort.* Advice based on the expenditure
of a large amount of money that buys analysis also carries a great deal more
weight, whatever distaste there may be for the policy implications of the
analysis. Under the circumstances, notwithstanding any comparative advantage it may appear to have in terms of political "neutrality" and its extensive
network of resident offices, UNDP cannot hope to compete on this limited
terrain of technical assistance and coordination with its much more meager
resources. Having recently gained approval for a general capital increase of
almost $65 billion, the World Bank plans to reach an annual lending rate
exceeding $20 billion by 1990. The other multilateral development institu-
tions, the regional development banks and the IMF also plan to make substantial increases in their lending and concessional aid programmes and to
devote a larger proportion to technical assistance. In contrast, UNDP is striving to reach a funding of about $1 billion by 1990, a target which in *real*
terms is lower than present levels.

UNDP is struggling to discharge its mandated responsibilities with a grab-
bag of programmes: the Short term Advisory Services (STAS) designed to
assist the developing countries in meeting their technical assistance requirements that call only for short duration assignments; the Structural Adjustment
Advisory Group (STAAG), which established a "talent pool" of high-level
experts under special contractual arrangements; and a Special Measures Fund
for the least developed countries (SMF) set up to bolster the capacity of the
Regional Bureaux to service their countries. (See Glossary)

The questions posed have been:

- Do these programmes fill the priority technical assistance needs of the
  third world at this time?
- If not, what role could UNDP play most effectively, especially with
  respect to the debt and environment issues that are unquestionably
  priority concerns?

UNDP has been urged to give high priority to addressing the specific
immediate needs of the debtor countries as they struggle with the so-called
"structural adjustment" process. In line with this, technical assistance would
focus on advising and training on the macro and micro aspects of policy-

making related to debt and environment management, and both in relation to aid coordination. This would include the information systems that are an integral part of an adequate management process. To assist these countries in this area, UNDP would have to build up its in-house competence beyond what is now required for its main role as a conduit for funds to the executing agencies of the United Nations system. Many of the organizational structural elements are already in place: the NatCAP programme, the Structural Adjustment Advisory Group and the Short term Advisory Service and the recent decision to strengthen the African Bureau with a substantial addition to its professional staff. But funding constraints will make UNDP's role a limited one.

UNDP cannot compete with the World Bank and the IMF in undertaking comprehensive country economic surveys and sectoral studies such as the annual series put out by the World Bank *(The World Development Report* and *World Debt Tables)*, by the IMF *(World Economic Outlook)*, and by UNCTAD *(Trade and Development Report)*, to name a few. In terms of documentation and commentary there is no shortage of well-prepared conferences and symposia focused directly or indirectly on the debt crisis and its broader implications. This need not preclude UNDP from tendering a valuable service in *offering debtor countries a ''respected second opinion'' in utilizing these surveys and recommendations*, particularly with respect to choosing from among the recommended institutional changes and policy options. In some cases, this may call for additional studies that could be done by UNDP, but such studies would be limited to filling in critical gaps deemed essential for UNDP's policy-advising role. UNDP-sponsored conferences could fill in other informational gaps, and at the same time, bring issues before a broader public.

SETTING UP THE UNITED NATIONS TO PLAY A GREATER ROLE IN THE GLOBAL ACTION AGENDA

The United Nations could help in setting the agenda for the deliberations along the following lines:

- At the global level, initiating and hosting meetings and conferences akin to the process undertaken during the early 1940s, before the United Nations was born, that led up to the Bretton Woods Conference of

1944 and the establishment of a "system" of rules for international trade and capital flows, and the complementary institutions such as the World Bank and the IMF;

- At the global and regional levels, initiating actionable programmes dealing with specific issues related to the debt crisis, such as the impact of structural adjustment lending, its underlying assumptions related to privatization, removal or reduction of trade-related subsidies and barriers, foreign investment regulations, and the host of measures that are suggested to help the debtor developing countries make more effective use of the capital provided, whether in the form of loans, investment or official aid.

Three problem areas with great potential are illustrative of what is likely to be high on the priority list, and at the same time, feasible to achieve in a reasonable time:

- Increasing South-South trade in goods and services well beyond the present levels, a change that likely would call for special agreements initially such as those already negotiated between Latin American and Central American countries with Brazil and Mexico playing pivotal roles;
- Decreasing dependence on the present mix of energy forms *while increasing the use of energy* so savings in foreign exchange can be achieved economically (especially when the value of foreign exchange is calculated realistically—"shadow priced") and so the devastating ecological damage from fuelwood dependance can be drastically reduced through the development of alternative fuels: solar, wind, geothermal, shallow gas and other forms of energy can relieve the pressure on fuelwood with its disastrous environmental implications. These technologies also can put energy at the service of those in the rural sectors outside the grid systems for more productive agricultural practises, for drilling for water for human consumption and for powering educational equipment and machinery in rural-based industrial estates, all leading to higher incomes, better health and improved education and training;
- Decreasing dependance on technical assistance in its present inefficient forms through the use of modern telecommunication technologies being used for teleconferencing and for "distance education;" "distance learning" through new communication technologies can create the "global classroom without walls" that relies on the inexpensive move-

ment of electrons rather than on the costly movement of instructors and students across vast distances; it holds the promise of revolutionizing technical assistance programmes.

The United Nations system, including the IFIs and the United Nations specialized agencies and UNDP, might then play a key role in the follow-through, with the hope of attaining a global economy that is growing on an environmentally and financially sustainable basis, and is at the same time, less beset with instability and inequity.

But beyond this, there is the troubling aspect of the Group of Seven summitry process preempting the role of the multilateral institutions. The authors of the WIDER report on *World Economic Summits: The Role of Representative Groups in the Governance of the World Economy* have correctly noted that:

> "It is already the case that many of the problems discussed by the Group of Five/Group of Seven and the Summit fall within the competence of one or more of the relevant international organizations, as does the responsibility for carrying through the proposed solutions...The truth is that, in political terms, international organizations are in a subservient position *vis-à-vis* the Summit, and cannot help competing among themselves for its favours..and, in doing so, be tempted to compromise their objectivity and their responsibility to the world community as a whole."[6]

This concern about the future of the United Nations system as an *effective* institutional arrangement for collective policy-making in the wide range of issues dealing with global economic management is widely shared. With the dominance of the Group of Three and with the *adhocery* that characterizes their attempts at cooperation, the global decision-making and programme implementing process has the appearance of relegating the United Nations system to a tertiary policy role and routine administration. The lop-sided nature of this arrangement leaves the other countries, particularly the third world countries, out in the cold. Accordingly, this situation has evoked calls for far-reaching reform to strengthen the system through elimination and mergers of the existing agencies and through special measures to alter the decision-making process.

This is not the first time that such concerns and suggestions for reform have been expressed. In the mid-1970s the United Nations Group on Restructuring was established and a report issued which came to very little.[7] In line with this the WIDER study recommends that the necessary reform exercise be undertaken by a newly-established World Economic Council that would

> "bring together the Five and the Non-Five. . . . to hammer out, through small negotiating groups, collective positions on specific and well-defined policy issues and to make agreed recommendations.. of a more realistic and intellectually coherent nature than those that have emerged from majority decisions (of the existing United Nations bodies). . . . and which therefore would carry greater weight."[8]

So far little has come of such proposals though there is greater concern about the nature of the trends with regard to the process of decision-making and to the substantive aspect that emerges from this process. In terms of effectiveness in dealing with the debt-related developmental issues that are central to the functioning of the global economic system, the United Nations system is, so to speak, withering on the vine. This trend jeopardizes the principle of global representation embodied in the United Nations system. It must be addressed if the resolution of the debt crisis is to go beyond the limited objective of avoiding breakdown, leaving in place the trends of increasing impoverishment and dimming the hopes for a better future for the majority of people on this planet.

THE RESPONSE OF THE UNITED NATIONS SYSTEM AND IFIs TO THE ENVIRONMENTAL CRISIS

The United Nations has long been active in the environmental field. UNDP dates its involvement back to 1973. Over the years since then it has financed in whole or in part about 2,000 projects with an allocation of over $1 billion, presently absorbing about 20 per cent of UNDP's total annual programme budget. The first dramatic involvement at the global level was the landmark United Nations Conference on the Human Environment in 1972 in Stockholm. The establishment of the United Nations Environment Programme (UNEP) soon followed with the Secretary of the Stockholm conference assuming the role of the Executive Director of UNEP. "Its mission" as cryptically described by one commentator, "is, quite literally, to save the world." Quoting Maurice Strong :

"This is the first time that the nations of the world, acting together, have recognized that something has gone wrong with the way man is managing his environment. . . . The present generation may hold the power to decide whether man can achieve the kind of changes in behaviour necessary to assure a continued healthy and flourishing life on this planet."

UNEP was established with headquarters in Nairobi, Kenya. It chartered its course slowly, starting with a global monitoring function working through governmental agencies around the world. An early warning system, "Earth Watch," was soon established to identify and warn of environmental change that might call for corrective action. UNEP has played a useful role of survey, research and public relations, but one limited by meager funding. Much of it was provided by UNDP which appointed UNEP as Executing Agency for environmentally-related projects. The United Nations followed up its environment conscious-raising efforts 10 years later with a conference in Nairobi in 1981 on the theme, "New and Renewable Sources of Energy." This UNCNRSE was a major initiative on the scale of the Stockholm Conference, and like that conference focused on measures to promote development with greater reliance on more environmentally benign sources of energy than fossil fuels and fuelwood. The reports of its 32 workshops, the national background papers and its action plan provide the basis for follow-up initiatives through national research programmes and projects, and at the international level through establishing a programme similar to the highly successful consultative group on international agricultural research (CGIAR).[9]

The 20-year anniversary of the Stockholm Conference is due to be marked by another United Nations conference on the environment to be held in Rio de Janeiro in early 1992 with the same man, Maurice Strong, at the helm. This time the stress will be on development, an emphasis that has been promoted by the World Commission on Environment and Development (The Brundtland Commission). The latter issued its report, *Our Common Future*, in 1989 after extensive hearings around the world. Its theme, "Sustainable Development," has become popular enough to be regarded as a cliche. Having raised environmental consciousness, the challenge is to give the idea operational traction if there is to be significant movement.

A *prima facie* case can be made for periodic and publicized reviews of the structure and *modus operandi* of any international institution. They need to be assessed in relation to the mandate at their inception and the circumstances at the time of the review. This applies with special relevance to the international agencies that date their birth from the end of the Second World War, almost a half century ago. The world has changed radically over the intervening years and of course the institutions have responded with some change, but the question is: have they adapted enough, not only as individual entities but as a system of agencies and ad hoc arrangements?

A need exists to "rationalize" the multitude of agencies involving changes of structure and process of the system of agencies viewed as a whole in relation to the debt and environmental crises and in relation to a global pattern of trade and capital flows characterized by greater equity and sensitivity to the maintenance of environmental quality. The changes also would likely involve cooperation and coordination with regard to macro policies and to specific international programmes involving research, data collection, technical assistance, project and programme implementation and appraisal, and national and global analysis, particularly those in support of global agreements on trade, financial and environmental issues. The agenda for the programme of action presents an ambitious challenge that can guide the process of change.

EPILOGUE:
RETORIC AND REALITY

"I caught a bear."
"Bring him here."
"He won't go."
"Then come here yourself."
"He won't let me go."

—Russian folk-wisdom

We are living through a period of far-reaching transition or transformation *forced* by several trends and severe constraints. We must face up to environmental limits. We have no choice about adjusting to the scientific-technological revolution that is ushering in the "information age." If we are to avoid a breakdown of calamitous proportions, it is imperative that we slow down and reverse some key trends with respect to the speed and manner of global growth in output, trade and capital flows. The danger is reflected in the persistently increasing burden of debt as a result of unsustainable trade and capital flow patterns, in the widening inequalities of income and of well-being between the industrialized and the developing countries and in the growing environmental damage on a planetary scale. The case is overwhelming for bold initiatives to get us off the present trajectory.

Instead, there seems to be a slow and reluctant adjustment to the new realities. The reasons are to be found in the power of inertia and of vested interests that favour the status quo, and in the factor of risk aversion in the face of uncertainties. The foot-dragging is rationalized on grounds of "realism" and "practicality." A clear example is provided by the creditors' practice of turning a figurative blind eye to the fact that many of the third world debtor countries have been piling up arrears that will never be paid;

the approach taken is euphemistically called a "policy of benign arrears." This process is not, however, benevolent; it still leaves most debtors' noses rubbing up painfully against the grindstone of debt. Some modest debt relief measures have been taken and a few of the debtors are beginning to see glimmers of light at the end of the tunnel of their despair, but, on balance, the verdict on the current muddling-through process must be a failing grade.

There are two principal grounds for this assessment: 1) this process has done little to assure that the necessary financial-economic conditions for a favourable *longer term* future outcome are in place, and 2) the pressures of the debt overhang continue to prevail with adverse global environmental implications as the impoverished debtor countries are being *forced* to focus on providing for their basic needs today rather than being concerned about tomorrow. In any case, the long-term path calls for them to embark on new environmentally benign patterns of development that they cannot finance.

The great degree of confidence by the policy makers of the industrialized countries about the essential "rightness" of the present world economic order is exceptionally dangerous and surprising. It is dangerous in so far as it induces a complacency that is misplaced. It is surprising in as much as it dismisses dire assessments of the short-term global economic prospect that have been made by the most authoritative sources of its own establishment. The normally cautious IMF in its *1990 World Economic Outlook* has characterized the present global economic and financial condition as "deteriorating," "serious" and "fragile." A 1991 study by the World Bank is hardly more encouraging. Table 21, in setting out the past trends and future scenarios forecast for the 1990s, reveals that as much as 40 per cent or more than 2 billion persons face dismal prospects with less and less hope of emerging from the thrall of absolute poverty.

Though the global trends reveal a persistent and widening gap between the rich and the poor and between creditor and debtor countries and a continuing gap between environmental rhetoric and action, no proposals are being put forward that could be considered as commensurate with the magnitude and urgency of the situation. To be sure, proposals abound for easing and resolving the global debt and environmental crises and their corollary, the crisis of increasing income polarization. But few of these proposals are spelt out in *operational* terms with their implications as to the necessary and sufficient institutional and policy changes.

Instead, we find a wide acceptance of a "steady-as-you-go" approach, an approach that consists essentially of doling out dollops of debt relief and debt forgiveness by the spoonful in the hope that the treatment will ease the stress for third world debtor countries and avoid the necessity of radical

Table 21: Growth/decline of GDP per capita in developing countries by regions. 1960-1990
(percentage)

Country group	Average annual rate of growth/ decline of GDP per capita		
	1960-1970	1970-1980	1980-1990
	3.3	2.4	0.1
Developing countries			
By regions:			
North Africa	8.2	1.2	−0.3
Sub-Saharan Africa	1.8	−0.4	−2.6
Western Asia	4.1	1.0	−4.3
South and East Asia	2.6	4.1	3.7
Latin America and the Caribbean	2.7	2.4	−1.1
Mediterranean	3.7	3.7	1.1

Source: United Nations, Department of International Economic and Social Affairs.
At 1980 dollars and exchange rates.

measures. The United States Treasury Secretary, Nicholas Brady, may advocate—as he did in early 1989—an approach designed ''to rekindle the hope of debtor nations that their sacrifices will lead to greater prosperity in the present and the prospect of a future unclouded by the burden of debt,'' but stripped of wishful thinking, this policy represents a continuation of the ''muddling-through'' approach. Imaginative financial embellishments have been introduced, but as Professor Edmar Bacha, a former Brazilian Finance Minister, has aptly noted this amounts to a policy of ''enhanced muddling-through.'' There is provision for modest amounts of new money and a significant measure of debt relief for a few debtors, but this approach fails to address the fundamentals that gave rise to the high and persistent debts of the third world and the United States.

In response to the economic-financial challenge of the times an ad hoc approach of ''leadership'' by summitry has evolved with Finance Ministers and central bank governors of the Group of Seven countries meeting periodically. Though these meetings have occurred often and regularly enough to be regarded as a ritual, there is little evidence of progress in establishing the required institutional base or the substantive policies and programmes. This should not be surprising since there are strongly divergent objectives and approaches among the members of the Group of Seven club, the self-appointed steering committee of the global economy. Even judged in terms of whether their attempts at policy coordination have achieved the limited objective of interest and exchange rate alignments and levels, their failure rate should make them very humble.

This "leadership" of the Group of Seven, but essentially of the Group of Three major economic powers, has been unable to sustain overall global growth and, at the same time, to even modestly modify its pattern to achieve environmental and equity goals; it has been unable to significantly increase the help to developing countries by providing more and cheaper capital and by reducing the discriminatory trade barriers they face; and, in a phrase, it has been unable to make the far-reaching *global structural adjustment* that is a necessary condition for getting the global economy back on track towards growth that is more stable, more equitable and more environmentally sustainable. The most critical role is that of the United States as the world's largest economy. Its persistent and historically high budget and trade deficits combined with low savings and productivity rates have made it the world's largest debtor and, with that status and all it implies, severely constrained its policy options to a point where it contributes more to the problem rather than to the solution. Nor are the Germans and Japanese, with the world's largest surpluses, able to exercise the kind of leadership required, beset as they are with problems closer to home that are absorbing much of their capital. The dismal record and the dim prospects for improvement have given rise, as Professor Paul Streeten has noted, "to widespread anxieties, the tremors from which could cause the walls of the existing system to crumble."[1]

There is not only a diminished capability. The situation is compounded by the reluctance to take action commensurate with the scope and danger of the crisis conditions on the part of the leaders of the major industrialized nations in the Group of Seven and of their bankers. They all support the muddling-through policy as the only feasible option—and as the desirable one. The beneficiaries of the present institutional arrangements are understandably fearful of the risks entailed in disturbing the status quo in any radical fashion. They are also inclined to indulge in wishful-thinking, entertaining the hope that their mild ameliorative policies are chartering a course that might yet see the global economy come through the storm. Besides, under the muddling-through approach a grossly disproportionate part of the pain of adjustment is inflicted on the third world's erstwhile borrowers who must continue to struggle with heavy debt burdens. There is, therefore, not likely to be much help coming from that quarter.

The events of the past decade have made it abundantly clear that the Group of Seven is not likely to fix itself either as a group or as individual countries pursuing their own agendas that are driven by short-term parochial domestic political pressures. Accordingly, it is incumbent *on the debtors* to get into the act in a more effective way. As members of the group of developing countries, together with non Group of Seven industrialized countries, they need to devise and fight for a long-term debt and environmental strategy that can provide the appropriate framework for short-term measures. Unless and until these countries are involved through some workable arrangement in the decision-making process related to designing and implementing both the debt and environmental strategies, the prevailing policies likely will be shaped by a leadership that is not confronting the key challenges of our times, a leadership that is drifting with the currents that are on present trends likely to pull all countries into the vortex of a global depression akin to that of the 1930s.

The first line of action would be to relieve the global economy of the debt overhang by an across-the-board series of measures involving a *significant* degree of debt relief. For some debtors the degree would be tantamount to debt forgiveness; for another group the appropriate degree might amount to a reduction of the present value of their debts by over 50 per cent. There is the precedent of the complete write-off of the debts owed by the poorest of African debtors that, in any case, were not being serviced and were unlikely to be, and in total amounted to only about 1 per cent of the third world's outstanding debt of $1300 billion. There is also the precedent of the Polish case where the United States, for geopolitical reasons, requested creditors to agree to a 70 per cent write-down and an agreement was reached by official creditors to write-off 50 per cent of their outstanding debt. The process needs to be generalized for fairness and for effectiveness in global terms. Qualms about "free riders" need to be put aside in deference to the great fairness issue of ending an asymmetric process that is exacerbating the division of the world between the rich and the poor. The scale is crucial.

At the same time, there must be a change of policies—and commensurate changes in the global institutional supporting system—that would lower real interest rates, dampen the volatility of exchange rates, lower protective barriers against third world exports and improve the terms of trade to favour the third world. This is a tall order. The Administrator of UNDP has correctly noted that "debt on this vast a scale cannot be addressed with further indebtedness. . . (and, therefore), requires structural solutions." If the objective is to avoid a breakdown of global dimensions, the structural adjustment must necessarily be global in scope, starting with each of the major economies and then, through cooperative agreements, applied to the global system.

There can be some grounds for optimism in the fact that, as yet, the global system has not broken down despite some tremors that have been short-lived occasions for fear and reflection. There is evidence as well of a will and capacity for bold institutional adaptation to changed circumstances. Western Europe provides an example where, after more than two decades of a consultative process, regional rules for trade and capital flows in the context of the movement towards union are being worked out with great prospects of success. In Eastern Europe and the Soviet Union the speed and manner of the painful transformation process is testimony to commitment to bold institutional change as a matter of deliberate policy.

At the same time, institutional change proceeds apace with the ad hoc ritual of summitry reaching a stage where it will be duly formalized with all the trappings of supporting secretariats. The tripolar leadership exercised by the Group of Three (Germany, Japan and the United States) is being institutionalized in a less formal way, but as the most important players on the international financial stage for influencing such key factors as interest and exchange rates and capital-technological transfers, there is pressure to move beyond the stage of ad hoc meetings. Their poor track record in policy coordination combined with the growing sense of danger inherent in the global economic-financial situation has given rise to calls for establishing the kind of constraining rules for international trade and capital movements that John Maynard Keynes and Harry Dexter White had in mind when negotiating the Bretton Woods agreement and which resulted in a flexible variant of the gold standard. This issue is on the agenda for discussions that come under the heading of the new Bretton Woods. As the old order, under stress and in crisis, gives way, there is reason to hope for more effective cooperative coordinating arrangements that can improve the odds of navigating the global economy out of the crisis conditions without capsizing.

This move towards cooperation is not being driven by the fear of a financial international breakdown alone. There is a growing awareness of the global environmental dangers and of the close connection between financial stress and environmental degradation. It is an issue that transcends borders. Attempts to tackle these threats have led to global and regional agreements on ozone depletion, on acid rain and on global warming. Some of these agreements are still under discussion and some have already been signed, though as yet they are largely without teeth or traction power.

Even if all the environmental targets set for the industrialized countries were achievable, there still remains the troubling aspect of the third world's ability to uphold their end while under intense pressure to service their debts and while contending with declining living standards and a growing sense of despair that makes them focus on the present to the virtual exclusion of concern for the day after tomorrow. In any case, their willingness and capability to opt for a new pattern of development dependent on energy forms that are environmentally more benign will require investment in research for the development of new technologies. The developing countries simply do not have the necessary investment funds to undertake the requisite research on alternative energy technologies that are cheap, virtually indestructible and simple to operate. Their expenditure on both basic and applied research accounts for about 1 per cent of the global total. Operating under the pressures of debt servicing, this deplorable situation will only be exacerbated.

The major onus must be placed, therefore, on the industrialized nations to re-establish a congenial milieu for the trade and capital flows that are a necessary condition for global recovery and for implementing environmental programmes of the required scope and scale. However, it is also clear that the broader participation of the global community-at-large is essential. The United Nations system with its universal representative character should be expected to play a key role in forging institutional changes and policies and programmes to lift the debt overhang that darkens the global future, programmes that will lead to new binding arrangements on debt and the environment that will institutionalize cooperation at the global level of governance.

Needless to say, to undertake this challenging programme it will be necessary to consider institutional modifications that rationalize the system of agencies to minimize overlapping responsibilities and to fill in the gaps. After all, the United Nations system was founded over four decades ago. Its original structural features have been changed over time in response to a rapidly and profoundly changing world, but with a lag and with untidy ill-defined compromises made in deference to established jurisdictional vested interests. New agencies, such as the United Nations Environmental Programme (UNEP) and the United Nations Conference on Trade and Development (UNCTAD), were added to the system. Their assigned functions, their operations and their budgetary resources were constrained, however, by resistance from established agencies which would not give ground in the ensuing jurisdictional battles. Thus there are calls for an over-arching review of the institutional arrangements to meet the exceptional challenge posed by the double-headed global crisis.

More and more voices are being heard that indicate a growing recognition that action to meet the environmental and debt threats requires *fundamental* change and this, in turn, has profound *political* implications in the larger sense of the concept of "politics." The current "eco-protest" phase draws attention to the need to change institutional arrangements in only the most general way, though there is now a widespread realization that the prevailing *systemic* arrangements are inimical to environmental objectives and action. This view flies in the face of the now ascendent privatization ethos that is

being so assiduously fostered by those who would maintain the status quo
or, better yet from their perspective, who would like to roll back the degree
of governmental involvement in all sectors that regulate and otherwise constrain the pursuit of profit. In democratic societies a great measure of popular
support is necessary to overcome this institutional-political resistance.

A broader range of questions must be placed on the public agenda. Martin
Ryle in his book, *Ecology and Socialism* (London, Radius, 1988) has made
a pertinent point about this political aspect of the environmental issue:

> "As the green movement develops out of eco-protest and formulates
> comprehensive programmes, it finds itself asking not just what kinds of
> social relations are ecologically viable, but what kinds are good; and so
> confronts the questions about justice, autonomy and hierarchy, public and
> private spheres, all of which have constituted political discourse since
> antiquity."

Attempts to secure the necessary level of support pose the temptation to
simplify and emotionalize the issues. Accordingly, the war metaphor comes
to mind, suggestive as it is of the intensity and seriousness of the precondition
for mobilizing adequate support. This dramatic metaphor was used not long
ago by the former editorial page editor of that radical journal, *The New York
Times*. Writing a signed editorial in the issue of 12 January 1989, entitled,
"Bush's shell game," John B. Oakes, wrote:

> "This is the time when environmental deterioration across the board —
> from ozone depletion and acid rain to deforestation and extinction of
> species—is at last becoming recognized as an even greater threat to life
> on this planet than the nuclear threat that it encompasses. This is a time
> when the National Academy of Sciences says environmental changes are
> putting 'the future welfare of human society' at risk. . . . *This war is too
> important to be left to the politicians.*"

The clarion call is clear but the tactic is not, unless what is meant is that
the battles must be led by statesmen, that is, politicians who have outlooks
that are longer-term and global and the courage to follow the implications of
their analysis to its logical conclusions. It would not be sufficient to win small
victories in the political arena but lose ground through heavy reliance on
private decision-making with its narrow financial and short-term perspective.

Nor will a slow incremental approach suffice in face of the impending danger. When the world's attention is focused on the two-headed global crisis issue and on the warning signs of breakdown, there appears to be a "window of opportunity" for action.[2]

To mobilize enough popular support and the large financial and other resources that are needed, it must be made clear to the voting public, who must ultimately endorse the allocation of resources to this end, that the two crises are global and mutually reinforcing and that, accordingly, we are grappling with what might be termed a "mega-issue," that is, one having to do with the evolving pattern of our global society or civilization: will it continue to grow given environmental and other limits, for how long and in what manner? Will this growth be shared "fairly" intra-generationally for the living generations and inter-generationally for those yet to be born?

One of the anonymous writers of *The Economist* suggestively described the situation in which we find ourselves by reference to a classical analogy:

> "The participants seemed to be unaware that they closely resembled the prisoners in Plato's legend of the cave, looking at shadows and believing that these were the real world."

There is a great deal at stake in finding our way out of the cave—soon. Anxiety is needed as well as understanding; any lessening of anxiety about the debt and environmental crises makes the present situation even more fragile and dangerous, especially if the community of nations, in trying to get out of the cave and into the sunlight , confuses shadow for substance and wishful-thinking for hard reality.

NOTES

Preface

[1] *Will They Ever Finish Bruckner Boulevard?* (Berkeley, CA, Univ. of California Press, 1987), p.4

Introduction

[1] These views are in an editorial of 20 April, 1983, entitled "What debt crisis?" and in the report of the 1989 IMF/World Bank meeting by a *Wall Street Journal* reporter writing in *The International Development Review* (Winter 1989/90) under the heading, "What if they declared a debt crisis and nobody came?"

[2] *World Debt Tables*, 1990-91: *External Debt of Developing Countries*, Vol. 1, Analysis and Summary Tables, (Washington, D.C., World Bank, 1990), p. 4; and World Bank, *World Development Report 1988*, p.32.

[3] Masaru Tamamoto, "Japan's search for a world role: the Japan that can say yes," *World Policy Journal* (Summer 1990), p.513. Professor Tamamoto observes that Japanese financial institutions have been regularly buying one third of United States Treasury bill issues and providing additional infusions of capital that have become critical to America's ability to run a large budget deficit and to sustain the United States leadership role in international economic/financial affairs.

Part I

Chapter 1

[1] For an illuminating succinct treatment comparing the 1930s and the present period, see World Bank, *World Development Report — 1982*, Box 2.2, pp. 20-21, and; Angus Maddison *Two Crises: Latin America and Asia: 1929-38* and 1973-83 (Paris, OECD, 1985), passim."

[2] *World Debt Tables, 1990*, table 7 (Washington, D.C., World Bank, 1990).

[3] Stephen Fidler, *The Financial Times* of 24 October, 1990. Since 1985, Brazil has paid out $55 billion in interest payments without making a dent in its total debt. The

situation has been described by a Brazilian official as "intolerable," echoing election declarations that threatened a partial repudiation of the debt.

[4] *IMF Survey*, 10 September, 1990.

[5] See OECD Development Centre Technical Paper (No. 32) by B. Hofman and H. Reisen, entitled *Linking Debt and Investment*. After undertaking empirical studies, the authors concluded that the weak levels of investment in heavily indebted countries arise from the capital supply side or a lack of new funds.

The decrease in investment has not been sufficient to replace depreciated capital in many African and Latin American debtor countries. In Africa the minimum necessary to replace depreciated capital is estimated at 13 per cent of GDP, in Latin America at 14 per cent. Seven sub-Saharan African countries and three in Latin America were not able to reach these investment levels in 1987. *Adjustment Lending Policies for Sustainable Growth*, World Bank Policy and Research Series No. 14, 1990, p.82.

[6] C. Fred Bergsten, Director of the Institute for International Economics, Washington, D.C., spoke and wrote of the second debt crisis early in 1985: "The second debt crisis is coming," *Challenge* (May-June 1985). Professor Gerald Epstein of the New School for Social Research has written about the third debt crisis by counting the United States budget and trade deficits as separate but related phenomena: "The triple debt crisis," *World Policy Journal* (Fall 1985).

[7] "Keeping a chicken in every pot," *The New York Times*, 6 February, 1991.

[8] Exports increased by over 25 per cent, in large part due to the relative decline in the value of the United States dollar while imports continued at their previous troubling rates of increase. When in 1990 the dollar appreciated, the impact was reflected in the slowing of the rate of increase in exports. Exchange rate changes have limited scope as a stimulant and have the disadvantage of being fragile and the attributes of a two-edged sword.

[9] "Between 1870 and 1929 productivity was remarkably stable, around 2 per cent, dropping to 1 per cent during the Great Depression, soaring to 4 per cent in the 1940s. By 1979 productivity growth rates had returned to a little below the 2 per cent norm. Between 1979 and 1984 productivity growth fell still further to 1.3 per cent, well below the long-term norm." Defree G. Williamson, "Productivity and American Leadership; a review article," *Journal of Economic Literature* (March 1991), pp. 53 and 54. Professor Williamson makes the point that the statistical record shows that "United States productivity exceeded the average of her fifteen competitors in every period from 1870 to 1950 save one, the Great Depression. I see the century 1870 to 1979 as falling into three regimes: 1870-1929, the United States always in the vanguard; 1929-1950, a transition; 1950-1979, the United States always in the rear. Lagging

American productivity is, to my way of thinking, very much a post-World War II event." (p.58). The article is a review of W. Baumol, S. Blackman and Z. Wolff's *Productivity and American Leadership: The Long View* (Boston, MIT Press, 1989). BBW's thesis is that United States productivity growth is still conforming to the historical average rate. According to Williamson, "BBW paint both an optimistic picture of America's lagging performance as well as (conveying) a sense of policy impotence as implied by the inevitability of these styled facts." (p.52).

[10] The direct investment abroad, being long established, is earning a higher rate of return than that of investments by foreigners in the United States. Thus, the concept of net debt is not clear-cut since its measurement depends on how these different investments are valued. If, for example, United States foreign investment were valued at current market prices the net United States debt would be greatly reduced, and the United States may, in fact, not be a net debtor at all. But what counts, for our purposes, is the trend: with trade deficits running in the $150 billion range, the debtor status of the United States is increasing very rapidly or the movement towards this status is very rapid.

Chapter 2

[1] Only about 1 per cent of the CO2 emission increase is derived from man-made activities per year, but, as this process is cumulative, the increase is estimated at about 25 per cent to 30 per cent above the normal levels of centuries past. A best scientific "guess/estimate" is that in 1987 fossil fuel combustion released 5.5 billion metric tons of carbon into the atmosphere. (Fossil fuels provide about four fifths of the global commercial energy output with oil accounting for one third of that, coal for about one quarter, and natural gas, about one fifth. The carbon content per unit of energy from coal is 75% higher than that for natural gas and 44 per cent higher than for oil.) Part of the increase is attributed to the destruction of tropical forests. In 1987 the cutting of tropical forested lands is estimated to have allowed the release in that year of as much as 1.65 billion metric tons of CO_2 *that would otherwise have been absorbed by the vegetation.*

[2] The table is from John Holdren, "Energy in transition", *Scientific American Special Issue: Energy for Planet Earth* (September 1990), p.160. A terawatt is equal to a billion tons of coal or 5 billion barrels of oil per year. The data were compiled by Professor Holdren, Energy and Resources Group, Berkeley.

[3] There are some who make a case for a no growth society, such as Ezra Mishan, in an interesting article entitled, "Ills, bads and disamenities: the wages of growth", *Daedalus*, 1973. This issue was devoted to The No-Growth Society.

[4] Christopher Flavin, *State of the World-1990*, (Washington, D.C., Worldwatch Institute, 1990).

[5] Based on an assumption that these countries will grow at the rate of 4.5 per cent, the World Bank's medium forecast, this would call for an increase in generating capacity of 1,500 gigawatts. *Power Shortage in Developing Countries* (Washington, D.C., USAID, 1988) and A. Churchill, "A look ahead to the year 2010: Outlook for energy and supply demand," *Finance and Development* (Washington, D.C., World Bank, 1988).

[6] "Electricity in the third world: A dark future", The Economist, July, 1988, p.82. The electricity bill for these countries has absorbed an estimated one fifth of their Government's budgets and accounted for as much as 40 per cent of their foreign borrowing. There is considerable scope for cutbacks in energy expenditures without losing the needed energy output, but, for various reasons, the high return energy efficiency route is not being taken as vigorously as it should and could be. It is too facile to regard aid policies as the culpable factor.

[7] The scope and the realism of the assumptions that underlie the "sustainable development" concept and the obstacles that lie in the way of making it operational and achieving its objectives are discussed in Chapter 8 and in Annex C where the concept of "sustainable development" is considered in somewhat greater detail.

[8] Shadow pricing is defined as "the value used in economic analysis for a cost or a benefit in a project when the market price is felt to be a poor estimate of economic value. . . . For final goods and services, this is the value in use, and for intermediate goods and services, it is the opportunity cost, that is, the benefit foregone by using a scarce resource for one purpose instead of its next best alternative use." J. Price Gittinger, *Economic Analysis of Agricultural Projects*, World Bank/EDI Series in Economic Development (Baltimore, Johns Hopkins Univ. Press, 1982), p. 499.

"Shadow pricing adjusts financial inflows and outflows to transform them into economic terms . . . which can be defined only by the effect of the project on some fundamental objectives of the economy. . . . This approach, like most applied welfare economics in other areas, emanates from the so-called new welfare economics of the 1940s." Anandarup Ray, *Cost-Benefit Analysis: Issues and Methodologies* (Washington, D.C., World Bank, 1984), pp.8 and 9.

Part II

Chapter 3

[1] For an early (1983) comprehensive modeling exercise see, William Cline, *Systemic Risk and Policy Response* (Washington, D.C., Institute for International Economics, 1984), passim.

[2] In 1989, the World Bank ventured two estimates for growth over the next decade, one predicated on "adjustment-with-growth" which asssumes policies that will be taken to lessen the macroeconomic imbalances within and among the industrialized countries, the other on a "low-growth" scenario predicated on little or no corrective policies being taken to bring down interest rates and lessen protectionist barriers. A survey of forecasts of leading international agencies and institutions reveals an average forecast of 2 to 2.5 per cent growth in the seven major industrial countries, the Group of Seven. The survey includes forecasts by the IMF, the German Institute for Economic Research, the Japan Economic Research Centre, the OECD and the UN as well as the World Bank. The IMF's forecast is contained in its *World Economic Outlook*, and the OECD's in its *Economic Outlook*, both of which are published annually.

[3] The average forecast of 150 forecasters polled by Consensus Economics for 13 of the largest OECD countries is 1.77 per cent, with the United States and Sweden at 0.1 per cent and Canada at 0.2 per cent at the bottom and Japan at 3.7 per cent and Germany at 2.9 per cent at the top. *The Economist*, 12/15/1990. All the forecasts were slightly lower than the 1990 rate of increase. The commentary states: "forecasters continue to grow gloomier about prospects in 1991". In October 1990, The Economist put forward its best guess of about 2.5 per cent for the 1992-95 period and 1.5 to 2 per cent for the medium-term. The downward revisions are attributable in part to factors such as the drastic fall in United States and Japanese real estate values, the collapse of "junk bond"-financed mergers and acquisitions, the costly "savings and loan" failures (sometimes referred to as "the trust fiasco") and the weakened condition of the United States and the Japanese banking systems that are directly related to the drop in the real estate markets.

[4] This has been the central contentious issue of the Uruguay Round of the GATT. The United States is estimated to have spent about $60 billion each year between 1986 and 1989 for direct subsidy payments to its farmers, and the European Community and Japan about $150 billion.

[5] *World Bank, World Debt Tables:1988-89* (Washington, D.C., World Bank, 1989), Box: "The heavy toll of protectionism," page xxvii; and an article based on a speech by the former World Bank President Barber Conable which he delivered in December 1988 on the occasion of the GATT's Uruguay Round meeting in Montreal, reprinted in "Free trade aground?", *World Paper*, February 1989.

[6] William Cline's model as elaborated in *Systemic Risk and Policy Response*, assumes that for every percentage point in the growth of the gross domestic product (GDP) of the OECD countries, export volume can be expected to increase by 3 per cent (i.e., an export elasticity of 3.0) and that export prices can be expected to move procyclically, that is, rise faster than the inflation rate.

The World Bank's reading of the statistical record reveals an export elasticity of 1.3 and 3.0 with respect to manufactured products. (Shahid Javed Burki, "Flows of international finance and the international financial system," *The Bank's World*, March 1985). Burki goes on to cite the ahistorical behaviour of commodity export prices, noting that "this is the first post-recessionary period in which revival of economic activity in developed countries has not resulted in an increase in commodity prices."

[7] *Transnational Corporations in World Development: Trends and Prospects* (N.Y. United Nations, 1989). For illustrations of this phenomenon see Robert Reich, "The real economy," *Atlantic*, (January 1991), passim.

[8] The significance of the level of interest rates was noted by Dragoslav Avramovic and Ravi Gulhati in the early 1960s in their World Bank study on third world debt. See Dragoslav Avramovic, Ravi Gulhati, and others, *Economic Growth and External Debt* (Washington, D.C., John Hopkins University Press, 1964).

[9] *Partners in Development*, the Commission on International Development, chaired by Lester B. Pearson, (N.Y., Praeger, 1969). pp. 74-75, 153 and 164-65.

[10] Dragoslav Avramovic, former UNCTAD and World Bank economist, in a paper on the debt problem entitled, "Interest rates, debts and international policy": "The rate to aim at should be perhaps around 2 per cent per annum in real terms, (which) in the words of the Council of Economic Advisers of the United States, (is) the historically typical real interest rate." The source cited by Dr. Avramovic is *The Annual Report of the Council of Economic Adviser*, Washington, D.C., (2 February, 1983). He goes on to note that according to the *Annual Report of the Bank for International Settlements* (June 1983), "the average real rate in the post-war period 1963-1982 in five leading countries — the United States, the United Kingdom, Japan, the Federal Republic of Germany and Switzerland — was lower, 1.1 per cent per annum."

[11] This issue will be taken up in Chapter 5 that focuses on the leadership aspect and in Chapter 11 where global-scale institutional change is considered.

[12] See B.B. Aghevli and J.M. Boughton, "National saving and the world economy: Why have savings rates declined since the early 1970s?", *Finance & Development* (June 1990), pp. 2-5; A.L. Bovenberg, "Why has United States personal saving declined?" Finance & Development, (June 1990), pp.10-11; and J.J. Polak, "The decline of world savings," *Economic Insights, Institute for International Economics*, Washington, D.C. (September/October 1990), pp.18-19.

[13] The 1985 Commonwealth Secretariat's Report on the *Debt Crisis and the World Economy* (also known as the Lever Report after its Chairman, Lord Harold Lever),

estimated the gap for oil-importing developing countries at $75 billion to $100 billion by 1987 and $100 billion to $120 billion by 1990;

The 1983 Brandt Commission Report, *Common Crisis: North-South Cooperation for World Recovery*, estimated the need of the developing countries at about $85 billion per year to restore their import capacity to 1980 levels on which basis they could hope to attain a minimally acceptable rate of investment and growth;

Rimmer De Vries, Senior Vice President of Morgan Guaranty Trust Inc., has put forward an estimate of a financial gap of roughly $60 billion per year or $180 billion over three years for the 21 most heavily indebted countries and of $16 billion through 1991 to meet the minimal financial requirements of the four biggest Latin American debtors (after assuming a 7 per cent net increase in commercial bank lending to those countries).

[14] This is discussed in Chapter 2. For the most up-to-date review of such forecasts, see the *Worldwatch's State of the World - 1990*, especially the section in Chapter 2 by Christopher Flavin entitled "Alternatives to fossil fuels," pp.22-27.

[15] "More is not enough", in *Mazingira Special Issue, The Growth-Environment Dilemma*, No.3/4, 1977. "The challenge we now face", he wrote, "is nothing less than that of creating (that) whole new approach, to the goals of growth, to the processes of growth and to the systems of incentives and penalties which determine our patterns of growth (and this, in turn, implies) . . . The real alternative to 'no growth' is 'new growth'—a new approach to growth both in the industrialized and the developing societies."

Maurice Strong now heads the forthcoming United Nations World Conference on the Environment and Development that is scheduled to take place in 1992 in Brazil.

[16] "Strategies for sustainable economic development", *Scientific American, Special Issue: Managing Planet Earth* (September 1989).

[17] Despite the fashion, the attribute of renewability is not essential. Gas deposits that can last say 50 years to fuel small local industry and provide heat and cooking fuel for villages are, *from a policy point of view*, perpetual. The discount factor makes its present value akin to that of a renewable source of energy.

[18] This aspect is discussed more fully in Chapter 11 in which consideration is given to such proposals of international scope as part of a global agenda of action.

Chapter 4

[1] France was the first recipient of a World Bank loan and Japan was among the recipients. It was only in 1989 that Japan made the last repayment on its loan from the World Bank. These loans were covered under the "reconstruction" aspect of the mandate of the World Bank, otherwise officially known as the International Bank for

Reconstruction and Development. The annual Marshall Plan contributions amounted to 1.3 per cent of the United States GNP and, in later years, much of the debt so incurred was forgiven.

[2] "Lending for adjustment: an update", *World Bank News*, April 1989, p.14.

[3] William McCleary, "Policy implementation under adjustment lending: a review of the experience with structural adjustment lending", *Finance & Development* (March 1989), p.32.

[4] R. Faini and J. de Melo, "Adjustment, investment and the real exchange rate in developing countries, *Economic Policy* (Washington, D.C., World Bank, 1990). They conclude, on the basis of a review of 83 developing countries, that since 1981, devaluation has not had any measurably discernable positive effect on their trade balances.

[5] *The Economist*, (24 November, 1990).

[6] See V. Thomas and A. Chibber, "Experience with policy reform under adjustment: how well have the adjustment programmes been working?," and William McCleary, "Policy implementation under adjustment lending: a review of the experience under adjustment lending," *Finance & Development* (March 1989), pp.28-34. The review covered 51 SALs and SECALs in 15 countries.

[7] The World Bank has undertaken studies on the social impact of SALS and SECALs. The resultant accentuation of poverty is readily acknowledged in these reports. See "Poverty and adjustment: issues and practises" by Elaine Zuckerman (March 1988) and prior studies written by other Bank staff members or consultants: A. R. Khan, *World Bank Operations and the Alleviation of Extreme Poverty*, 1986; Guy Pfeffermann, *Poverty in Latin America: The Impact of Depression*, 1986; Huan and Nicholas, *Protecting the Poor During Periods of Adjustment*, 1987; and Demery and Addison, *The Alleviation of Poverty Under Structural Adjustment*, 1987. There are other World Bank publications that are forthcoming, written by M. Schacter and others on Bolivian and other case studies.

On this aspect, see also, Giovanni Andrea Cornia, Richard Jolly and Frances Stewart, *Adjustment with a Human Face: Protecting the Vulnerable and Promoting Growth*, (Oxford, Clarendon Press, 1987).

[8] Having been a staff member of the World Bank in the Special Projects Division and in the Policy Planning Division in the mid-1970s and as Executive Director in the early 1980s, the views on this issue derive from first-hand involvement.

[9] K. Burke Dillon and L. Duran-Downing, *Officially Supported Export Credits: Developments and Prospects*, World Economic and Financial Surveys, (Washington, D.C., IMF, February 1988).

[10] This special capital sourcing approach is also considered in Chapter 11. See also M. Miller, *"Coping is not enough"* The International Debt Crisis (Homewood, IL, Dow Jones Irwin, Inc., 1986), pp. 230-240.

The Brandt (1980 and 1983) and Manley (1985) Commission reports and the Development Committee Task Force's Report on Concessional Flows contain proposals on tapping non-traditional forms of aid.

[11] Reported by Leonard Silk in *The New York Times*, 8 May, 1987, "Reconstructing the world system".

[12] *Voluntary Approaches to Debt Relief* (Washington, D.C., Institute for International Economics, September 1988), pp. 33-38.

[13] Professor Richard Gardner of Columbia University has noted that every 1 per cent diversion of this increment could yield about $3 billion annual flow. Cited by Leonkil ("The global appeal of capitalism," *The New York Times*, 23 May, 1986) in a report on a meeting of the trilateral commission in Madrid, Spain. Professor Gardner also drew attention to a study which showed that the rate of return of a weighted stock index of nine developing country stock exchanges was more than double that of a similar index for industrialized countries.

[14] The fragility of the Japanese financial system is described in "Downbeat: a survey of Japanese finance," *The Economist* (December 8, 1990). "The reasons for the bursting of the biggest speculative bubble seen this century can be found in the idiosyncrasies of Japan's long regulated, long cosseted and highly cartelized financial system." The key factor is the falling real estate and stock markets that have underpinned a fragile over-extended financial system.

[15] The debt-for-scholarship swap involves Harvard University's purchase of $5 million of Ecuadoran debt for $750,000 which is given to an Ecuadoran educational fund to administer. The debt-for-good works swap is designed to provide non-governmental organizations with local funds to help the rural population of an African debtor country to install wells in remote areas where they are desperately needed. The debt-for-dignity swap suggestion is contained in a column by Paul Knox entitled "Giving lopsided Latin economies the right push: why not help out Latin American governments that make a serious attempt to feed, house and educate their people?", *The Globe and Mail*, 10 December,1990. The idea is to ensure that the funds made available through the swaps would go to the poor, that is, to projects that feed, house and educate those in the debtor countries that are presently unable to obtain these basics.

[16] Quoted in Judith Evans, "What if they declared a debt crisis and nobody came?," *International Development Review* (Winter, 1989/90),.p.46. This is in line with the statement of a Vice President of the Royal Bank of Canada who, in relation to third world debt, declared that to indicate a willingness to forgive such debt is tantamount to proclaiming the end of banking.

Chapter 5

[1] "The developing country debt problem," *International Debt and the Developing Countries - A Symposium* (Washington, D.C., World Bank, 1985), p.117.

[2] "Public goods" or "collective goods" are defined as "that class of goods (or services) like public works where exclusion of consumers may be impossible, but in any event consumption of the good by one consuming unit—short of some level approaching congestion—does not exhaust its availability for others." In the international sphere the primary public good is the restoration and maintenance of peace. In the economic sphere the list would include: "an open trading system, well-defined property rights, standards of weights and measures that may include international money, or fixed exchange rates, and the like." "International public goods without international government," *The American Economic Review* (March 1986).

Dr. Sylvia Ostry, former Director of the OECD's Economics Department, asserts that the primary "international public good" of the multilateral trading system is stability and that greater harmonization or coordination of trade policies among the major economies will increase global stability and, thereby, global welfare. In *Governments and Corporations in a Shrinking World: Trade and Innovation Policies in the United States, Europe and Japan* (N.Y., N.Y., Council of Foreign Relations Press, 1990)

[3] Mancur Olson, "The productivity slowdown, the oil shock, and the real cycle," *Journal of Economic Perspectives* (Fall, 1988), pp. 43-69.

[4] *The New York Times* headlined a story on book publishing in 1989 that signalled a cultural shift with the end of the Reagan presidency: "In books, greed is out, environment is in."

[5] Benjamin Friedman, "Financial fragility and the policy dilemma", *Challenge* (July/August, 1990). Professor Freidman elaborates on this theme in an interview about his book, *Day of Reckoning: The Consequences of American Economic Policy under Reagan and After*, (N.Y., Random House, 1988).

[6] Fred Bergsten, Director of the Washington-based Institute for International Economics, reflects this line of thought when he notes that: "Today, given the emerging tripolar structure of the world economy, it's not easy for the United States to take the

lead unilaterally. There will have to be a more collective tripolar management. . . . The three economic powers certainly have a history of cooperation on economic issues, although not necessarily one of putting together a stable system. At least they got together to avoid crises and total breakdown. . . . We need to get back to global negotiations on a new world monetary system, as well as on trade, international investment, and policy coordination. . . . (recognizing that) systemic reform takes a long time. "A new big three to manage the world economy," *Challenge* (November-December 1990).

[7] Flora Lewis, "Japan joining the world?" and "Japan's moral crossroads," *New York Times* (7 May and 11 May, 1986). She added, "those who think beyond method, such as tax reform aimed at reducing the incentive to save or increasing government spending, talk of forcing a change of society (that) could be as great as the change brought by America's Commodore Perry, who battered open Fortress Japan and led to the 19th century renewal of the Meiji Emperor's supremacy, or by General Douglas MacArthur's occupation regime. . ."

[8] "Japanese finance: falling apples," *The Economist* (8 December, 1990), p.3, as part of a special feature section entitled, "Survey of Japanese finance: downbeat."

[9] To judge by the United States/Canada Free Trade Agreement, the scope goes far beyond trade (to include rights with respect to oil, water and other resources) and, in the final analysis, has the aim (from the United States perspective) of easing its adverse trade balances. It has, after more than a year of operation, succeeded with Canada's positive trade balance with the United States shrinking dramatically. The current target is Mexico and then the rest of Latin America where cheap labour is the critical factor and, with respect to some of the countries, oil. See M. Miller, "El Acuerdo de Libre Comercio entre Canada y los Estados Unidos: lecciones para América Latina," *Integracion latinoamericana*, revista mensual del Instituto para la Integración de America Latina (INTAL), Buenos Aires (enero-febero 1990), pp.24-34.

[10] Bergsten, ibid, p.24; Robert Reich: "Commentary on 'Globalization and the Nation-state", *Review '90, Outlook '91* (Ottawa, North-South Institute, 1991), p.21: "Among the most important new issues is direct investment....Some sort of agreement on appropriate strategies, on inducements and even on appropriate steps when a nation wants to thwart investment, is desperately needed."

Part III

Chapter 6
[1] In an interview published in the *New Environment*, premier issue, Toronto, 1990.

[2] A United States government report, *National Energy Strategy, Interim Report (Compilation of Public Comments)*, has recorded testimony from various governmental and non-governmental parties about the estimated costs, observing that these are necessarily very tentative since such factors as emission-control technologies are not yet well developed and research costs and the findings of the research are even more indeterminate. See also P.Hoeller, A. Dean and J. Nicolaisen, "A survey of studies of the costs of reducing greenhouse-gas emissions," *OECD Working paper* No. 89, Paris, 1991.

[3] Jim Mac Neill, et al. *Beyond Interdependence: The Meshing of the World's Economy and the Earth's Ecology* (N.Y. Trilateral Commission, 1991). These estimates are derived from studies by McKinsey and Co. and other sources, many of which were prepared for the Brundtland Commission. They cite other estimates as amounting to the equivalent of one to five per cent of the United States GNP for the United States programme alone.

[4] Jeremy Rivkin in an article entitled, "Put the 'green dividend' to work on tomorrow," *International Herald Tribune*, 9 May, 1990. The following items are included in this estimate: $110 billion for cleaning up the worst hazardous waste sites of which $30 billion is for radioactive waste alone, about $40 billion to reduce acid rain emissions, $100 billion to implement the Clean Air Act, $7 billion for reclaiming strip-mine lands.

[5] Professor William D. Nordhaus, "Greenhouse economics: count before you leap," *The Economist* (7 July, 1990). These effects do not, however, take into account the random occurrence of catastrophic events. Only with some basis for establishing the probability of such events, is there an actuarial foundation for calculating what "climate insurance" should cost.

[6] The subtler advertising that goes under public relations takes the form of Mobil sponsoring Masterpiece Theatre and public policy "think-pieces" in the op-ed pages of *The New York Times*, Exxon sponsoring other public broadcasting programmes such as the McNeill/Lehrer Report, and Olympic competitive events shown on TV networks. These companies thereby get to reach audiences inexpensively through the guise of a sponsorship ("charitable") contribution rather than paying straight advertising rates when they can direct their tax-deductible sponsorship to specific programmes that publicly acknowledge their contribution. It is a process that becomes a form of subliminal advertising, portraying the companies as exercising good citizenry. It reinforces what William Ruckelhaus, former director of the Environmental Protection Agency of the United States, called "the culture of unsustainability."

[7] Paul Klugman, "Proposals for international debt reform," *International Debt and the Developing Countries, a World Bank Symposium*, (Washington, D.C., World Bank), p. 92.

[8] Amory and Hunter Lovins, in an op-ed article in *The New York Times* of 3 December, 1990, "Make fuel efficiency our gulf strategy," point out that "higher gasoline taxes are a weak incentive to buy an efficient car . . . but the 40-mile-per-gallon difference for cars and light trucks (which is now technically possible and can be made a regulatory requirement and/or can be made an inducement by "feebate" incentives to buy fuel-efficient vehicles) represents more than twice America's imports from the Gulf (which when all costs of the military operation are calculated) now costs in excess of $100 a barrel."

[9] In a paper entitled, "Energy and the sustainable society," prepared for the *Globe 90 Conference*, the Canadian physicist, Fred Knelman, notes and decries the governmental bias towards subsidization of research for conventional energy technologies. To meet "the distortion of the energy market" he proposes "counter-distortions and reversal of role-playing on the part of energy suppliers.. (by means of granting credit) for durability, life cycle cost, efficiency and reduced social and environmental debt through a combination of incentives and disincentives, tax credits and penalties that can catalyze the transition towards environmentally-benign energy technologies. He cites the record in Canada which shows cuts made by the Canadian government in research on passive solar heating and other renewable energy technologies, and cuts in energy conservation programmes as well as cancellation of oil substitution and home insulation programmes, while, at the same time, the financial support for the oil, gas and nuclear industries increased from levels that were already very high.

[10] Christopher Flavin, in Worldwatch report, *State of the World-1990*, cites a count of 130 bills introduced into 22 United States state legislatures in the first half of 1989. He provides a useful list of proposals now being debated in various national legislative bodies, p.33.

[11] "Sustainable development: an overview", in Development, Special Issue, *"Sustainable Development: From Theory to Practise"* (February, 1989).

[12] A recent study of the changing patterns of trade by I. Walter and J.H. Loudon, "Environmental costs and the patters of North-South trade," has shown that the products these developing countries have been exporting have tended to be characterized by "higher than average environmental and resource-damage costs." Cited in *Our Common Future*, p. 80.

[13] "By early 1985, UNCTAD's commodity price index was 30 per cent below the 1980 average. . . . These countries are turning the terms of trade against themselves,

earning less while exporting more, (leading) to cases of unsustainable overuse of the natural resource base." *Our Common Future*, p. 80. While the commodity price index has since made a slight recovery, many of the exportable commodities on which the developing countries depend for their foreign exchange have not as yet recovered.

Part IV

Chapter 7

[1] Related by Professor Trygve Haavelmo, University of Norway, in a submission to *Economic Policies for Sustainable Development* (Asian Development Bank, 1990).

[2] "Managing the debt crisis in the 1990s: the resumption of sustained economic growth should be the priority", *Finance & Development* (June, 1990), p.24 ,World Bank and IMF, Washington, D.C. The authors, at the time of publication, were respectively, Vice President, Economics Department and staff member of that department.

[3] *WRI Issues and Ideas*, (Washington, D.C., World Resources Institute, January 1990).

[4] Professor David Bigman, "A plan to end LDC debt and save the environment too", *Challenge* (July/August 1990), p.34. Referring to the Brady Plan and variants thereof, he observed, "few rational individuals are going to put their money on this lemon, and others are not likely to put enough money to make any noticeable difference."

[5] For a catalogue listing and description of the items on the "market-based menu," see the World Bank's pamphlet, *Market-Based Menu Approach*, prepared by the Bank's Debt Management and Financial Services Department (January 1988).

For an earlier (1985) treatment of this subject, see Donald R. Lessard and John Williamson, *Financial Intermediation Beyond the Debt Crisis*, (especially Chapter 4, "Financial instruments," pp. 49-88, (Washington, D.C., Institute for International Economics, September 1985).

[6] David L. Bock, former Director of the World Bank's Debt Management and Financial Advisory Services Department, "The Bank's role in resolving the debt crisis," *Finance & Development* (June 1988), pp. 7–8. He hedged this statement with the phrase, "wherever the strength of adjustment programmes and the countries' circumstances warrant such support."

[7] The Commission on International Development, *Partners in Development*, chaired by Lester B. Pearson (N.Y., Praeger, 1969), pp. 74-75, 153, 164-65.

[8] Dr. Dragoslav Avramovic, one of the authors of the Pearson Report, has suggested that "the rate to aim at should be around 2 per cent per annum in real terms, (which is still higher than) the historically typical real interest rate. "The source cited by Dr.

Avramovic is *The Annual Report of the Council of Economic Adviser*, Washington, D.C., (2 February, 1983). He goes on to note that according to the *Annual Report of the Bank for International Settlements* (June 1983), "the average real rate in the post-war period 1963-1982 in five leading countries — the United States, the United Kingdom, Japan, the Federal Republic of Germany and Switzerland — was lower, 1.1 per cent per annum" "Interest rates, debts and international policy", *Trade and Development*, an UNCTAD Review, 5 November, 1984, pp. 361 and 363. Professor Rudiger Dornbusch has calculated that during the period from 1930-80, the real rate of United States government bonds was less than 2 per cent. As already noted, the authors of the Pearson Report, Partners in Development, suggested as early as 1969 that rates for official development assistance loans be "no more than 2 per cent with a maturity of between 25 and 40 years with grace periods of from 7 to 10 years."

For a convenient summary listing on the range of estimates, see M. Guerguil, "The international financial crisis: diagnoses and prescriptions," *CEPAL Review* (December 1984), p. 166.

[9] Both proposals are presented in *The Economist*. Zombanakis' proposal is contained in his article entitled, "The international debt threat: a way to avoid a crash," (30 April, 1983); Sir Harold Lever's proposal is set out in "The international debt threat: a concerted way out," (9 July, 1983) and in the book he co-authored with Christopher Huhne, *Debt and Danger - The World Financial Crisis* (Boston, Atlantic Monthly Press, 1986).

[10] Professor Kenen attempts to answer the objections of Bulow and Rogoff in his article entitled, "Organizing debt relief: the need for a new institution," *Journal of Economic Perspectives* (Winter 1989). He challenges the Bulow and Rogoff argument against a facility to facilitate debt buybacks and other debt relief measures on the grounds that their assumptions are faulty when they assert that (1) debtors and creditors hold identical views about the future, and (2) there are existing unexploited investment opportunities in the debtor country that are prejudiced by the allocation of funds for debt reduction schemes.

[11] Professor Jeffery Sachs, "A strategy for efficient debt reduction," *Journal of Economic Perspectives* (Winter 1989), pp.19-29.

[12] This scheme offered the holders of Mexican debt an opportunity to trade the Mexican debt on their books in exchange for 20-year United States Treasury zero-coupon bonds at a discount with Mexico reserving the right to reject unacceptably low bids. Most of the major creditors refused to submit to the debt/bond conversions at the prices prevailing on the secondary market. Thus, Mexico was able to accept only $3.67 billion in bids from banks.

[13] The buyback option is an important part of the Brady Plan, but it is subject to a serious drawback in as much as the repurchase pushes up the secondary market value. In the case of Bolivia, in March 1988 it bought back about half of its $670 million debt when the market value was 6 cents, but on spending $34 million to buy back $308 million of its debt the remaining debt rose in value to 11 cents for a market value of $40 million.

[14] Leonard Silk, the economics editor of *The New York Times*, ventured the most plausible hypothesis to explain the seemingly paradoxical United States behaviour in rebuffing earlier Japanese initiatives and then endorsing their key feature of using the IFIs as guarantors: "The Administration is unwilling to see its role as world leader and lender taken over by the Japanese who have emerged as the world's strongest financial power. The United States, on other occasions, has urged Japan to use its vast resources to help solve the world's problems, but when the Japanese offered their debt plan in Berlin, the Americans opposed vehemently. Similarly, the United States opposed the idea of the managing director of the IMF, Michel Camdessus, that the burden of the dollar as a reserve currency might be eased if a greater role were given to special drawing rights (SDRs), the internationally created money; *apparently, the Administration is fearful of seeing the SDR dilute the role of the dollar.*" (italics added)

"A strident United States at I.M.F. talks, *The New York Times*, 30 September, 1988. Mr Silk goes on to observe that "if the United States hopes to retain its leadership role in the world, it will have to do two things: work with others to develop the resources required to hold the world economy together, and face up to the urgency of fiscal actions to repair its own heavily indebted position, at home and abroad."

[15] Masaru Tamamoto, "Japan's search for a world role: The Japan that can say yes". *World Policy Journal* (Summer 1990), p. 514.

[16] For an elaboration of the procedures, the regulatory legislation and the policies and history of the process, see World Bank, *World Development Report 1987*, pp. 22-23, Box 2.2; and UNCTAD's *Trade and Development Report 1986*, Box 7.

[17] For a detailed assessment of the Chilean case, see F. Larrain and A. Velasco, *Can Swaps Solve the Debt Crisis? Lessons from the Chilean Experience*, Princeton Studies in International Finance #69, 1989.

[18] *Financial Intermediation beyond the Debt Crisis* (Washington, D.C., Institute of International Economics, 1985). They estimate an investment flow of about $10 billion per year might be achieved through this means.

[19] *Exchange Participation Notes: An Approach to the International Financial Crisis* (Washington, D.C., Georgetown University Center for Strategic and International Studies) (mimeo), and in *The Economist* (18 February, 1983).

Close variants are set forth by Allan H. Meltzer, "A Way to Defuse the World Debt Bomb," *Fortune* (28 November, 1983), and Christine Bogdanowicz-Bindert, "Debt beyond the quick fix," *Third World Quarterly* (October 1983).

[20] This scheme has been put forward by the Director of the French Scientific Research Council, Professor Moise Ikonicoff, in an article in *Le Monde* of 2 August, 1988, entitled, "Dette ou Democratie? The idea of this debt/local currency swap evokes memories of the United States food programme called P.L. 480 where the United States was "paid" in local currency that was at the disposition of the United States government for use in that country. This proposal would be limited in its scale by the availability of surplus food and of other products and by its adverse impact on the farmers in the debtor country who might be affected.

[21] Andrew Whitley, *Financial Times (U.K.)* , (28 August, 1985).

Chapter 8

[1] Peter Passell, "Washington offers mountain of debt to save forests: plan could offer big increase in funds for Latin conservation," *The New York Times* (22 January, 1991).

[2] Professor David Bigman, "A Plan to end the LDC debt and save the environment too," *Challenge* (July/August 1989), pp.33-37. The more detailed elements of the plan are set out in Annex E.

[3] Paul Knox, "Should Brazil pay for first world sins?," *The Globe & Mail (Toronto)* (2 March, 1989).

[4] Reported by Marlisle Simons, "The Amazon Forest: Brazil wants its dams, but at what cost?", *The New York Times* (12 March, 1989).

[5] The latest state of play of this debt-for-nature swapping idea is summarized in *The Economist*, (6 August, 1988), "Greensback Debt," p. 62-63.

[6] *The International Conservation Financing Project* (Washington,D.C., World Resources Institute, 1989).

[7] In March 1991 the World Bank's management recommended that its Board grant about $33 million from its fiscal 1990 surplus or "profit" for the establishment of a trust fund for the Global Environment Facility. The GEF is a tripartite arrangement between the World Bank, UNEP and UNDP. In the words of Ernest Stern, a senior Vice President of the World Bank, this is "a coordinated approach to environmental management. The GEF is an umbrella structure which permits the bank to accept funds in trust to assist developing countries with projects affecting the global environment." Two trust funds are envisaged at the outset. The first is an ozone projects trust fund to help implement the Montreal Protocol on the Protection of the Ozone

Layer. The second is a pilot facility called the Global Environment Trust Fund for which commitments of about $1.2 billion have been received to be used over a three-year period. It will provide concessional funds to developing countries for projects that will reduce activities having undesirable impact on the global environment or promoting or enhancing biodiversity and other desirable environmental goals. To provide the best available information and advice, the establishment of a Scientific and Technical Panel is envisaged.

"The global environment facility," *The Bank's World* (April 1991), pp. 9 - 10.

[8] All of these are phrases that have been used by such spokesmen for "the movement" as William Ruckelhaus, Maurice Strong, and Jim MacNeill, all of whom have had - and still have - close relationships with institutions at the national and international levels of governance.

[9] William Ruckelhaus, ibid.

[10] Robert D. Hamrin, *Policy Control Options for A Comparative Air Pollution Study of Urban Areas*, World Bank Environment Working Paper, No. 28, (April 1990), p.1.

[11] Barrett Hardin, *The Tragedy of the Commons*, and Ezra Mishan, "Economic and political obstacles to environmental sanity," *National Westminster Bank Quarterly Review* (May 1990).

[12] William U. Chandler, *Energy Productivity: Key to Environmental Protection and Economic Progress*, Worldwatch Paper No. 63, January 1985, p.43. Chandler observes that "the overall conservation response could have been greater but the United States was slow to decontrol oil prices, still controls the price of half of all natural gas used, and prices electric power at average costs which are typically below the cost of new power." He cites the experience of Canada and other countries, noting that Canada's energy demand in 1982 was a third lower than would have been expected if pre-1974 trends had prevailed and that two-thirds of this reduction can be attributed to higher energy prices. After reviewing the pricing practices in a host of other countries, Chandler observes that "energy scarcity alone (as reflected in higher prices) may not be enough to encourage a level of conservation measures consistent with a low energy future."

[13] Chandler, op. cit., pp. 43-49. In a section entitled "Preparing for an energy efficient future," he cites various studies indicating that because of policies related to maintaining the "profitability" or to limiting the subsidies of parastatal utilities or for policy reasons related to income distribution, "the role of markets in determining energy prices (continues to) diminish."

[14] For a succinct treatment of this tax issue, see Paul Wallich and Elizabeth Corcoran, "Carbon levies," *Scientific American Special Issue: Energy for Planet Earth* (September 1990), p. 171. Also C. Flavin, op.cit., p.28-29.

[15] T. Tietenberg, "Using Economic Incentives to maintain our environment," *Challenge* (March-April, 1990). He cautions, however, that "transforming an existing industrial structure to reposition it for the future will be an expensive proposition."

[16] Marc J. Roberts, "On reforming economic growth," *Daedalus, Special Issue: The No-Growth Society* (Fall, 1974), p.123. There are very few who would advocate a "no-growth" objective as a desirable one. One articulate economist who espouses this view is E. J. Mishan: *The Costs of Economic Growth* (Penguin, 1980), and "Ills, Bads, and Disamenities: The Wages of Growth," *Daedalus Special Issue: The No-Growth Society* (Fall 1974).

Chapter 9

[1] "Building a bridge of hope to our Latin neighbours," *Washington Post* (24 June, 1985).

[2] "Interest rates, debts and international policy", *Trade & Development: An UNCTAD Review*, No. 5, 1984.

[3] Peru's current economic plight with rampant inflation and severely depleted foreign exchange reserves and an almost complete cut-off of credit can be attributed only in part to its strong stand on the debt issue. A large part of the blame can be placed on grave mistakes in its economic management and its internal civil strife.

[4] *Notes on the Provision of Debt Relief*, a paper prepared for the North/South Roundtable, New York, 13 December, 1985. He added that neither debt forgiveness "nor interest rates have been reduced by more than modest cuts in spreads." Since then there has been some movement on both aspects.

[5] See Angus Maddison, *Two Crises: Latin America and Asia 1929-38 and 1973-83* (Paris, OECD Development Centre, 1985).

[6] For some relevant commentary on this point see David Crane, "History does give clues how to solve the debt crisis," *The Toronto Star* (8 June, 1988); and Anatole Kaletsky, *The Costs of Default*, (New York: Twentieth Century Fund, 1985); Chandra S. Hardy, *Rescheduling Developing Countries Debts, 1956-1981: Lessons and Recommendations*, Monograph 15, (Washington, D.C.: Overseas Development Council, June 1982), p. 41; and John Maynard Keynes' 1919 classic, *The Economic Consequences of the Peace.*, which contains some insightful observations on this theme.

[7] His experience as an advisor to the Bolivian and Polish Governments may have influenced his specific recommendation that the scale of the interest forgiveness be set at five years for 35 countries. His list of countries includes all Latin American countries except the major debtors, all sub-Saharan African countries and the Philippines. He estimates the commercial bank creditors would have to lose approximately $6 billion and United States banks would face a reduction of capital of about 8 per cent. *World Economic Problems.*, op.cit., p.191-2. and "The IMF and the developing country debt crisis," *Harvard International Review* (Winter 1990), pp.14-17.

[8] The United States forgiveness initiative regarding Poland amounted to 70 per cent of its $3-8 billion debt, but the 50 per cent forgiveness by other official creditors applies to $33 billion. The Japanese opposition was based not on this asymmetry but on an issue of principle. The Japanese Ministry of Finance indicated its displeasure at this pressure by refusing to approve a $500 million loan that had already been promised by the Japanese Prime Minister. The Japanese position was characterized by a United States official as "unconscionable" and "coldly financial." The Japanese have countered by proposing an easing of the debt burden by an increase of special drawing rights through the IMF to obviate the geo-political factor in debt relief.

[9] *The Washington Post*, 10 March, 1986. He also suggested "capping repayments at 25 per cent of exports." The average discount is now 50 per cent.

Part V

[1] *International Economic and World Order*, the Motta Lecture, Washington, 24 Sept, 1984. Reprinted in op-ed page of the Washington Post, "International trade: it's time to change the rules of the game" (22 Nov, 1984).

[2] "The cost of keeping cool", *The Economist* (26 January, 1991), p.59. The article reviews two recent studies, "A Survey of studies of the costs of reducing greenhouse-gas emissions", by P. Hoeller, A. Dean & J Nicolaisen, OECD *Working Paper No. 89*, and The International Incidence of carbon taxes", by J.Walley and R. Wigle, Univ. of Western Ontario.

Chapter 10

[3] Professor Richard Cooper, "A monetary system for the future," *Foreign Affairs* (Fall 1984). There are some, such as Anthony Solomon, formerly a governor of the Federal Reserve Bank of New York, who dispute the designation of "system" to this arrangement or agreement since it did not have an enforcement provision, that is, it was based on "an understanding."

[4] Professor Gerald K. Heilleiner, "An agenda for a new Bretton Woods," *Foreign Policy Journal* (Winter 1984), p.367.

[5] The central banks of 19 countries issue the statistics on currency trading, making an effort to avoid double-counting so far as possible. Thus the numbers for 1989 of $431.1 billion a day, and over $500 billion for 1990 (up from $196.5 billion in 1986), are to be treated as rough approximations. The trends are, however, indicative of a rate of increase that, according to one report, "even awed central bank officials."

In an article in *International Development Review* (Winter 1989/90) entitled, "The market no one could control," by Sandra Salmans and Kevin Rafferty, the authors quote a Tokyo financial analyst: "The sums the central banks have been pouring in are peanuts compared to what the big players have at their disposal, as, for example, the 22 giant Japanese life insurance companies that have about $300 billion between them to put into foreign currency investments."

And another currency dealer declares, "when it gets its head, the market tends to run away, and in such circumstances the efforts of Governments to influence the market don't make much sense."

[6] See Sandra Salmans and Kevin Rafferty, "The market no one could control," *International Development Review* (Winter 1989), pp. 22-26.

[7] Purchasing power parity (PPP) is believed to underlie the movement of exchange rates towards an equilibrium relationship to each other over the long-term since it equates the prices of internationally traded goods. The rates would move, as well, in line with relative inflation rates. However, over the short term, the factor of capital movements in response to differentials in interest rates and expectations about future movements of exchange rates makes the PPP less of a force, especially as the capital movements are about 20 to 25 times larger in the global economic/ financial picture.

[8] Stephen Marglin and Juliet Schor, ed., *The Golden Age of Capitalism: Reinterpreting the Postwar Experience* (London, Clarendon Press, 1990).

[9] Professor C.P. Kindleberger "International public goods without international government," *The American Economic Review* (March 1986).

[10] "International adjustments 1985-90: What have we learned?: a review of an IIE conference, October, 1990," *International Economic Insights* (Washington, D.C., Institute for International Economics, November/December 1990)

[11] This raises the question of calculating trade balances in terms of ownership, by which measure the United States trade deficit of $144 billion in 1986 becomes a surplus of $14 billion. This points to the decreased relevance of nation-states as world economic and financial integration proceeds at an unprecedented speed. "The state of the nation-state," *The Economist*, (22 December, 1990), pp.43-46.

See also Robert Reich, "The real economy," The Atlantic (February 1991), pp.35-52.

[12] *World Economic Summits: The Role of Representative Groups in the Governance of the World Economy*, WIDER Study Group Series No. 4, Helsinki,1989, p.11. The Group of Five has since become the Group of Seven when Italy and Canada were invited into that exclusive club.

[13] Reported in *Washington Post*, (12 March, 1986). The committee report characterized the prevailing system governing exchange rates as a "nonsystem," and "broke" and recommended an international monetary conference, one objective of which would be to consider fixing it with an agreement to establish a target zone approach.

[14] Reported in a Reuters report from Brasilia, "Mitterand backs Brazil on debt issue," *International Herald Tribune* (October 18, 1985). President Mitterand is also quoted as stating that "developing country debtors should not have to repay at the cost of unemployment and recession; it is indefensible that developing countries be left with no other options than recession and stagnation over the next 15 to 20 years."

[15] Reported in *The New York Times*, (10 May, 1983).

[16] *The Reform of the International Monetary and Financial System: Revised Programme of Action*, Intergovernmental Group of 24 on International Monetary Affairs, Task Force on Reform of the International Monetary and Financial System, 2 September, 1983.

[17] "Build a new economic stability," *The Wall Street Journal* (9 August, 1985). See also, "A new chance for the economy," *New York Review of Books* (24 April, 1986).

[18] "Muldoon Outlines Priorities of a Second Bretton Woods: Wants Global Monetary Structure Revamped," *The Washington Post*, (26 February, 1984).

[19] Professor Gerald Helleiner, "An agenda for a new Bretton Woods," *Foreign Policy Journal* (Winter 1984), p.374. In this article he summarizes the ideas contained in the 1983 Commonwealth Secretariat report *Toward a new Bretton Woods*. He notes that "process must begin with or without the United States . . . (but) to be sure, if negotiations are to succeed they must eventually include the United States."

[20] Op.cit., p. 15.

[21] Interview in *Challenge* (November/December 1990). "Recent history," he went on, "leads one to be fairly optimistic that a tripolar world can evolve in a cooperative and harmonious way, but the longer sweep of history leads to a pessimistic outlook, the world never having been managed successfully by a committee of nations." The concept underlying the word "management" is, of course, in need of clarification with regard to scope. Presumably, management refers to key financial aspects that need the cooperation of all the major parties to improve on the present situation with its volatility, fragility, etc.

[11] "International Monetary Indiscipline and the Debt Problem," p. 173.

[12] *International Economic and World Order*, op.cit.

Chapter 11

[1] OECD's *1990 Economic Outlook*. At the same time it was noted that in the OECD countries total savings as a percentage of GNP are far below the average levels of the 1960s and 1970s. For a concise popular treatment of this aspect of the global picture, see James Fallows, "Getting along with Japan," *The Atlantic Monthly* (December 1989), pp.53-64, and A. Lans Bovenberg, "Why has United States personal saving declined?," *Finance and Development* (June 1990), pp.10-11.

[2] "The bane of nations," *The New York Times* (28 November, 1990), op-ed page. The focus of the column is on the European movement to a common market, in the course of which she observes apropos France that "it is a deep wrench for a proud old nation, but the French realize they have no choice: . . . they cannot assert sovereignty separately." It is the illusion that some nations have on this score that is "the bane" to which she refers. This, of course, applies to the United States in the global context.

[3] The reasons for these divergent patterns of trade and capital movements and for their undesirable impact on global real interest rates can be found, in large part, in an examination of United States policies. Although those policies have deep-seated underlying causes, it may suffice to confine the analysis to the policies themselves. On this score, the comments of Hans-Werner Simm (in a paper entitled "American economic policy and the international debt crisis," National Bureau of Economic Research Working Paper 3532, (December 1990) are appropros: "The combined effects of a very restrictive monetary policy, an exceptionally expansionary budget policy and a massive investment incentive scheme led to a truly explosive increase in American real interest rates." (p.22). He added: "As a result of American policy the driving forces of economic growth were shifted away from the less developed countries and the rest of the world to the U.S.A."

[4] For a concise broad-brush synopsis of the dynamics of the process of European integration, see Sylvia Ostry, "Learning the real lessons from Europe," *The Globe & Mail* (Toronto), (7 February, 1991.

[5] C.M. Aho and B. Stokes, "The year the world economy turned," *Foreign Affairs* issue entitled, *America and the World 1990-91*, Vol. 70, No.1, 1991, pp. 172-3. The authors observe that "greater symmetry among the major economies has strengthened the case for closer economic policy co-ordination" and use words such as "externally imposed," "enforce" and "dictate."

[6] Aho and Stokes, *op.cit.*, p. 176. The authors go on to suggest "new procedures to ensure follow-up and monitoring of economic summit agreements," the establishment of "a permanent secretariat to scrutinize economic summit pledges" and the creation of "a new World Trade Organization as a successor to GATT to implement the results of the Uruguay Round and help in the adoption of new rules on trade and investment."

[7] Of the total lending programme a larger percentage is being directed towards quick-disbursing "structural adjustment" loans and towards the poorer, most hard-pressed debtor countries, particularly those in sub-Saharan Africa who have been the beneficiaries of targeted programmes such as the Special Facility for sub-Saharan Africa administered by the World Bank and the Enhanced Structural Adjustment Facility of the IMF. Together these facilities are channelling an additional $2 billion annually to the low-income African countries. As well, concessional lending through the World Bank's "soft window," IDA, has increased with the sub-Saharan African percentage increasing from about one third to about one half of IDA's concessionary funding. Much of this pledged funding has been a diversion from bilateral aid, not an addition to the normal ODA programmes.

[8] In terms of the percentage of GNP devoted to aid, Japan still ranks below many other nations such as the Scandinavian countries, Holland and France. The Japanese Government announced a commitment to recycle $30 billion in the form of untied public and private funds to the developing countries over the next several years through its own aid programme, the World Bank, the Asian Development Bank, the Inter-American Development Bank and through special funds and co-financing arrangements.

[9] "The transformation of United States banking and economic instability: a systemic dilemma," *Hearings before the Congressional Committee on Banking, Finance and Urban Affairs* (6 April, 1977), p. 8.

[10] "Building a bridge of hope to our Latin neighbors," *The Washington Post*, 24 June, 1985.

[11] "For a Japanese equivalent of the Marshall Plan," *The Washington Post* (3 May, 1986). See also, "A costlier yen is not enough," *The New York Times* editorial, (7 April, 1986).

[12] "The new chance for the economy," *New York Review of Books*, (24 April, 1986), pp. 20 and 21.

[13] "Using its surpluses to advantage: a proposal for enhancing Japanese and world security," *Nihon Keizai Shinbun*, (2 July, 1986). Dr. Okita's proposal is also contained in the WIDER report of April of that year that he authored with Arjun Sengupta and

Lal Jayawardena. Its main thrust would have Japan's surplus divided three ways: (1) to sustain the United States economy that has "turned into an economic 'black hole' sucking in savings from Japan, Europe and elsewhere" and by virtue of "its massive fiscal and trade deficits, (cannot be expected) to act as the mover for world economic growth," (2) to stimulate domestic demand, and (3) promoting economic growth in the developing and debtor countries that needs long-term low-interest capital.

[14] *Developing Country Debts in the mid-1980s: Fact, Theory and Policy*, paper submitted to the 48th Pugwash Symposium on Foreign Debts and International Stability, Lima, Peru, (Feb 1987). Sidney Dell has also advanced a similar proposal in an article entitled, "The Case for World Economic Recovery", *United Nations Journal of Development Planning*, No. 14, 1984, p.23.

[15] With a stock of some 20 billion, an increase of 10 to 15% would amount to about $3 billion, an amount that William Cline notes "would not go far even if the German concern about inflationary consequences were overcome and the distribution of new SDRs were concentrated on debtor countries rather than in proportion to IMF quotas as in the past". *World Development Problems*, p. 177.

[16] *North-South: A Programme for Survival* The Report of the Independent Commission on International Development Issues (Cambridge, Mass., The MIT Press, 1980).

[17] R. Dobell and T. Parson, "A world development fund", *Policy Options Politiques* (December 1988), pp.6-8. The article discusses the issue of funding and addresses the objections of skeptics.

[18] Michael Manley, *Global Challenge — From Crisis to Co-operation: Breaking the North-South Stalemate* (London, Pan Books, 1985), p. 207. The report goes on to state that "we should be spending a trillion dollars a year more than now on additional resources to sustain global development and transform the current global crisis."

[19] Ruth Leger Sivard, *World Military and Social Expenditures*, (Washington, D.C. World Priorities, 1989).

[20] Clyde Prestowitz and Robert Jerome, "GATT's not where it's at," *The New York Times* (6 December, 1990).

[21] "The year the world turned," Vol. 70, No. 1, 1991, p. 176.

[22] "The state of the nation-state", *ibid.* p.46.

Chapter 12
[1] *Our Common Future* (Oxford, Oxford Univ. Press, 1987), Chapter 10, "Managing the commons," pp. 261-289.

[2] Like CGIAR, the new institution would be a financing arrangement for raising and disbursing funds for research, but in this case, to accelerate the development of "stand alone" energy sources that are especially appropriate for the rural sectors and would therefore take pressure off the ecologically damaging dependence on fuelwood. See Jim MacNeill, David Runnalls and John Cox, *CIDA and Sustainable Development*, (Ottawa, IRPP, 1989), especially page 28 and 29 for an elaboration of the proposal. See also the programme of action of the *Report of the United Nations Conference on New and Renewable Sources of Energy*, (N.Y., United Nations, 1982).

[3] As is being undertaken by the Global Environment Facility. See footnote 8-7.

[4] Despite the pledges made in a solemn, well-publicized ceremony after almost a year had elapsed, four of the 53 countries that signed the agreement had paid their full share of the $54 million in annual contributions to the newly-established funds. The $3 million pledged by the Nordic countries were paid early, the rest delayed to a point where UNEP's Executive Director, Mostafa Tolba, expressed exasperation and concern.

[5] Philip Shabecoff, in an article entitled "A 'Marshall Plan' for the environment," *The New York Times* (3 May, 1990) reports on the proposals adopted at a Washington conference of legislators from 42 countries. The ones pertaining to the developing countries envisaged a substantial allocation of aid funds for environmental-enhancing projects and programmes through a Marshall Plan type of programme or by establishment of a "Bank for Sustainable Development".

See also J. McNeill et al. *Beyond Interdependence: The Meshing of the World's Economy and the Earth's Ecology* (N.Y., A task force report to the Trilateral Commission, 1991).

[6] See Jeremy Warford, *Environment, Growth and Development*, (Washington, D.C., The Development Committee, World Bank and IMF, 1987), especially the chapters entitled "National policies and instruments for environmental management" and "An agenda for action," pp. 17-33. Also, Robert Repetto, *Economic Policy Reform for Natural Resource Conservation*, World Bank Environment Department Working Paper, No. 4, May 1988. Also D. Pearce, *Environmental Policy Benefits: Monetary Evaluation* (Paris, OECD, 1989).

[7] Jeremy Rivkin in an article entitled, "Put the 'green dividend' to work on tomorrow," *international Herald Tribune* (9 May, 1990) See also, F. Knelman, op.cit., Appendix A: "Global problems need global solutions."

[8] D. Helm and D.Pearce op.cit. believe that "the issue of 'side payments' will dominate the 1992 United Nations Environment Conference in Brazil." The analysis rests heavily on the options and outcomes of the situation found in the "Prisoners' Dilemma" and in the "Problem of the Commons," (the atmosphere being a global

commons measured by a quality index), both of which provide useful analytic analogues for identifying the trade-offs from cooperative and non-cooperative actions and for judging the preferred outcomes.

In another article in the same issue, D. Dasgupta writes on another aspect of the same issue:

[9] P. Dasgupta, "The environment as a commodity", *Oxford Review of Economic Policy*, vol. 6/1, p.55

Chapter 13

[1] Sidney Dell, "The international monetary system: some reflections on institutional reform," *Crisis of the '80s*, ed. Khadija Haq, (Washington, D.C., North-South Roundtable, S.I.D., 1984).

[2] Before 1982 less than 10 per cent of the World Bank loans were programme loans as contrasted with project-based loans. Until the mid-1980s, the elapsed time from departure of an appraisal mission to a board presentation ranged from 11 weeks to over 200, with the median being over 40. Counting all the time involved, the median staff weeks required was in excess of 60. - "World Bank lending approaches," *World Bank News*, (April 1986), p.9. Also V. Baum, *The Project Cycle*, (Washington, D.C., World Bank, 1975).

[3] These loans were designed to provide foreign exchange to meet emergency needs for spare parts and maintenance to keep existing projects operational despite the severe shortage of foreign exchange, but it was limited in total amount to only $500 million during a trial two-year period. This type of loan played a critically important role in breaking bottlenecks in over 250 projects threatened by foreign exchange shortages and enabled additional disbursements to be made amounting to almost $5 billion on projects in process.

[4] This can be illustrated with the example of the outcome of petrocycling when lending and borrowing were carried to a point of crisis: "...loan pushing and subsequent pulling led to all lenders being on the run (at which time) the borrowing country has nowhere to borrow and no one can be repaid. Bankers forgot the sections in their elementary economics courses dealing with the fallacies of composition." M.I.T. Prof. Lance Taylor, "The theory and practise of developing country debt: an informal guide for the perplexed," *Journal of Development Planning, No. 16,* (N.Y., United Nations,1985), p.205.

[5] Jeremy Warford, and Zeinab Partow, *World Bank Support for the Environment: A Progress Report*, Development Committee Report No. 22, (Washington, D.C. World Bank, September 1989)

[6] Barber Conable, President of the World Bank, "Giving the environment its due at the World Bank," *Environmental Protection Agency Journal* (September 1987), p. 17.

Chapter 14

[1] During the recent past donors have tended to allocate more technical assistance to multilateral lending institutions and to United Nations specialized agencies. In the late 1960s a very low percentage of the regular budgets of the specialized agencies were allocated to technical assistance, but by 1985 the allocations for this purpose amounted to about 20 per cent of the regular budget or about $300 million. The shift with respect to "extra-budgetary" resources is more dramatic. In 1968 the specialized agencies secured about $20 million in trust funds for technical assistance, an amount that comprised about 10 per cent of the UNDP's funds. By 1985 their trust funds exceeded $400 million or almost 70 per cent of UNDP's expenditures in that year. Thus the overall impact is reflected in the decline of UNDP's share of total United Nations funding from 65 per cent in 1968 to about 25 per cent by 1985. The downward trend still continues.

[2] The list includes the United Nations Programme for African Recovery and Development (UNPAARD), the Substantial New Programme of Action (SNPA), the United Nations Trust Fund for Sudano-Sahalian Countries (UNTFSSC), the Special Measures Fund for Least Developed Countries (SMF/LDC), the Special Action Programme for Administration and Management (SAPAM) .

[3] Shiv Kapur et al. NatCAP-*National Technical Cooperation Assessment and Programming: An Initial Review* (N.Y., UNDP, June 1987), mimeo.

[4] In 1981 at the United Nations Conference on Least Developed Countries, UNDP and the World Bank were designated as the agencies responsible for organizing donor meetings for the 36 poorest countries. Consultative Group meetings were to be organized by the World Bank and round table meetings by the UNDP, but the division of labour was not spelt out. Roughly half of these countries opted for the Round Table process. NatCAP is the programme designed to carry the UNDP responsibilities in this regard.

[5] UNCTAD, which has a debt monitoring and financial analysis unit to help third world countries strengthen their debt-related data bases, is seeking UNDP financing. UNITAR has undertaken programmes for training "high-level experts" in debt management. The World Bank also offers a training course in external debt monitoring for "debt office staff" under the auspices of the International Finance Division of the International Economics Department. The option of developing an in-house UNDP capacity to deliver this type of technical assistance does not seem to be under consideration.

[6] *Op.cit.*, p. 24. The report goes on to suggest the long-run objectives and strategy for achieving "genuine institutional reform involving the negotiation of new or amended charters, articles of agreement, conventions; the downgrading or elimination of some organizations, and the strengthening and possibly the merging of others. . . . (as a way of) improving the existing United Nations policy-making system."

[7] *A New United Nations Structure for Global Economic Co-operation*, Report of the Group of Experts on the Structure of the United Nations System, (N.Y., United Nations, 1975). There were also other groups charged with similar tasks, such as the Group on Supplementary Financial Measures arising out of an UNCTAD conference in the mid-1960s and the Committee of Twenty which was formed by the IMF and World Bank to consider reform of the international monetary system and which issued a report entitled, *International Monetary Reform: Documents of the Committee of Twenty on Reform of the International Monetary System and Related Issues* (Washington, D.C., IMF, 1974)

[8] WIDER Study Group Series No. 4, op,cit., p.24. The study contains detailed proposals, particularly in the Appendices by Stephen Marris entitled "A proposal to create the 'group of the non-five'" and by Lal Jayawardena entitled, "Towards improved decision-making in the United Nations system," pp.34-120.

[9] This analogous institution focused on energy and the environment could be tentatively labeled $CGIE^2R$. A feasibility study as to its justification, its funding, its modus operandi and such has been proposed both at the UNCNRSE and at the World Bank. No progress has been made on this idea.

Epilogue

[1] Paul Streeten, Professor Emeritus at Oxford and Boston Universities, in a talk at Harvard University on the subject of "pax Americana" identified three key attributes of hegemonic power, apart from the military: size (so that the economy is crucial to the world's economic operations), a healthy trade balance, and a corresponding strength in not being very dependent on capital imports. The United States, he pointed out, is unable to claim the last two attributes. Reported by Leonard Silk, "Reconstructing the world system," *The New York Times*, (8 May, 1987).

[2] Professor Oran Young in *International Co-operation: Building Regimes for Natural Resource and the Environment* (New York, Cornell University Press, 1989), p. 230, has written of the "windows of opportunity for those concerned with the development of coherent socially desirable regimes," "regimes" being defined as "sets of implicit or explicit principles, norms, rules, and decision-making procedures around which actors' expectations converge in a given area of international relations." The heading of the relevant section of the book is aptly titled: "Seize Opportunities."

ANNEXES

THE CONCEPT OF "CRISIS" AS APPLIED TO THE CURRENT GLOBAL SITUATION

There are various views of the meaning and significance of "crisis." The Greek word from which crisis was derived means decision or "to decide." The *American Heritage Dictionary* defines crisis as "1) a crucial point or situation in the course of anything; turning point, 2) in political, international or economic affairs, an unstable condition in which an abrupt or decisive change is impending, 3) in pathology, a sudden change in the course of an acute disease, either towards improvement or deterioration, 4) in literature, the point in a story or drama in which hostile forces are in the most tense state of opposition."

James O'Connor in *The Meaning of Crisis: A Theoretical Introduction*, (Basil Blackwell, 1987), distinguishes between an "objective" historical process such as, for example, the turning point in an illness over which the victim has no control, and a "subjective" historical process such as a "time when it is not possible to take for granted 'normal' economic, social and other relationships; a time for decision; and a time when what individuals do counts for something." In his view, this latter perspective is "congruent with the classical Greek meaning of crisis as the moment for deciding between uncertain and arguable evaluations of a disease or illness." The distinction is significant in the sense that one is a deterministic view and the other is more interpretative or containing an element of voluntarism or choice.

For our purposes, it suffices to interpret "crisis" as a situation that is unsustainable on the basis of present trends with, therefore, a denouement that will be either ''hard'' or ''soft'' but, in either case, transforming. The only element of choice is related to how the transition could be handled, not whether—once the crisis is ''resolved''—there will be a return to the status quo ante. Two examples of what is not meant might suffice to clarify the concept and illuminate the importance of understanding what we do mean when we talk of ''crisis'' and its resolution.

One extreme interpretation of crisis is reflected in a view expressed in an editorial of *The Wall Street Journal* at a time when ''the international debt crisis'' was a matter of almost universal concern. An editorial writer, in the 20 April, 1983 issue of that newspaper, posed the question, ''What debt crisis?,'' and went on to attribute the mood of panic in the summer of 1982 and the months following to a conspiracy concocted by officials of the International Monetary Fund (IMF) to shake down the American people for an increase in their contribution to that international organization. The editorial suggested that ''debtor nations, bankers, IMF officials and others with a vested interest in bailouts like to scare the public with such specters as the $600 billion or so owed to industrialized countries by the non-OPEC developing countries.'' Since the situation was the basis for a requested quota increase by the IMF's management, the editorial went on to suggest that the sense of urgency and emergency was generated by that institution as ''a way of permanently augmenting the power of the IMF bureaucracy.''

More recently a similar view was articulated by Judith Anderson, a reporter for the same journal, writing in *The International Development Review* (Winter 1989/90), in an article entitled, ''What if they declared a debt crisis and nobody came?'' In her view (as she interpreted the views of the delegates to the 1989 Joint Annual Meeting of the IMF and the World Bank),

''the crisis has become exclusively a national crisis: Argentinian, Algerian, Brazilian, Nigerian and Peruvian. . . . Behind the muscle-flexing of the private bankers is the conviction that the LDC debts are no longer a tangible risk to the international financial system. 'With the threat no longer there' said a major United States bank economist, 'concern about a solution has disappeared'. . . . This year it became clear that the international foreign debt crisis is over; it receded not with a bang but with a whimper.''

From this perspective the crisis issue revolves around the question of whether the major American, European and Japanese banks that lent heavily to the third world countries were at risk should their loans to these countries not continue to be serviced, whether this was likely, and whether, if large-scale defaults by these debtors were to occur, this would pose a danger to the continued "normal" functioning of the prevailing international financial system. The global financial crisis that erupted in 1982, in this view, amounted to nothing more than "an old-fashioned banking panic": the major banks had been weakened by their orgy of third world lending in the 1970s, but they had almost all survived. *Thus*, the global debt crisis, if it ever existed, has already faded into history. We can go on as before.

Then there is the view of another school of thought typified by the World Bank's management. At the end of 1990 in a World Bank report, *World Debt Tables 1990-91: External Debt of Developing Countries*, they noted that "the debt crisis is far from over." From this perspective the state of crisis that dramatically erupted in 1982 will be over when the overwhelming majority of the larger debtors are "creditworthy," that is, when the debtors have attained a status *in the eyes of the creditor community* that will enable and entice the resumption of the flow of investment capital and commercial bank lending so that there is a large net flow to the third world debtor countries. The World Bank's *World Development Report 1988*, reflecting that institution's basic policy thrust, states that

"the main objective (of the World Bank's programme to address the third world debt crisis) should be, first, to enable debtor countries to allocate more resources to investment and consumption, and, second, to strengthen their creditworthiness, thus eventually permitting a resumption of voluntary commercial lending."

Accordingly, the prescribed cure is a measure of debt relief provided by the creditors and "structural adjustment programmes" (SAPs) by the debtors so as to restore their economies to a condition of economic-financial health that would once again attract foreign investors and lenders.

In line with this, during the 1980s the proportion of lending of the World Bank devoted to "structural adjustment loans" (SALs) increased, accounting for about a quarter of Bank lending by the end of the decade. The conventional SAL contains a package of policy "recommendations" (that are conditionality items) comprised of some or all of the following: lowering or eliminating trade and investment barriers, privatizing state enterprises and down-sizing the civil service, placing greater reliance on "market forces" which calls for reducing subsidies, real wages, and other measures such as are required to "get the economic house in order," a state of affairs that is measured by their trade balance and other indicators related to "creditorworthiness" in the eyes of private lenders and investors. Thus would the global system return to a sustainable condition, out of danger of breakdown. Then the crisis would be over.

This, too, implies a narrow definition of the global debt crisis—and of the environmental crisis in so far as the debt servicing pressures impact on the debtors' policies with respect to the environment. Leaving aside the issue of whether this SAP-type effort by the debtor countries would suffice to achieve that nebulous status of "creditworthiness," there is a question about whether this "achievement" would resolve the crisis conditions of instability and fragility of a global system in which the growth of income and well-being is slow or even negative for most of humankind, in which the income-well-being gap between the rich and the poor is widening and in which the pattern of development is environmentally damaging and thus, over the longer-term, unsustainable.

The Build-up to
the Debt Crisis

It is rather banal to observe that the clue to the genesis of the crisis is to be found in an examination of the period of its gestation. But it bears pointing out that a retrospective review of the policies of that period of gestation and of its supporting financial-economic system can shed light on the institutional changes that incubated the crisis. Such an historical exercise can then guide policymakers who need to answer the question as to whether further changes are necessary both to avoid the worst-case scenarios of a "hard landing" and to get over the crisis and put our global system onto the path of growth consistent with equity and environmental goals. What the nature and scope of those changes might have to be to get us there is an issue that follows.

Looking back, *from the perspective of the borrower* the period beginning in the late 1960s through to the late 1970s was one characterized by a favourable combination of conditions, principally low *real* rates of interest and rising prices for primary commodity exports. Real interest rates were averaging under 1 per cent and at times were negative; the primary commodities that the developing countries exported were fetching historically high prices so that, for a time, their export earnings were increasing at a rate of 20 per cent a year.

A temporary and manageable setback occurred in 1973 with the impact of the so-called "oil price shock" that in one year turned the average $13 billion annual collective surplus of the oil-importing developing countries into a deficit of about $37 billion. By the end of the 1970s their current account deficits stood at about 2 per cent of their collective gross national product (GNP), a comfortable or manageable ratio. Thus the policymakers of those countries had few qualms about continuing to borrow to cover both the increased price of the imported oil and the greater quantities of imports needed to sustain growth rates that were averaging above 5 per cent per year.

During this period, *from the lenders perspective*, there were few qualms about lending to these willing borrowers. Ample capital was available to lend,

particularly after the first oil shock of 1973 when the collective surplus of
the members of the Organization of Petroleum Exporting Countries (OPEC)
jumped from an annual level of about $1 billion in the years before 1973 to
almost $70 billion in 1974. Because these countries did not have the capacity
to absorb this amount of capital, the private commercial banking system rose
to the occasion, acting as intermediating agents in the process of what came
to be called, "petrodollar recycling." The volume of bank lending to developing countries expanded exponentially, quadrupling between 1970 and
1975, from $3 billion to $12 billion, and doubling again to almost $25 billion
by 1980. The annual expansion rate was more than 30 per cent, so that by
the end of the 1970s commercial banks were responsible for almost two thirds
of the total flow of capital resources to the developing countries. The editor
of *The Economist*, Rupert Pennant-Rea, summarized the process succinctly:

> "Some people who borrow money prefer to cloak what they are doing in
> euphemisms. The thickest cloak of all was used in the 1970s: 'recycling.'
> How simple it all seemed: on one side, billions of petrodollars piling up
> in banks; on the other, countries with big deficits to finance. Recycle the
> cash from one to another, and the problem would be solved. Actually, it
> was created."

By 1977 both the lenders and borrowers began to display signs of nervousness. Voices were heard suggesting that the lending-borrowing pace
should begin to slow down. But under conditions where oil prices had leveled
off and negative or near-negative interest rates prevailed, these were voices
in the proverbial wilderness. The nervousness was more than offset by both
the temptation and the bandwagon effects. It was only toward the end of the
1970s that the spigot began to be turned down. Net transfers of short-term
lending (net payments of profit and interest minus the net inflow of capital)
to developing countries went down after 1980 and by 1982 had become a
transfer *from* the developing countries. In 1983 in the Latin American region
alone—the region that accounted for about three fourths of the capital repayment flow—the negative transfer reached about $20 billion, not counting
flight capital that went unrecorded. With some minor fluctuations from year
to year, the statistically registered flow from the region to the creditor countries
increased to where it stands today at roughly $30 billion. By 1990 the flow
from all the developing country debtors to the creditor countries was running
at about $40 billion, over $30 billion of which was a net transfer from the
17 most highly-indebted developing countries. The total outflow thus repre-

sents an amount almost comparable to the inflow of official development assistance (ODA) to these countries.

Both lenders and borrowers had been playing the odds, counting on a continuation of rising commodity prices, a depreciating dollar and low or negative real interest rates. The event that broke the back of the proverbial camel was the "Volcker shock" of 1979. In order to counteract the inflationary effect of the second oil shock of 1979 when oil prices had been boosted once again, the then Chairman of the United States Federal Reserve System, Paul Volcker, raised nominal and real interest rates to unprecedented heights. He slammed on the brakes by a combination of policy measures and the rest of the world went through the windshield. By the summer of 1982 the debt crisis had arrived in dramatic fashion.

The policy decision to apply the Volcker shock treatment as a means of addressing the inflationary pressures of the late 1970s and early 1980s had a draconian impact. Its rationale and its consequences can best be understood and assessed within the institutional context of the times when the decision was taken, that is, by examining the prevailing system or "international order" in which the debt crisis was nurtured. The institutional changes of the 1970s have by now become deeply imbedded in the structure of the global system for trade and capital movements. *It is the prevailing structures and processes that incubated the global debt crisis.*

SUSTAINABLE DEVELOPMENT: A CLICHÉ OR A USEFUL OPERATIONAL CONCEPT?

Many of the proposals that have come in great profusion to address the environmental issue have used a phrase, "sustainable development," as the key to unlock the seemingly inherent conflict between growth and concern for the environment. But few have attempted to give it substance in a real-world context, that is, to concretize the concept in terms of policies and programmes.

This state of affairs prompted one writer of *The Economist* to make the following tart observation in a September 1989 issue reporting on that elusive concept:

"sustainable development is ultimately a frustrating idea (when one tries) to turn it into a usable concept,(that is), to apply it to investment decisions or national accounts . . . (but this fact has not, however, discouraged) every environmentally-aware politician from being in favour of 'sustainable development'. . . . *but what on earth does the phrase mean?*"

Another commentator, Terence Corcoran, in *The Globe and Mail* (Toronto) of 23 March, 1990 in a column entitled provocatively, "Sustainable development: a dumpsite for ideas?," ventured an answer in the same skeptical spirit:

"Sustainable development," he wrote, "is fast becoming a landfill site for every environmental idea. . . . (with), for the most part, nobody seem-

284

ing to care what the words mean, or whether they even have any real meaning.''

He added the barbed question: ''have we reached a point where sustainable development has become a hazardous concept?'' The viewpoint reflects that of a segment of the business community who are wary of the costs associated with the operationalization of the concept, costs they feel they will be expected to bear.

The recent surge of popular support for the idea can be interpreted as the public's concern for the future in reaction to fears about impending environmental catastrophes akin to the oil spills of the Torrey Canyon and the Exxon Valdez, the nuclear accidents at Three Mile Island and at Chernobyl, and the gas tragedy in Bhopal. These remain very much in the collective consciousness. The political climate for action, would therefore, appear to be ripe.

However, there can be little doubt that few of those who declare themselves supporters have more than a vague idea about the meaning of the ''sustainable development'' phrase, nor even of the term, ''good environmental management.'' Even fewer are aware of the implications of the kind of political-social-economic changes that such support implies. For example, a mid-1990 poll taken to assess the Canadian public's understanding of ''the environmental issue'' revealed that only one Canadian in 10 could make the connection between fossil fuel emissions and global warming. The support should be regarded, therefore, as softer than appears at first sight.

The critical limit to growth or development is the limited capacity of the water, land and air to act as garbage disposal sites. Thus there is a sharply focussed concern about the carbon emissions and other effects of human activity, especially those that can be changed by reducing the environmentally-harmful activities or transforming them so they are environmentally benign. Policies and programmes can be devised to address these options, especially with respect to energy use and energy sources. To be effective on the requisite scale, these policies and programmes may, in turn, require radical changes in the institutional framework or system, that is, the decision makers, their criteria for decisions, the scope of their decisions, the evaluation of their social impacts and the like.

However, the environmental movement under the banner of ''sustainable development'' has also taken on a different Malthusian cause related to ''resource depletion'' as a threat to future welfare without a sharp focus on what is meant by a resource. The word is transmuted into ''ecological capital'' in the Malthusian paradigm, as though we can measure ecology (the beauty of a landscape and the utility as a watershed reducing the frequency and scope of flooding) and need to put it into economic terminology as "capital" that has meaning and measurement for economists only in terms of the flow of income that it can generate.

This "economic" aspect of the concern for the future is, therefore, a conceptual cul-de-sac, weakening the legitimacy of the limits related to the capacity of the air, water and land to absorb pollutants and wastes. The economistic emphasis is a harmful diversion since it is also operationally woolly and politically naive. The Malthusians have been shouting false warnings for centuries, and in doing so, have been serving the established order of things by pointing the accusing finger of impending disaster at "nature's niggardliness" and at human proclivity for procreative activities, when it is the institutional order that should be singled out as neither sustainable nor equitable. Since their warnings about food and energy (wood, coal and oil) shortages have proven false time after time, the Malthusian credibility is very low. The environmental limits are tainted with the same skepticism when the concept of limits is extended to the concepts of "natural resources" or "ecological capital."

It would be preferable to let the limits of the garbage can capacity of the air, land and water to absorb pollutants stand on its own. This way the idea of limits breaks from the liabilities of the traditional Malthusian sense of limits that has been applied time and again for several centuries to the productive capacity of land and water and air to provide the food, materials and other necessities of life and the industrialized form of civilization. Using this environmental concept there is a basis to argue *that those earlier developed nations that have already utilized much of the limited capacity should be obliged to pay a rent for the percentage use of this global commons that they have "enjoyed"* in a rather wanton fashion. This would help address the capital transfer problem, especially in relation to environment-enhancing programmes and projects such as, for example, the Brazilian tropical rain forest. In a case such as this one can get around the seeming reversal of the "polluter pays" principle and the sense that the world is being held hostage by Brazil. The idea is simply paying "rent for the global commons."

GLOSSARY OF TERMS

Compensatory Financing Facility (CFF): This is a funding arrangement under the IMF that is designed to provide immediate liquidity to countries suffering from a sudden unexpected deterioration in their balance of payments.

Development Committee: The Development Committee's formal name is the Joint Ministerial Committee of the Board of Governors of the Bank and the Fund on the Transfer of Real Resources to Developing Countries. It meets at the time of the Annual Meetings (usually in the autumn) and in the spring. The agenda of the committee's meetings are not structured to focus on key issues though papers are prepared on various themes. Each participant gives a prepared speech and there is no exchange of views. The pattern changed at the Annual Meeting in Seoul in 1987 when its duration was extended to two days, thus providing opportunity for less formal afternoon sessions that enabled some interaction on agenda items. The committee at present has no analytic/writing staff resources of its own and no mandate or capacity for decision-making by virtue of its ambiguous mandate, its lack of staff and the way the meetings are conducted. Its issue papers are prepared by the staff of the World Bank and the IMF. The Committee has a potential usefulness in so far as it can be strengthened to provide an opportunity for Governors to place some items on the global agenda.

Debt Service: The payment of interest and principal on loans in accordance with the obligations assumed by the debtors when the borrowing arrangements were made. In practice, debt servicing is what is paid, an amount that may not include the payments against principal, nor even all the interest due. To the extent there is a shortfall, there is a **default**.

Eurocurrency: The funds held in accounts outside the country in whose currency they are denominated. This has enabled banks to operate outside the constraints of their own country's regulations and has given rise to the **Euromarket**, an international capital market in which are traded Eurobonds, Euro syndicated credits, etc.

Extended Fund Facility: This is a funding arrangement under the IMF that is designed to provide support of structural adjustment programmes for three years.

General Agreement to Borrow (GAB): This was established in the early 1960s by the large quota members and, until 1983, was available only to them. When after 1983 the GAB was broadened, special constraints were set to limit access by claimants on the regular funds of the IMF in the event that several countries with large quotas applied at the same time.

General Agreement on Tariffs and Trade (GATT): This institution might also be included in the company of international institutions, though it is a small secretariat that prepares studies, organizes discussion "rounds" or negotiating conferences, and monitors the agreements which incorporate the rules that have been agreed upon. Its coverage with respect to trade is limited and an issue in the "rounds" of discussion is the extension of coverage to include such items as intellectual property, services and other items related to international trade in goods and services.

General Capital Increase (GCI): See Sustainable Lending Level (SLL). The conditions that major donors attach to their agreement for a GCI is one of the most effective ways in which they can influence World Bank policy. The tactic is a form of "hostage-taking" whereby the World Bank is held hostage to the major donors. It is effective when the World Bank has reached the SLL and the needs of the developing countries call for its increase, especially in light of the amounts that the borrowers have been paying back on previous loans, that is, the net disbursements (which are lower than lending commitments that are paid out over time in frances).

The authorization for a GCI is needed from time to time as the Bank comes up against the limits of the SSL, and the World Bank's Articles of Agreement limit its lending and guarantees to an amount no greater than the sum of the paid-in capital, the callable capital and the retained earning or reserves. This is the so-called "one-to-one gearing ratio." Changing the ratio is therefore a costless option which would increase the "sustainable level of lending," that is, the level of lending which is sustainable in perpetuity without any additional capital.

Thus there is little validity in any country pleading budgetary constraints as the reason for its resistance to the GCI. The "fact" is that this commitment regarding callable capital would be required only on the occasion of one eventuality, namely, the winding up or the insolvency of the Bank, an extremely unlikely occurrence. In any case, should matters come to that extreme distress on a global scale, this would be the least of anyone's worries. (For an illuminating account of the issue, see Shereen Benzvy Miller, *The Challenge of Control of an International Organization: the World Bank*, April, 1983, Osgoode Hall Law School, York University, Toronto, mimeo.)

Global Environment Facility (GEF): A funding arrangement to finance environmental projects or programmes, the GEF was established in November 1990 as a three-year $1.5 billion pool of capital to be managed by three agencies: UNDP, UNEP and the World Bank. Its 1991 work programme, as agreed upon in May 1991, included 15 projects costing $214 million and 11 technical assistance programmes costing $59 million. The range of activities include preserving biodiversity, protecting international waters, preventing ozone depletion and reducing carbon emissions that contribute to global warming. UNEP has established a 14-person **Science and Technical Advisory Panel (STAP)** that will establish scientific and technical criteria for the use of GEF funds. More than 20 countries, eight of which are developing countries, have contributed to the funding. Over 20 non-governmental organizations (NGOs) are associated with the first projects and programmes being undertaken with GEF's financial and technical assistance.

Gold Trust Fund: This funding arrangement under the IMF was established after the 1973 "oil price shock" in response to a need for new windows of concessional aid. Through the Gold Trust Fund $1.3 billion was lent out over four years.

Gross National Product (GNP):   The value of all goods and services produced in an economy during a specific period, usually a year.

Interim Committee: The Interim Committee was once known as the Committee of 20. Its official name is Committee of the Board of Governors on Reform of the International Monetary System and Related Issues. It meets at Annual Meetings and on an ad hoc basis when decisions have to be made.

International Development Association (IDA):   This is the so-called "soft window" of the World Bank, the subsidiary that is only a bookkeeping entity and lends at zero interest (but with a low "administration fee") and long grace periods before repayment commences. Its recipients are the countries with annual incomes under $700 per capita. When a country's income is above that level it is said to have graduated. Many countries get both WB loans and IDA loans, referred to as "mixed blend" countries. IDA funding is done on a pledging basis every three years.

As of early 1990, the total pledges had reached $15 billion with Japan and Italy leading the way in offering greater contributions *if their voting shares would be adjusted accordingly.* The voting share arrangement came through when the United States made a "concession" on veto power after agreement was reached to lower the veto power on voting with respect to changing the Bank's Articles of Agreement to 15 per cent. As the United States voting strength dropped below 20 per cent to about 18 per cent they were thus still able to maintain veto power over amendments to the Articles of Agreement. (There is no such veto power with regard to the normal operations of the institution. In fact, there is rarely a vote on any issue. If the major shareholders hold a common position, it is know and there is no need for votes, but often one or more of them stand alone on an issue and it is merely recorded)

International Financial Institutions (IFIs):   the International Monetary Fund **(IMF)** is included along with the World Bank and the other MDBs. The IFIs differ from the MDBs in so far as the emphasis of the former is on financial health while the latter is on longer-term development, but not to the exclusion of the financial aspect in the short-term.

International Monetary Fund (IMF):   Established in 1944 at the Bretton Woods Conference to assist developed and developing countries counter short term balance of payment problems.

International Trade Organization (ITO):   At the Bretton Woods Conference of 1944 that established the "Bretton Woods twins," the World Bank and the IMF, there was a proposal to establish "triplets," the third one being the ITO. The opposition of the United States to the proposal transformed the idea of a full-fledged trade promoting agency into GATT.

London Interbank Offered Rate (LIBOR):   The rate at which prime banks offer to make Eurodollar deposits with other prime banks for a given maturity from overnight to 5 years.

Multilateral Development Banks (MDBs):   The MDBs include the **World Bank**, the **African Development Bank**, the **Asian Development Bank**, the **Inter-American Development Bank** and the **Caribbean Development Bank**.

Multilateral Investment Guarantee Agency (MIGA):   This body is sponsored and housed within the World Bank. It was only operationalized in 1989 when the requisite endorsement of Governments and their subscriptions of capital had been attained. Its track record has yet to be established.

Oil Facility: This funding arrangement under the IMF was established after the 1973 "oil price shock" in response to a need for new windows of concessional aid. Between 1975 and 1977, through the Oil Facility window, the IMF lent out $8.2 billion to over 100 countries at lower rates and longer maturities.

Programme Lending: This is contrasted with **project lending**. It usually takes the form of **structural adjustment loans (SALs)** or **sectoral adjustment loans (SECALs)**. These loans can be quickly implemented from conception to disbursement while project lending goes through a "project cycle" of identification, preparation and appraisal, all within the context of sector and country analyses undertaken on a periodic basis for each borrowing country. The process of project-based lending takes a great deal of time, especially as the projects are worked out in an iterative fashion with the recipient countries.

Quota Entitlement: This refers to a membership share that is held on deposit with the IMF and is available in tranches, the first of which is 25 per cent given automatically upon request while other tranches are available with conditions incorporated in so-called "standby agreements" which set out the policy proposals agreed upon in negotiations for that tranche. These agreements specify monetary and other targets and are meant to correct the balance-of-payments imbalance that prompted the standby agreement. The funds under the agreement are not paid out at once and can be stopped in the event of non-compliance. Each member's quota is based on its gold and dollar reserves, its average imports and exports, and their ratio to its national income. On joining the IMF each country pays in 25 per cent of its quota

in gold or dollar equivalent and the remainder becomes callable in its own currency.
The quota determines the member country's voting strength; on that basis the United
States has 126,000 votes and 40 African countries have an aggregate vote of less
than 35,000.

Real Rate of Interest: The rate derived by subtracting the rate of inflation from
the nominal rate of interest.

Secondary Market: The market for the sale and purchase of outstanding debts that
are held by creditors as assets. The value of these assets at any point in time before
their maturity depends on what a buyer is willing to pay. The debts of almost all
third world countries are discounted in accordance with the assessment of their
ability and willingness to service their debts, the discount being reflected in their
valuation in the secondary market.

Special Drawing Rights (SDRs):   A composite currency unit issued by the IMF
that has become the IMF's official unit of account. Their valuation is based on a
basket of five currencies. SDRs were first introduced in 1970 to provide a source
of liquidity other than the United States dollar. The SDR is also known as "paper
gold."

Standby Credit: This is an IMF provision to provide support for a jointly negotiated
economic adjustment programme for one or two years.

Sustainable Lending Level (SLL):   The "sustainable lending level" sets the limit
of World Bank lending capacity. Since the World Bank lends on a one to one ratio
(unlike commercial banks that can operate on very much higher ratios), the SLL
is determined by the World Bank's paid-in and callable capital, plus retained earnings
that year-by-year go into the reserves against which the World Bank can lend. By
this conservative policy the Bank enjoys a higher rating on capital markets and thus
borrows at lower rates, which, in turn, means that its borrowers can enjoy lower
rates. Thus it is important for the Bank to get authorization for a "general capital
increase (GCI)" from time to time. Only a tiny fraction of that GCI need be paid
in, giving the donors a powerful leverage of expanding lending capacity for each
dollar paid.

Authorization for a General Capital Increase (GCI) is needed since the World
Bank's Articles of Agreement limit its lending and guarantees to an amount no
greater than the sum of the paid-in capital, the callable capital and the retained
earning or reserves—the so-called "one-to-one gearing ratio." Changing the ratio
is therefore a costless option which would increase the "sustainable level of
lending," that is, the level of lending which is sustainable in perpetuity without
any additional capital.

United Nations Development Programme: A special arm of the United Nations
that is funded through triannual donations, and which is disbursed to third world
countries through projects and programmes for which, in most cases, a specialized

agency or IFI or MDB acts as executing agency. In addition, the UNDP conducts programmes on its own account and has established special programmes such as the **United Nations Programme for African Recovery and Development (UN-PAARD), the Substantial New Programme of Action (SNPA), the United Nations Trust Fund for Sudano-Sahelian Countries (UNTFSSC)**, the **Special Measures Fund for Least Developed Countries (SMF/LDC)**, the **Special Action Programme for Administration and Management (SAPAM)**, the **National Technical Cooperation Assessments and Programmes (NatCAP)** and the Round Table programmes. **Short-term Advisory Services (STAS)** was begun on a two-year trial basis in mid-1985; by April 1987, STAS had completed 25 assignments in 13 countries and based on an evaluation of its performance, the programme has been deemed to be worth continuing. The **Structural Adjustment Advisory Group (STAAG)** has a roster of experts that could be available on short notice to respond to requests by African countries for assistance in managing and monitoring financial aspects of structural adjustment issues, particularly those related to debt management and negotiations. The **Special Measures Fund for the Least Developed Countries (SMF)** was established under a 1985 Governing Council resolution and in 1986 secured contributions amounting to $10.59 million. 80 per cent of the fund has been allocated to the various bureaus to enable them to assist the countries within their area of responsibility to strengthen their capacities to undertake macro-economic analysis in support of the activities of UNDP connected to preparations for Round Table meetings, NatCAP exercises and other aid coordination programmes.

United Nations Specialized Agencies: principally, the **Food and Agricultural Organization (FAO)**, the **United Nations Industrial Development Organization (UNIDO)**, the **United Nations Conference on Trade and Development (UNCTAD)**, the **United Nations Educational, Scientific and Cultural Organization (UNESCO)**, the **United Nations Environment Programme (UNEP)** and the **World Health Organization (WHO)**.

United Nations System: The system in its developmental role consists of the United Nation itself with its units—the economic and social field and with UNDP and UNITAR, the "specialized agencies" for health, agriculture, industry, education and culture, environment, etc., and the IFIs and MDBs. These latter institutions such as the World Bank and the IMF are part of the United Nations system, but with a difference in so far as they have distinctive constitutions ("articles of agreement") with weighted voting, relative freedom from hiring staff on a quota basis, and, most importantly of all, vastly greater financial resources. UNDP funding is provided to other agencies of the UN System for the implementation of projects for which they act as "executing agency."

World Bank (or officially, the **International Bank for Reconstruction and Development**): This institution is the first and largest of the MDBs. By the end of

1990, the paid-in capital from all member Governments had amounted to $3.2 billion which enabled the Bank to make loan commitments of over $180 billion and disburse about $100 billion (which nets out at about $45 billion when allowance has been made for repayment of principal). All this has been financed by borrowings in private capital markets (mostly outside the United States) at market rates of interest, amounting to $80 billion in total since 1968 and by 1995 to about $140 billion. That "market" rate has, of course, been well below what developing country borrowers could obtain—if they could obtain such sums at all—yet with a slight mark-up of a fraction of 1 per cent, the World Bank has been profitable, a profit that accrues to the developing countries in so far as it adds to reserves and expands the "sustainable lending level."

SALIENT FEATURES OF CURRENT PROPOSALS FOR DEBT RESTRUCTURING AND DEBT RELIEF

ADVISORY GROUP REPORT OF THE UNITED NATIONS SECRETARY-GENERAL, FINANCING AFRICA'S RECOVERY.

Reschedule all payments of principal and interest due over the next three years on terms that are more favourable with regard to grace period, maturity and interest rates; in effect reducing the present value of the debt by an amount that reflects their discount on the secondary loan market—(applicable to those sub-Saharan African debtors that have impaired debt-servicing capacity).

- Continue the prevailing process of the Paris London Club reschedulings on a year-to-year or multi-year basis, but with commercial bank creditors and Governments agreeing to rescheduling at below-market interest rates (but higher than IDA rates) with the "subsidy" entailed in the rate differential being financed as part of official development assistance (ODA) programmes—(applicable to other sub-Saharan African debtor countries)

- Provide permanent but partial debt relief by exchanging outstanding bank claims for long-term debtor bonds of the same face value but at a lower interest rate - (applicable to "excessively indebted countries")

- Encourage and facilitate debt-equity swaps and debt-for-nature swaps as well as swaps for the debtors' commitment to allocate a specified amount of local funds to finance UNICEF programmes;
- Request a 20 per cent increase in concessional flows through bilateral ODA in the form of quick-disbursing generalized balance-of-payments support;
- Enlarge or replenish concessional multilateral programmes of the IMF, the World Bank, the African Development Bank and the EEC through the following means:
  —repayments to the IMF's Structural Adjustment Facility (that was recently increased from SDR 2.7 billion to SDR 9 billion) be re-negotiated to achieve softer terms:10 years, 5 1/2 years grace period and 0.5 interest;
  —an External Contingency Facility (ECF) in the IMF be established to meet contingencies such as unexpected interest rate increases and natural disasters (to replace the use of the existing Compensatory Financing Facility (CFF) for this purpose, thus enabling the CFF to offset cyclical rather than secular trends);
  —the World Bank's Special Facility for Africa (SFA) be replenished at a three-fold higher level and used to subsidize interest payments on non-IDA loans to "some of the hard-pressed low-income sub-Saharan African countries";
  —the European Community's Stabex Scheme that provides grants to counter shortfalls in export revenues be replenished.
- Establish joint committees of senior representatives of the debtor Governments and their major donors to improve the monitoring and co-ordinating of "recovery and reform programmes" and the implementation of the commitments of the donor community.

AFRICAN DEVELOPMENT BANK
—(prepared by S.G.Warburg & Co.)

- Establish an entity whose board would be representative of the African Development Bank, the World Bank and the IMF that would have the responsibility to ensure that debtors adhere to the IMF conditionality that would be a precondition for eligibility;

- Issue long-term (20-25 year) securities through this entity for the full face value of the loans but carrying below-market rates; these would be exchanged for existing debt obligations with the repayment guaranteed through the establishment of a "redemption fund" into which the debtor would pay an agreed sum each year at terms compatible with the debtor's debt-servicing capability; this sinking fund, over time, would build up the capital required to redeem the securities at maturity.

FRED BERGSTEN, WILLIAM CLINE, JOHN WILLIAMSON
— (Institute for International Economics)

- Authorize the World Bank to offer guarantees to commercial bankers for new lending and to enable debtors to capture the discount on their debts in the secondary market when the creditors opt for "exit bonds" that are priced to reflect the discounted value of the debts.

(The recently authorized General Capital Increase for the World Bank will enable it to tie up some of its capital for such guarantees which constitute contingent liabilities without constraining its normal lending; the guarantees would apply for short terms to cover the years but only until *the World Bank reaches its new sustainable lending level.*)

DAVID BIGMAN
— (Hebrew University)

- Debtors would secure a 50 per cent discount on their commercial bank debt from all creditors on an identical basis, and would pay 75 per cent of the remaining outstanding debts in local currency, half of which would be made available to a new international agency, the Environment Fund (EF) that would have a responsibility for implementing and supervising measures for environmental protection, the other half allocated under the supervision of the World Bank and the IMF to finance population control projects and programmes;

- Debtors would pledge future export earnings as collateral for the payments that are due on its remaining debt in foreign currencies, but the principal and interest would be guaranteed by a Guarantee Fund (GF) set up in the IMF. Banks not willing to participate in the settlement would not be paid under more favourable terms, nor have access to the guarantee arrangements;

- Financing for the Environment and for the Guarantee Funds would be derived from a special tax on fossil fuels (five cents per gallon for all countries) with part of the funds of the EF devoted to research on environmental problems and part of the funds of the GF devoted to cover annual payments to the creditor banks as agreed upon in the settlement between the debtors and creditors.

BILL BRADLEY AND PAUL SARBANES, ET AL.— (Senators and Congressmen Obey, Kennedy, Schumer, La Falce, Morrison and Fauntroy)

- Establish an International Debt Management Authority to operate as a self-supporting entity, with the aim of providing across-the-board debt relief amounting to over $40 billion through a 3 per cent reduction in interest rates for three years and an annual write-off of 3 per cent of the loan principal for the next 3 years.

- Secure for debt relief purposes, an annual increase in ODA and lending from the developed countries amounting to $3 billion.

(Conditional on debtor countries taking appropriate reform measures including reduction of subsidies, restrictions on foreign investment and on capital flight, and other policies to promote economic growth)

NICHOLAS BRADY —(United States Treasury Secretary)

- Relaxation of United States opposition to an increase in the IMF quotas and other enhancements of IMF resources for assisting debt-distressed countries to be accompanied by parallel financing from the Japanese Import-Export Bank;

- Creation of special facilities within the World Bank and the IMF that could be used to expand debtor country access to the financial resources of these institutions for purposes of reducing debt and debt-servicing;

- Endorsement of the guarantee role for theseinstitutions that has to date only been pursued cautiously in light of the previous United States policy of opposition to this practise;
- Endorsement of negotiation to remove the sharing and negative pledge clauses in existing agreements between creditors and debtors (whereby all leading banks are guaranteed equal ranking in claims on debtors) so as to facilitate individual banks negotiating debt reduction arrangements on their own.

(Put forward in a speech on 9 March, 1989, as suggestions rather than as a formal planned programme, the following ideas were heralded by some as an innovative approach. They were more accurately represented by others as a break from the initiative put forward by his predecessor in that post, James Baker III, in as much as its emphasis has shifted to the hitherto "unthinkable" idea of debt or debt-servicing reduction and guarantees involving the transference of risk to the public treasuries from the private creditor banks rather than on pleas for commercial banks to increase their lending.)

JEREMY BULOW AND KENNETH ROGOFF
—(Stanford University and University of California, Berkeley)

- Divorced development aid from debt negotiations (and, therefore, opposed to establishment of debt discount facility that offers guarantees to induce creditors to convert debt to guaranteed bonds: this conversion process entails governmental financing directly or through guarantees, a process characterized as "a black hole for aid funds yielding only minimal efficiency benefits"; "the less creditor-country Governments are involved in the bargaining over private bank debt, the better. . . . since they tend to ossify negotiations"; the debt overhang is not a major impediment to debtor country economic recovery and "debt elimination would be no cure-all");

- Establish an International Citizenship Fund (ICF) as a new grant-making arm of the World Bank to tie aid to debtor country performance in areas such as environment policy, drug interdiction, population control programmes, and other areas where third world actions create major externatilities: if the IFC aid is not be entangled with existing World Bank or IMF lending operations, reform of the financial structure of these institutions is necessary so that the debts owed them are written-down, forcing the donor countries to assume the Bank's bond liabilities directly and putting the costs of the discounts on the official loans "on the books."

- Reverse a number of legal and regulatory measures affecting United States banking practices that were made in the 1970s to encourage lending to the third world countries.

BENJAMIN COHEN—(Tufts University's School of Law and Diplomacy)

- Provide significant debt relief to reflect each debtor country's underlying capacity to pay;
- Place a ceiling on interest payments, the ceiling to be determined by factors such as export earnings, improved economic management, incentives for new capital formation, etc.

RUDIGER DORNBUSCH ET AL.—(Committee of 20th Century Fund) - (Harvard University)

- Establish an "American Fund" or a Debt Restructuring and Refinancing Trust (DRRT) that buys up the debt held by United States banks of all countries—except for those of Venezuela, Argentina, Brazil, Mexico and the Philippines—on a quota basis for each country determined by economic and political considerations;

- The American Fund would restructure the commercial bank debt (possibly including debts held by foreign banks) to capture the full secondary market discount amounting to about $8 billion for the benefit of the debtors—which would reduce their debts by as much as 20 per cent—and provide guarantees to underwrite the bonds that would entail about a $2 billion contingent liability for the United States directly or through the World Bank with the participation of other governments that would subscribe to the arrangements, in which case, a new facility might be called for that is independent or beyond the reach of the United States Treasury;
- Banking regulations would be eased to enable smaller banks to exit completely.
- For large debtor countries like Mexico, interest recycling involving debt-equity swaps on the interest payments rather than the principal could be helpful for the debtor seeking to achieve growth and stability and facing the dual problems of budget foreign exchange constraints;
- For Mexico that faces only a foreign exchange constraint—and must take the initiative unilaterally with no option for the creditors but to accept:—half of its interest due would be paid in local currency that creditors can invest in an unrestricted manner except for repatriation which is allowed only after 10 years— about one-quarter of the debt payments due would be capitalized automatically with a rate equal to Mexico's per capita growth and United States rate of inflation, thus freeing up capital for domestic investment and avoiding a ballooning of debt-service obligations, the remainder would be paid in dollars.

Jonathan Eaton
—(University of Virginia)

- Establish an international legal environment that includes a supranational judicial system with adjudication and enforcement functions that does not put Governments in the role of implicit or explicit guarantor as a step towards avoiding another debt crisis and encouraging future private investment in developing countries —("contract enforcement, bankruptcy procedures and the protection of private property rights need to be distanced from political decisions'');

- Oppose in principle establishment of debt discount facility and other measures of converting privately-held lending into foreign aid, especially as banks and middle-income debtors are not the most deserving recipients of such aid and considering that there is no assurance that this form of aid will benefit the poor in the debtor countries. But if the public money is to be spent in this bailout process, it might be preferable to establish a new institution that could make the expenditure more visible and separated from normal foreign aid.

IRVING FRIEDMAN
—(former official of the IMF and World Bank, United States Treasury, banker)

- Commercial banks should establish a new financialinstitution to buy loans at an appropriate discount (as the Japanese banks have done on a limited scale), with the entity holding the loans until maturity with the original discount taken as income or make them available for debt-equity swaps or conversion into marketable securities— (''a sort of international factoring service'').

MILTON FRIEDMAN AND ALLAN MELTZER
—(University of Chicago and Carnegie-Mellon University)

- Debtors and creditors should work out their own arrangements without any government intervention, such intervention having the effect of prolonging the painful adjustment process to no net social advantage, but a possible gain for the parties involved that would thus escape the consequences of their own mistakes.

HANS-DIETRICH GENSCHER
—(German Foreign Minister)

- Donor countries increase aid with broadening and easing of terms, particularly for the poorest countries through provision of grants and "tangible debt-servicing relief";
- Establish international laws for crimes against the environment to prevent industrialized nations ("northern overconsumption societies") from tempting third world to sell rights for their countries to become "poison-garbage depots".

KEITH GRIFFIN
—(University of Sussex)

- Debtors should collectively take unilateral action to bring about a comprehensive negotiated settlement with the aim of achieving total or partial repudiation of their debts.

INSTITUTE FOR INTERNATIONAL FINANCE
—(Bankers' association)

- Provide debt relief through a process that involves governmental intermediation to provide guarantees and other inducements, but which must be voluntary. (If the banks are coerced, rather than coaxed, to do what is necessary, the banks will take legal action to protect their right to handle their debtors as they see fit.)
- Change government regulations and taxing of banks so as to enable the creditor banks to adopt a more flexible approach to writing down their debts in negotiation with each debtor on a case-by-case basis or to opting out through the "exit bond" door.

Sheik Jamer al-Ahmed al-Sabah,
—Emir of Kuwait

- Creditor nations write off interest on their loans to debtor countries, including foregoing payment on principal for the poorest;
- IMF and World Bank reconsider "their stringent conditions" on lending, showing more flexibility;
- Expansion and regulation of scientific and technical assistance with concerted efforts aimed at conservation of natural and human resources.

Japanese Bankers

- Establish a debt-clearing agency dealing with Latin American debt financed by the banks in proportion to the debts they hold. (Twenty-eight banks holding over $50 billion in developing country debts have established such an agency).
- Agency buys debt at market discount rates enabling the banks to take a tax loss equivalent to the discount.
- Distribute interest collected by the agency to the banks as dividends that would be taxed at a lower rate than income derived from interest.

Professor Peter Kenen
—(Princeton University)

- Establish an International Debt Discount Facility (IDDF) that would issue long-term bonds in exchange for debt;
- The IDDC (guided by the secondary market prices) would choose the rates at which the debt would be discounted, allowing each debtor to choose the one for its own obligations, the degree of discount correlated to policy conditionality provisions.

- The creditor banks that choose to use the IDDC—and they must decide within a limited period whether or not to do so—must agree to discount all debt uniformly at a uniform fraction of its total claims on all the debtor countries on which it has claims;

- The debtors must also decide whether or not to use the offices of the IDDC, but only those that have prior policy agreements with the IMF and the World Bank would be eligible, and, in the event that policy commitments are not met, the IDDC would be authorized to grant relief provisionally and modestly at first by reducing the interest rate payable to the IDDC or writing down the claims themselves;

- Marketable bonds issued by the IDDC would likely be amortized over 30 years, starting five years after issue, and bear an interest slightly higher than the then-current rate on long-term United States government bonds;

- IDDC bonds would have a secondary market and the IDDC would be empowered to redeem them and issue new ones to holders of maturing bonds;

- IDDC profit might be held as a reserve or used for selective interest rate relief;

- Debt to the IDDC might be amortized over a 25-year period, after a 5-year grace period, bearing interest at 50 basis points above the average rate on IDDC's own bonds.

(The updated variant of Professor Kenen's 1983 proposal ("Third world debt: sharing the burden, a bailout for the banks", *The New York Times*, March 6, 1983) is contained in the *Journal of Economic Perspectives*: Winter 1989), "Organizing debt relief: the need for a new institution". He asserts that his proposal is not a "bailout" of the commercial banks, that it limits the "free rider" problem by offering incentives for banks to participate and penalizing those that don't since they would likely have to take large losses later since arrangements would be made for the IDDC to appropriate most of the increase in the value of the debt that results from the debt relief measures.)

PEDRO-PABLO KUCZYNSKI
—(Chairman of First Boston International)

- Provide debt relief for large debtors greater than those now being offered by at least 30 per cent;
- Divide loans into two tranches:
  —Tranche A would be paid on a scheduled basis and carry an interest rate that is normal LIBOR plus spread, its quality being enhanced by the two-tranche arrangement to a degree that would make it unnecessary for guarantees to be provided;
  —Tranche B would carry no interest or amortization and would be payable through "the Agent" if and when—after year 2—certain conditions come into being that would enable such payments without constraining growth, such as the level of the debtor country's foreign reserves exceeding projected debt servicing.

    (The premise is that debt relief proposals by themselves are not capable of resolving the debt crisis since the key ingredients for such an outcome are reform within the debtor economies and substantial capital inflows on terms that are well below prevailing interest rates and of longer maturity.)

FRANZ LUTHOF
—(Swiss banker)

- Debtors would have the discretion to automatically capitalize interest payments, but would undertake to make enhanced payments on the basis of objective indicators such as increased export receipts due to favourable price changes for their exports.

PRESTON MARTIN
—(former Vice-Chairman of the United States Federal Reserve Board of Governors)

- Cap should be put on interest rates to financially ailing debtor countries;
- Some of debt owing United States banks should be converted into equity;
- World Bank and IMF should swap bonds guaranteed by them for some of the third world. debt.
- (Paul Volcker, then Chairman of the Federal Reserve's Board of Governors, reacted strongly by characterizing Martin's proposals as "incomprehensible, unfortunate and unrealistic in suggesting that there are unorthodox approaches to deal with the international debt problem". He added, "what is hopeful and promising is that so many countries are coming to grips with necessary and difficult adjustment efforts, as, for example, Argentina." - (Reported in *The Washington Post*, 21 June, 1985)

GOVERNMENT OF MEXICO

- Swap commercial bank debts for Mexican bonds with a 20-year maturity, the principal to be repaid with the proceeds of 20-year zero-coupon United States treasury bonds which Mexico will have purchased using its own foreign exchange reserves.
- Accept bids tendered through an auction procedure with Mexico reserving the right to reject those bids that are deemed to be too low.
- Mexico under this arrangement assumes all the risks with respect to increases in interest rates and undertakes to set aside part of its foreign exchange reserves to secure the United States treasury bonds.

PERCY MISTRY—(Fellow of Oxford University and former World Bank adviser)

- Establish a Debt Restructuring Facility (DRF) as a World Bank affiliate that would issue long-term (25-30 years) bonds which would be exchanged at a significant discount for developing country debt held by commercial banks— and thereby enable about $400-450 billion of third world debt to be retired if the discount averaged 25-30 per cent.
- The DRF would be capitalized by the United States, Japan and OECD countries at $30 billion (with 10 per cent provided as paid-in cash and 90 per cent callable guaranteed capital) and would operate with a gearing ratio of 10:1 so that over the next three to five years the DRF could issue bonds up to a value of $300 billion;
- Through swaps with commercial banks, the DRF would acquire the developing country debts of those debtors prepared to adhere to an IMF/World Bank conceived and monitored ''appropriately structured policy reform package'' at prices that reflect the discount on these debts, thus passing the discount on to the debtors;
- The DRF would convert this debt into fixed-interest loans at a time when the interest rates are low, thus securitizing and unloading a part of its assets in the secondary market with greater flexibility and establishing a secondary market in its own bonds.

(Though this proposal is similar in concept to all the others that are centred on debt conversion, it has been described as ''bold financial engineering'' by virtue of its high leverage feature. This scheme is seen to have the advantage of having a significant impact both in terms of the amount of debt that would be retired quickly, thus enabling debtors to become creditworthy more rapidly than otherwise, and in terms of strengthening of the secondary market with greater liquidity, thus enabling creditors to improve their options for handling developing country debts.)

FRANCOIS MITTERAND
—(President of France)

- Forgive one-third of the public and state-guaranteed commercial debt owed by the poorest 21 countries of sub-Saharan Africa;
- Reschedule part of the remaining twothirds at normal market rates of interest with repayments stretched out to a maximum of 25 years and another part at preferential interest rates of less than half the market rate with a repayment period of about 15 years.

KIICHI MIYAZAWA
—(Japan's former Minister of Finance)

- Similar to that of the debt-bond swap of Mexico in that the debtor nation would securitize part of its debt with the principal guaranteed by foreign exchange reserves and receipts from the sale of assets deposited in a trust account at the IMF. The balance of the debt that is not securitized would be rescheduled on more favourable terms.
- There are, however, two key differences:
  —the debtor is obliged to agree to structural adjustment conditionality as worked out with theIMF;
  —the commercial bank creditors are not obliged to take a loss in executing the swap whereas theMexican scheme called for deep discounting of the debt with the discount being captured by the debtor.

(Ostensibly because the losses would be incurred by taxpayers rather than bankers and because its institutional modalities were not spelt out, the proposal met with a cool reception when it was first put forward to other members of the Group of Seven at the Toronto summit in the summer of 1988. The opposition, particularly by the United States, may have had more to do with geo-political considerations than with the proposal itself.)

Saburo Okita, Lal Jayawardena and Arjun Sengupta
—(United Nations University (UNU)/ World Institute for Development Economics Research (WIDER))

- Establish a debt reconstruction facility with ties to the World Bank (to be located in Washington or Tokyo) that would initially act as a Japanese Trust Fund (JTF) to raise resources for debt reduction purposes from the Japanese capital market.
- The amount raised by JTF would be $125 billion over 5 years, $10 billion annually recycled through collateralized lending from the JTF against the collateral of zero-coupon bonds issued by the Japanese Government, $10 billion through loans guaranteed by the Export-Import Bank of Japan for untied co-financing deals with the World Bank, and $5 billion raised in the Japanese market by the IMF for lending to low-income developing countries with an interest rate subsidy from the Japanese Government. (The magnitude reflects the capacity of the Japanese economy to recycle part of its annual trade surplus and the need for a critical mass of capital flow to make a significant reduction in debt so as to start a "virtuous circle" that would enable the debtor countries to achieve reasonable rates of growth.)
- Access to the funds for debt reduction would be conditional on policy reforms as set out in consultations with the World Bank and the IMF.

James Robinson III
—(President, American Express Co.)

- Create the Institute of International Debt andDevelopment ($I^2 D^2$) as an entity jointly operated by the World Bank and the IMF with seed capital and contingent financial support from major developed countries;
- $I^2 D^2$ would purchase debt at a discount on the secondary market, paying banks with the Institute's perpetual bonds and participating preferred stock in the Institute that would pay dividends when the debt service

payments to the Institute exceed its own service obligations on its consols;

- I^2D^2 would negotiate with each country the scope of the structural adjustments that are a necessary condition for participation.

FELIX ROHATYN
—(partner, Lazard and Freres Inc.)

- Establish an entity backed by government guarantees as a separate agency or as an affiliate of the World Bank or the IMF to purchase the developing country loans from commercial banks in exchange for low-interest long-term bonds;
  —the agency or affiliate would, in turn, make loans at 6 per cent interest with maturities of 15 to 30 years;
  —the resultant losses would be absorbed by the banks and the creditor countries in a ratio to be negotiated on a case-by-case basis.
- Japan would allocate about $175 billion of new money over five years for Latin American debtor countries through an increased contribution to the General Capital Increase (GCI) of the World Bank and to IDA and other international financial institutions and through making a commitment of $20 billion per year and interest rate reductions amounting to $15 billion per year.

EUGENE ROTBERG
—(former World Bank Treasurer)

- Commercial banks would lend new money to major debtors, equivalent to a substantial fraction of the interest due for a period of 20 years based on tranched and conditioned structural adjustment loans, with a substantial "balloon" on the payments on principal after 20 years;
  —the World Bank would provide to commercial banks a "put" at par on all principal payments exercisable only after 20 years;
  —if and when the banks, after 20 years, exercise the put, it would

receive par from the World Bank in exchange for the notes due from the debtor;

—this would then be relent to a World Bank affiliate which, in turn, would be in a position to repay the World Bank;

—the commercial bank would then receive from the affiliate the three-month T-bill rate for the succeeding 20 years.

(This proposal, in effect, would switch the exposure of the commercial banks to a World Bank affiliate financed from several sources: the World Bank, some governments and those commercial banks that stand to gain from this arrangement and would, therefore, be prepared to participate.)

PROFESSOR JEFFREY SACHS
—(Harvard University)

- Establish an International Debt Facility. The IDF would be charged with organizing a comprehensive package, linking debt reduction to policy reforms in debtor countries, and providing official guarantees on the reduced interest payments due after the debt reduction package is operational;

- The IDF would be lodged in the World Bank and the IMF;

- The IDF would press for a comprehensive settlement between debtors and creditors according to the extent of debt reduction deemed "necessary" as judged by market indicators and World Bank medium-term scenarios, the debt reduction taking the form of cuts in interest rates to sub-market levels;

- The IDF would call for the participation of all creditor banks (but once about 80 per cent agreed) the IDF would provide those participating banks full guarantees, and the others would accumulate arrears under the protection of the IDF.

L. WILLIAM SEIDMAN
—(Chairman of the United States Federal Deposit Insurance Corp.)

- Establish an international debt discount facility for conversion of debt to financial instruments guaranteed by the debtors themselves, rather than by the facility's funds.
- The required capital would be elicited from the IMF, the World Bank, Governments and commercial banks. The banks would be charged an annual premium to insure their holdings of the debtor's bonds.

(This proposal was published in The New York Times of 10 July, 1989. Professor Peter Kenen has noted a disadvantage in this idea in as much as a large number of new bonds would be issued, each with its own market, as contrasted with his proposal for an International Debt Discount Facility (IDDC) that would issue its own bonds, thereby enabling these bonds to have one market that would operate more efficiently and, also, making it less tempting and more difficult for banks to block bond issues by debtors.)

ARJUN SENGUPTA
—(Indian Executive Director to the IMF

- Create an IMF Debt Adjustment Facility (DAF);
- Write-off by creditor banks of a portion of debt of participating debtors and exchange another portion for long-term, low interest bonds from the DAF;
- DAF purchases existing debts at prevailing discounts on the secondary market and passes on the discount to the country thereby converting existing debts into new debts with the same repayment period and interest rate for the bonds issued to banks;
- Debtors agree to adhere to new growth-oriented policy package that thereby should upgrade country's credit rating and attract new investment and lending.

PAUL STREETEN
—(University of Boston)

- Establish an international central bank capable of creating liquidity and global reserves at a pace that is neither too inflationary nor deflationary;
- Establish an international income tax that would be levied automatically and progressively on all countries;
- Establish an international investment trust to channel capital from rich surplus countries to the developing ones.

H. JOHANNES WITTEVEEN, ET AL.
—(WIDER Study Group on Debt Reduction)
—(former Managing Director of the IMF)

- Secure funds for debt reduction through an IMF quota increase, through Trust Fund arrangements, the proceeds of World Bank structural adjustment loans, and through voluntary contributions of $50 billion from countries in surplus such as Japan and Germany through the use of IMF Trust Fund arrangements to achieve a debt reduction of at least $125 billion (as a tentative estimate of what is required to restore creditworthiness) using a variety of techniques, particularly buybacks and collateralization;
- All banks must participate with choice as to various options, some of which would be guaranteed by multilateral agencies and Governments, but the maximum participation is required to achieve critical mass and enable the orchestration of a comprehensive settlement with creditors;
- Access to the IMF Trust Fund would be conditional on the usual IMF macroeconomic conditions and commensurate with the need of the debtors for debt reduction.

MATRIX OF DEBT
CRISIS PROPOSALS

Proposer (Source)	Key Elements	Institutional Innovative Feature	Assessment
Africa – U.N.'s SG Advisory Group Report ("Financing Africa's Recovery")	• Reschedule payments with more favourable maturity and interest rates. • Exchange outstanding bank claims for debtor bonds. • Encourage debt-equity swaps, b-o-p support, etc.	External Contingency Facility within IMF	Offers some modest improvement to ease the current situation for African debtors but offers little for long-term change that is necessary condition for avoidance of breakdown and recovery.
Alfonsin, Raul (former President of Argentina)	• Commercial banks reduce interest rates on outstanding debt by 4%. • Reschedule existing credits for 30 years. • Official creditors (ie. Wold Bank) increase lending.		Offers to ease pressure but likely to be limited in scope given banker's lack of commitment.

Bigman, David	• Debtors secure 50% discount from all creditors, paying 75% of remainder in local currency, half of that available for use by Environment Fund for environmental projects and programs; • Principal and interest payments on conversions guaranteed.	Environment Fund & Guarantee Fund to be set up under the WB and the IMF auspices	Funds to be financed in part by globally uniform carbon tax; the debt conversion with guarantees not tied to conditionality a la Brady; merit of tying debt reduction to environment ends.
Bailey, Norman	• Creditor banks swap existing loans for new Exchange Participation Notes that provide lenders with a pro-rata share of the debtor's annual foreign exchange receipts.		Debtors unlikely to accept given inflexible features; nor would bankers accept deep discounts on EP Notes.
Baker, James (former Treasury Secretary)	• Plea for commercial creditor banks and MDBs to lend additional funds to 13 most heavily-indebted LDCs. • U.S. support (unspecified) contingent on debtors undertaking str. adj. policies (privatizing, deregulat..)		Bankers unreceptive to pleas for further lending and MDBs unable without much larger GCI and IDA.
Bergsten, Fred	• Authorize WB to offer guarantees to banks for new lending		
Bolin & Del Canto	• Establish new institution (Export Dev. Fund) to provide loans up to 15 years maturity to enable debtors to import essentials for renewal of development programs.	New Export Development Fund to work with W.B.	Calls for new financing, unlikely to be acceptable to donor creditor countries.

315

Proposer (Source)	Key Elements	Institutional Innovative Feature	Assessment
Bolivia	• Debtors purchase commercial bank loans at heavily discounted secondary market prices.		Anticipate cool reception and resistance from banks.
Brady, Nicholas (U.S. Treasury Secretary)	• Write off part of the Third World debts and pass benefits of discount directly to debtor nations and grant temporary waivers on the repayment of interest and principal for up to 3 years. • IFIs asked to play bigger role with U.S. sanctioning offer of guarantees from institutions to commercial bank lending. • Additional funding promised from U.S. and Japanese for IMF and parallel financing by Japanese Import Export Bank along with more IMF lending.		Greater debt relief will ease situation but impact not likely to be significant.
Bradley, Bill (Senator)	• Reduce interest rate on official U.S. government loans by four percentage points. • Enable debtors to swap outstanding debts for low interest, long-term securities. • U.S. government to guarantee interest and principal payments on these newly issued securities.		Offers possibility of significant improvement since scale of proposals are commensurate with situation; however G-7 resistance remains strong.

Brazil	• Secure new bank loans, including co-financing with support of World Bank and from medium-term trade deposit facility. • Limit payments to 2.5 percent of GNP. • Increase scope of debt-equity swapping transactions • Issue exit bonds at fixed low interest rates (6%) with long maturities (25 years).	Temporary easing for Brazil but does not address critical conditions and probability of recurrent crisis are still strong. Banks and creditor governments must still agree.
Castro, Fidel	• Debtors cease paying interest (moratorium/repud?). • Creditor governments assume obligations, paying interest due directly to commercial banks.	Offers temporary easing of situation but long-term calls for broader approach. (Castro has not taken own advice.)
Davidson, Paul	• Central banks take over non-performing loans from commercial banks in exchange for stock in the Central Bank. The Central Bank then sells loan securities to the government in exchange for government bonds. • Govts then negotiate write-downs with banks.	Promises improvement if governments are willing to assume losses, leaving banks off the hook. Not likely.
De Carmoy, H.	• Creditor governments and multilateral development banks make new loans at concessional rates. • Private commercial lending limited to project and trade finance.	Would transfer risks away from banks; calls for additional funds and constrains usage. Unlikely to be acceptable to any of the parties.
New International Action Committee		

Proposer (Source)	Key Elements	Institutional Innovative Feature	Assessment
de Cuellar, Javier Perez	• Creditor gov'ts convert all bilateral aid loans into grants. • Reschedule official trade debts at soft loan rates comp. with those of IDA.		
de Gortari, Carlos Salinas (President of Mexico)	• Creditor governments provide funds to enable provision of guarantees for zero-coupon bonds to secure favourable conversion terms of existing debt to enable debt reduction and new money, the options being open for the creditors to decide.	The guarantee could be ext. collectively via the World Bank or IMF	Creditor governments may not accept fully
Dornbusch, R. (M.I.T.)	• Allow LDCs to pay all or part of debt servicce in local currencies. • Banks would be required to reinvest the local currency in the country for a set number of years.		Offer some improvement if creditor banks resumed lending.
Frimpong-Ansah, J. (Std Chartered Bank London)	• More permanent and ongoing debt relief by creditors while adjustments in debtor countries are made.		Too high conditionality, debtor countries likely to oppose imposition of adjustment programs.

Source	Proposal		Comment
Fullerton, D. (Canadian Imperial Bank of Commerce)	• Provide debtor countries with incentives to continue interest and capital payments (ie. incentive) • Creditor govts, not banks, must assume responsibility to provide new lending to LDCs.		Offers improvements but banks must agree.
Garcia, Allan	• Debtors limit total interest payments to 10% of export earnings and only pay those creditors making new loans.		Not workable as a solo act; freeze by lending institutes inflicts increased pressure.
Genscher, Hans-D.	• Increase ODA to the poorest country debtors. • Commercial banks resume voluntary lending.		Donors unlikely to oblige.
Gorbachev, M.	• 100-year moratorium-poorest countries. •tailoring of repayment installments to debtors means.	Int'l Guarantee Agency repurchase debt at discount	
Group of Seven (G7) (Summit/Sept.,88)	• Forgive ⅓ debt of 21 poorest African nations.		Helpful, but of limited scope.
Grubel (Princeton Essays on International Finance)	• Establish International Deposit Insurance Corporation to insure loans not currently covered under existing national arrangements (not specifically applicable only to LDC lending).	Int'l Deposit Ins. Corp. (akin to MIGA?)	Doubtful that reluctance to lend can be significantly overcome with only risk factor addressed this way.

Proposer (Source)	Key Elements	Institutional Innovative Feature	Assessment
Ikonicoff, K. ("Dette ou Democratie?" – Le Monde, Aug. 2, 1988)	• Transfers debtors payments into fund that creditors can utilize for investment in debtor countries. (Precedent is P.L. 480, the U.S. Food Program, that gave U.S. funds in local currency in exchange for food.)	Establishment of Local Currency Funding Banks in each country	Entails losses for creditors and process likely to be so cumbersome as to be of very limited application.
Feldstein, M.	• Keep muddling through. • Concessions on interest rates and capital inflows		Offers improvements but increase the total debt.
Jaber al-Ahmed al-Sabah, Emir of Kuwait	• Creditor nations write off interest on their loans for a specified period and possibly forego a portion of principal. • Debt rescheduling, lowering of interest rates and related measures in Africa.		Would likely be helpful but unlikely except as part of a broad package of proposals. Should be part of a broader international effort to rescue Africa.
Japanese Bankers	• Establish a debt-clearing agency dealing with Latin-American debt. • Creditor govts purchases debt from banks at market discount rates with int. payments going to banks.	Debt-clearing agency	Calls for banks to take losses and for governments to play role; politically difficult.

Kaufman, Henry	• Convert portion of banks LDC portfolio into higher yielding securities at value of securities established by the secondary market.		Resistance of banks likely given the discounts this calls for.
Kenen, Paul	• Establish International Debt Discount Corp. to buy debts at discount in exchange for long-term bonds. • IDDC then lends to debtors at lower int. rates	Create new International Debt Discount Corporation (IDDC)	Offers some modest easing but transfer of risks and shouldering of costs of new arrangements poses problems.
Knox, David (Former VP of World Bank)	• Latin American debtors undertake serious structural adjustment reform programmes and creditor governments provide guarantees so debts can be converted at large discounts due to the reduced risk.		Some improvement possible but debtor countries may resist type of reform programs.
Kuczynski, P.P.	• Increase capital flows and debt relief according to program reform in LDCs • Loans to be divided into two branches with LIBOR plus spread interest ratess, and with no interest.		Offers some improvements.
Griffin, Keith	• Debtors take collective action to negotiate comprehensive settlement of outstanding debts, with threat of total or partial repudiation.		Offers significant easing of pressures for African countries but banks and IMF-WB must agree.

Proposer (Source)	Key Elements	Institutional Innovative Feature	Assessment
Latin American Free Trade Association	• Barter deals. • Members to pay for trade among themselves in units called Central American Import Rights.		Offers savings of foreign currency but limited to a more dynamic international trade.
Lever, Lord Harold	• Export credit agencies insure new commercial bank lending. • Reschedule loan principal.		Unlikely to elicit significant reponse from banks with no incentive or guarantees.
Lever & Hume	• Increase lending from commercial banks. • Reduce interest rates and lengthen maturities. • Write off loans from debtors that cannot possibly pay.		Desirable but improbable under prevailing conditions.
Lindbeck	• Transformed outstanding debt into long-term bonds. • Debtors issue "priority bonds" for new money with precedence over old bonds.		Not likely to have much appeal to bankers.
Lizano, E. (Central Bank of Costa Rica)	• Convert $1.5 billion commercial debt into 25 year bonds with interest capped at 6 percent of Costa Rica's debt.		Not probable, banks have opposed it.

322

Lovejoy, Thomas	• Debt for nature swap. • Buy discounted Brazilian debt denominated in dollars and exchanged in Brazil for bonds denominated in local currency. • Bonds are donated to an environmental institute.	Would ease some percentage of total public debt but has been rejected by Brazilian government.
Lutoif, F. (Swiss Bank Corp.)	• Temporary grace on interest payments. • Postponement of amortization until exports of debtors recover.	Offers relief to debtor countries but banks likely to resist.
Mailson Nobrega (formerly Brazilian Finance Minister)	• Conversion of debt into investment equity. • Take advantage of discounted debt paper "secondary market". • IMF purchase disc. debt paid by special IMF drawing rights. • Trade debt for long-term "exit bonds" with guar. govt. payments	
Menem, C. (Pres. Argentina.)	• Suspension of all payments on the debt of Argentina during a five-year grace period.	Introduce relief during the suspension period but uncertain in the long run; debtors gov'ts and banks unlikely to accept.
Mexican–Morgan Guaranty	• Debtor repurchases its commercial bank loans at secondary market prices with securities collateralized by U.S. zero coupon bonds.	Could be significant if banks were willing to take the once-for-all losses.

Proposer (Source)	Key Elements	Institutional Innovative Feature	Assessment
Mistry, Percy	Establish a Debt Restructuring Facility (DRF) to issue 1–t (25–30 yrs) bonds to be exchanged at a significant discount for LDC debts held by commercial banks.	Debt Restructuring Facility (DRF)	Not likely to have much appeal to creditors unless sweetened by government support
Mitterand, Francois (President of France)	• Creditors forgive poorest African debtors one-third of their debts and reschedule the remainder at current interest rates for 10 years. • Reschedule their entire debts at commercial rates for 25 years or reschedule the debts at less than half the market rate of interest for 15 years.		Feasible for governments as creditors and thus of limited applicability; while helpful, scale is not adequate to achieve significant improvement over long term.
Miyazawa, Kitchi (Japanese Minister of Finance)	• Establish an IMF special trustee fund to be composed of foreign currency reserves donated by debtor countries, the funds of which would be used to guarantee bonds that the debtor nation would swap for discounted bank loans.		Creditors taking losses and debtors having to contribute for reserves make it unlikely to be acceptable even if the prospect for swapping would be a little more bright due to guarantees.

Source	Proposal		Comments
Monroe-Davies, Robin (MD of IBAC Banking Analysis Financial Times London)	• Series of bilateral agreements between debtors and lenders. • A portion of the debt would be forgiven if certain economic reforms are carried out.		Offers a balanced proposal of part forgiveness and part structural reform.
Morgan, J.P. and Company	• Commercial Banks swap portion of troubled Mexican loans for new marketable securities from Mexico. • Swap requires bank to write-off part of loan • Mexican securities backed by 20-yr, zero coupon U S Treasury bonds.		Has been tried; while reducing debt slightly has provided little new money yet absorbed valuable foreign exchange as collateral for bonds.
Morgan, Grenfell Company	• Creditors Banks sell loans to a new agency at face value and receive non-interest bearing bonds.	New Agency	
Obey, D. (D-Wis) Sarbanes, P. (D-Md)	• Establish special facility at IMF or WB to purchase loans from banks at discount, then pass discount along to LDCs • Surplus countries would finance the facility.	New special facility at IMF or WB	Surplus countries unlikely to take all transfer cost.

Proposer (Source)	Key Elements	Institutional Innovative Feature	Assessment
Okita, Sabura (former Japanese Foreign Minister)	• Establish a Japanese Trust Fund to borrow funds on Japanese financial market at commercial rates of interest and relend the proceeds to debtor nations at concessionary rates of interest. (The resulting interest subsidy to be financed from part of the expected increase in Japanese official development assistance).	Japanese Trust Fund	If Japanese funds were to be forthcoming on large scale the scheme would work and ease pressures, but does not address the larger problems.
Pereira, C.Bresser (Former Minister of Finance, Brazil)	• Swap half of Brazil's $68 billion in foreign bank debt for bonds that would be sold to investors at a fixed discount		Could offer easing of pressures but bonds would need to be deeply discounted; debtors gov'ts and banks unlikely to accept.
Perez, C.A. (President of Venezuela)	• Write off half of the Latin American debt and forgive African loans. • International organization to take responsibility for debt.	International Debt Organization	Offers significant relief but banks will resist.

Please, Stanley	• Banks sell loans to IMF facility at "underlying value" – defined as the price that reduces debt-service payments to "sustainable" levels compatible with pre-1982 growth rates.	IMF facility to purchase commercial loans.	Creditors not likely to be receptive unless incentives offered.
Quereshi, Moeen (World Bank's Senior Vice Pres. Operations)	• Debt reduction strategies in next phase of debt workout strategy. • Increased role for governments and international agencies. • More concerted and long-term investment and lending efforts by banks and financial institutions.		Enhanced muddling-through approach; helpful but far from enough until "increased rule" and "concerted efforts" are specified.
Ritchie, G. (Bank of Nova Scotia)	• Negotiate reduction of interest payments to all debtors by an amount determined on basis of debtors' annual export earnings. • World Bank increase lending substantially.	Interest Insurance Fund	Transfer costs of rate reduction from commercial banks to public treasuries; self-serving
Robinson, James (President of American Express)	• Establish an Institute of International Debt and Development to purchase existing loans at secondary market prices. (Countries complying with IMF programs to be permitted to negotiate new commercial bank loans).	(IIDD or I2D2) Institute of International Debt and Development	Variant of Mistry and other proposals with similar drawbacks and prospects.

Proposer (Source)	Key Elements	Institutional Innovative Feature	Assessment
Rohatyn, F. (Chairman of New York Municipal Assistance Corp.)	• Establish government-backed agency or IMF or WB affiliate to purchase the LDC loans from commercial banks in exchange for low-interest long-term bonds. (Funds would come largely from Japan five year allocation of $175 b. for L.A. debtors).	Gov't backed agency ("Big Mac") or affiliate of IMF	Calls for additional funds if the incentives are to be in place that would make it attractive and workable.
Rohatyn & Altman	• U.S. banks swap Mexican debt for securities offered by new U.S./Mexican Development Finance Authority that carry lower interest rates. • Increase flow of direct foreign investment.	US/Mexican Finance Authority	Calls for government financial support to provide guarantees but response not likely on large scale.
Rotberg, E. (Former World Bank Treasurer)	• Commercial banks increase lending sufficient to keep debtors up-to-date on existing debt-servicing obligations thru arrangements whereby the principal payments are rescheduled with a 20-yr balloon feature.	World Bank affiliate to extend guarantees.	Would be of marginal help.

Sachs, Jeffrey	• Establish Int'l. Debt Facility charged with organizing comprehensive package and guarantees, pressing for debt reduction that takes the form of cuts in interest rates. • Reliance on co-operation of creditor banks would no longer apply with compulsory participation of at least 80% of banks. (non-participating banks would not benefit from guarantees.)	International Debt Discount Facility located within the World Bank & IMF	Helpful. Similar to other conversion proposals (especially Kenen's); Positive features are comprehensiveness (no longer relying on creditor banks volunteering and penalizing non-participants) and substantial reduction of debt burden by forgiveness of large portion and by interest rate reduction.
Streeten, Paul	• Establish int'l. central bank to assure adequate global liquidity; • Establish a progressive int'l. income tax, levied automatically; • Establish int'l. investment trust to facilitate capital transfers.	International Central Bank and International Investment Trust	Calls for government to subsidize the losses entailed in the forgiveness feature. Could be marginally helpful unless done on large scale.
Seidman, William (Chm. U.S. Federal Depost Ins. Corp.)	• Establish int'l. debt discount facility for debt conversions to be guaranteed by debtors themselves, rather than by facility's; • Capital from ins. premium charged banks for guarantees.	Int'l. Debt Discounting Facility funded by bank insurance premiums	

Proposer (Source)	Key Elements	Institutional Innovative Feature	Assessment
Schirano, Louis (Senior Vice-Pres. First Interstate Bank Ltd.)	• Securitize remaining debt with liberal usage of World Bank guarantees. • Phased write-downs. • Western governments must support the bank and provide capital increases promptly. Japan must play larger role in future of World Bank.		Greater debt relief will ease situation but improvement not likely to be great.
Schumer, J. (Congressman)	• Banks restructure loans with longer-term, lower-interest rates.		Plea without carrots or stick features to make it go.
Sengupta, A. (Executive Director IMF, India)	• Commercial banks exchange a portion of their loans to eligible debtors for low interest bonds issued by a Debt Adjustment Facility.	Free-standing Debt Adjustment Facility (or IMF?)	Another variant on the same theme, no outstanding new wrinkle.
Shan, Pu (Chinese Academy of Social Sciences)	• Supportive policy on the part of industrial countries. • Immediate debt relief • Special issue of SDRs for developing countries. • South-South cooperation.		Offers improvements.

Social Democratic Party (Germany)	• Targetted debt forgiveness in specific cases. • Extension of repayment terms, long-term agreements and upper limits on interest rates, and limitation of debt service to a certain proportion of export earnings.	Framework for int'l mediation analogous to domestic bankruptcy law.	Some improvement possible but resistance from banks to set upper limits on interest rates.
Soros, G. (President Soros Fund)	• Convert existing debt into 25-year bonds paying a fixed rate of interest, with a portion of the margin's proceeds being placed in a premium account. Borrowers would contribute extra 1.5% of margin into escrow account. This combined percentage return would form an insurance fund—International Lending Agency (ILA).	International Lending Agency (ILA)	Could be helpful but dim prospect as debtors not likely to want to contribute to insurance funding for the benefit of creditors.
Taylor, Allan (Pres. Royal Bank)	• Increase long-term lending from the major multilateral lending institutions.	IMF and World Bank	Pleas from bankers ring false: Do as I ask, not as I do.
Ul Haq, Mahbub (formerly with WB U.N. and Pakistan Minister of Finance)	• Establish IMF Debt Refinancing Subsidiary to provide resources for extending maturities, reducing interest payments to maintain them at a percentage of export earnings so as not to stifle growth.	IMF Debt Refinancing Subsidiary	Another variant on the same theme; no new features to make it more attractive to creditor countries or banks.

Proposer (Source)	Key Elements	Institutional Innovative Feature	Assessment
UNCTAD	• One time 30% reduction in existing debts of 15 most heavily indebted countries (equivalent to 25% of debt) • Debt relief tailored to each country's circumstances		Boosts both growth and significantly improves debt indicators, thus putting the countries on a new and sustainable level. Banks likely to resist.
Urquidi, V. (Colegio de Mexico)	• Split interest payments into two parts: LIBOR rates less current inflation rate paid in foreign exchange case; difference from the market interest rate paid in the debtor's currency which is used by foreign creditor banks for domestic lending.		Offer some debt relief. Weak feature is creditor banks must agree, and this is not likely.
Wallich, L.	• Encourage more lending by insuring the banks for cooperative bank lending to LDCs.		(Similar to Soros proposal)
Warburg & Co.	• Issue long-term securities for the full face value of the loans but carrying below-market rates in exchange for existing debt.		Issue unresolved as to who pays and who carries risk; unlikely to be much help.

Weinert, L.	• World Bank to swap bonds for bank loans at below market rates.	Another variant with World Bank role specified; not a role that is appropriate (similar to Mistry proposal).
W.I.D.E.R. (Okita Sengupta and Jayawardena)	• Establish a debt rediscounting facility very with a high gearing ratio to purchase LDC debts in exchange for long-term bonds.	
Williamson, J., Bergsten, F., Cline, W.	• Exit bonds with some form of international guarantee to be effective.	International Credit Guarantee Fund (ICGF). (Similar to Soros and Wallich proposals)
Witteveen H. Johannes (Former M.D. IMF.)	• Establish an International Debt Guarantee Fund (ICGF) to guarantee bank loans with premiums and percentage insured to be fixed according to the need of borrower.	Similar to other conversion proposals. Positive feature is sensitivity to debtor stress.
World Financial Markets	• Encourage banks to provide additional lending either through establishing an insurance pool or through links between World Bank and commercial bank lending.	Reduces risks for banks but diminution of risk not likely to be enough to get them back in as voluntary lenders.
Zombanakis, Minos	• IMF to extend adjustment programs by 10–15 years. • Banks to reschedule loans compatible with program.	Familiar plea that is likely to fall on deaf ears.

333

Index